I0793685

IMAGES
of America

HELEN

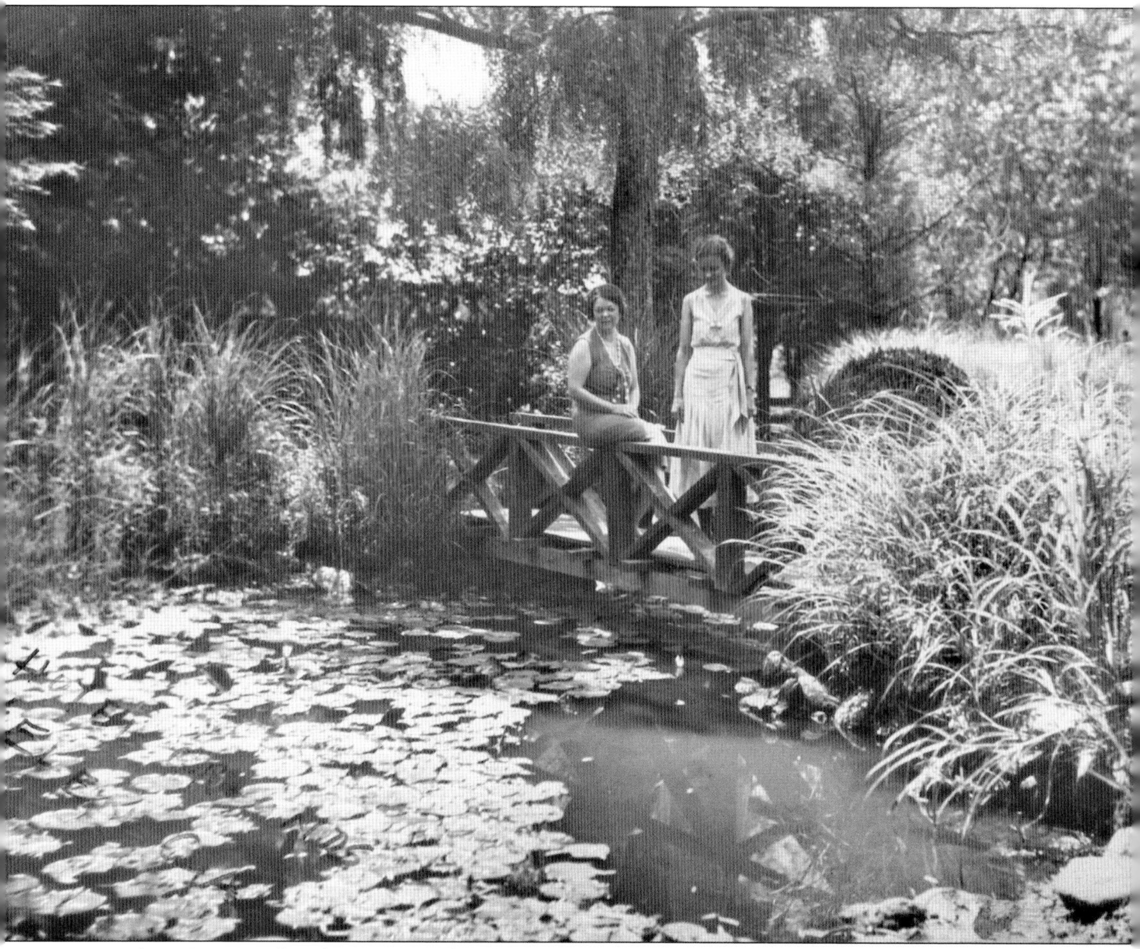

Helen, Georgia, has been a popular destination for visitors to the northeast region of the state since it was founded in 1913. Photographed here about 1936, visitors take a moment to enjoy the lily pond at the Mountain Ranch Hotel. John Mitchell, an associate of the Byrd-Matthews Lumber Company, built the hotel and was responsible for the development of both Helen and Robertstown. (Courtesy of David Greear.)

On the Cover: John Fields Greear and son Josh look out over the northern Helen Valley toward Robertstown around 1940. The Chattahoochee River flows toward downtown Helen on the lower right. In 1914, the Gainesville & Northwestern rail line that served the huge lumber mill in Helen came through this bottomland before reaching its terminus in Robertstown. With the knowledge of how to lay rail line switchbacks (zigzag track patterns), which he learned in his home state of Virginia, John Greear came to Helen as a civil engineer to survey rail lines into the difficult mountainous areas for the Morse Brothers Land and Lumber Company. (Courtesy of David Greear.)

IMAGES
of America

HELEN

Chris Brooks and David Greear

ARCADIA
PUBLISHING

ISBN 978-0-7385-9197-1

Published by Arcadia Publishing
Charleston, South Carolina

Printed in the United States of America

Library of Congress Control Number: 2011945066

For all general information, please contact Arcadia Publishing:
Telephone 843-853-2070
Fax 843-853-0044
E-mail sales@arcadiapublishing.com
For customer service and orders:
Toll-Free 1-888-313-2665

Visit us on the Internet at www.arcadiapublishing.com

Contents

Acknowledgments 6

Introduction 7

1. Settlement: 1800–1900 9
2. A New Century: 1900–1932 27
3. Quieter Times: 1933–1969 55
4. Images of Tourism in Northeast Georgia: 1860–1969 81
5. Helen's Alpine Conversion: 1969–Present 95

Bibliography 127

Acknowledgments

The authors wish to thank the following individuals and organizations for their assistance in the research and production of this book. We are deeply indebted to Dr. Tom Lumsden for his advice and the use of his John Martin Photograph Collection as well as other local historians and authors: John Kollock, Shirley McDonald, Caroline Crittenden, Richard and Jimmie Tinnius, Bernd Nagy, Mike and Ann Banke, Dottie Jackson, Jerry Vandiver, Matt Gedney, the Helen Arts and Heritage Center, the Sautee Nacoochee Community Association, the White County Historical Society, and the archival collections of Western Carolina University.

We encourage readers who are interested in learning more about the history of Helen and White County, Georgia, to read the works of Garrison Baker, *In the Shadow of Yonah*; Matt Gedney, *Living on the Unicoi Road* and *Helen and Thereabouts*; Dr. Tom Lumsden, MD, *Nacoochee Valley, Its Times and Places*; Carroll Proctor Scruggs, *History of Helen, Nacoochee and Robertstown*; and Emory Jones, *Distant Voices—The Story of the Nacoochee Indian Mound.*

INTRODUCTION

Few visitors strolling through Helen today are aware of its dramatic history. Some are curious and ask about the origins of the alpine motif. But few would imagine the area as a lush riverside bottomland home to pioneer families and their crops and livestock, or imagine cannons of high-pressure water blasting hillsides away and the sound of stamp mills pounding ore continuously to release gold. Most are unaware of the profound imprint left by lumber industries that arrived, stripped acres of old-forest timber, then left scores of people without jobs. And most would hardly imagine the troubled times that prevailed for years when the mill quit the area. Helen's history and that of the surrounding areas begins with some of the earliest native hunter-gatherers in North America. They formed advanced native chiefdoms with monumental architecture and intensive agriculture. Included are stories from the Colonial period, where traders, settlers, and militia units first interacted and clashed with Cherokee towns and villages. Helen has experienced the passage of early pioneers traveling by wagon to settle in the fertile valleys, followed by the gold miners seeking their fortunes, then the lumber barons seeking theirs, and the dark days that followed. But the story of Helen is also a story of survival and rebirth, as this visual history shows.

Located in White County at the foot of the Blue Ridge Mountains, the town of Helen, Georgia, is approximately 90 miles north of Atlanta and 40 miles south of the North Carolina border. Using the pre-Columbian Mesoamerica scale, the first evidence of human habitation in the valleys dates from 10,000 through 2,000 BC—the Paleo-Indian through the Archaic era periods. During this time, agriculture and the first permanent settlements developed. Artifacts of the period indicate the development of stone grinding, drilling, and pottery. Stone spear points were fashioned to hunt large game. By the year 1,000, the Woodland era, native inhabitants had established rituals and ceremonies, various living structures, burial mounds, vast trading networks, and the bow and arrow. The Mississippian era peoples of the 1400s left the largest and best-known artifact, the Nacoochee Mound, which stands in a field at the southern entrance into the Helen Valley and has been a landmark for countless travelers, including the earliest European explorers to the area. During a time when many farmers would plow down mounds or haul off their rich soil, Capt. J.H. Nichols saw Nacoochee Mound as a historical feature to preserve, and he constructed a gazebo on the summit. While some objected to the structure, believing it a desecration, its presence nonetheless has preserved the mound for the last 130 years.

In 1813, the Unicoi Turnpike Company opened a vehicular toll road over part of an ancient trading path, connecting the coastal populations with the new settlements in eastern Tennessee. In operation by 1819, the road brought European American settlers into Georgia on the heels of the Georgia Land Lottery in 1820. In 1822, a party of 61 settlers from North Carolina came into the valleys along the upper Chattahoochee and began to plant corn, build houses, and establish legacies that endure to the present.

The town of Helen can trace its birth to 1911, when in Sikeston, Missouri, A.R. Byrd, the owner of 36,000 acres of virgin northeast Georgia timberland, met with C.D. Matthews to form a company that would become one of the largest band sawmills east of the Mississippi River. The Byrd-Matthews Lumber Company chose to locate their mill in the bottomland along the Chattahoochee River and set about establishing a company town to house and accommodate the workers. One of the partners, R.M. McCombs, named the town Helen, after his daughter.

The lumber company built a 37-mile standard-gauge railroad to connect the town and mill to the outside world. Beyond the mill, additional track was placed to haul logs from the woods to the mill. By March 1913, the Gainesville & Northwestern Railroad was complete from Gainesville to Helen, and the first shipment of finished lumber left Helen in January 1914. The lumber company had borrowed heavily to construct the mill, the town, and the railroad and used the timberland as collateral. The approach of World War I, falling lumber prices, and the loss of the anticipated workforce to the war effort forced Byrd to relinquish his interest to Matthews.

To salvage his investment, Matthews joined forces with Morse Brothers Land and Lumber Company, located just west of the Byrd-Matthews holdings. The Morse Brothers leaders were experienced mountain loggers, owned 18,000 acres, and had timber but had no mill or rail connection. They decided to replace Matthews's standard-gauge rails with 42-inch, narrow-gauge equipment and used machinery and methods modified for maneuvering logs through mountainous terrain. The Morse Brothers Land and Lumber Company operated profitably for 20 years, clearing nearly 56,000 acres, until most of the available lumber had been harvested. In 1931, the sawmill was closed, dismantled, and shipped to Mexico. Shortly thereafter, with the help of visionaries Charlie Maloof and Arthur Woody, the land harvested by the lumber companies became the core of the Chattahoochee National Forest.

When the mill left the town in 1931, many of the residents associated with the lumber business were also forced to leave Helen to find work elsewhere. The Depression had begun, and Helen went into a slow decline. A local resident converted the lumber mill's former brick powerhouse building into a small, hardwood-flooring mill. Helen also attracted two small textile industries, including one of the few argyle socks manufacturers in the United States. The railroad was abandoned after the lumber mill closed, but tourists still made the trek to the mountains, now by automobile. When the highways improved after World War II, and tourists could travel farther into the mountains, Helen became just a stopover for gasoline or a few groceries. Those who remember this difficult period also recall the remarkable sense of community that helped neighbors persevere. When someone needed help, everyone pitched in. It drew people closer. A spirit of trust and communion was pervasive, and nobody worried about locking their doors. It was peaceful.

In January 1969, three Helen businessmen, Jim Wilkins, Pete Hodkinson, and Bob Fowler, met at a local restaurant and began discussing the idea of refurbishing the town to entice tourists to stop on their way north to the mountains. Hodkinson consulted an acquaintance for ideas, artist John Kollock from Clarkesville, whose family had deep roots in the area. Agreeing to draw up some sketches, Kollock knew almost immediately what he would propose. When he had been stationed in the Army in Germany, he had become fascinated with the similarity between the Bavarian Mountains and those in North Georgia. There, he drew many sketches of alpine villages he saw, including detailed renderings of the trim, features, and colors used, believing the ebullient style was the perfect backdrop for tourists. "How great," he recalled, "if there could be some spot in our mountains that could reflect this image for the vacationer." Kollock's instincts proved auspicious. His resulting sketches were well received by Helen's citizens and merchants, and by the fall of 1969, Helen had reinvented itself. Many of the old buildings had been refashioned with alpine attitude, and the following leaf season brought new visitors as well as new merchants. Helen has not looked back. Over the next 40 years, the town grew dramatically, evolving new ventures, shops, and venues; some successful, some not. Helen's remarkable rebirth and success was wrought by the creativity and dash of its citizens, a spirit of local entrepreneurship, and a demonstration of civic cooperation that united a dying lumber town and became Georgia's third most visited city.

One

Settlement 1800–1900

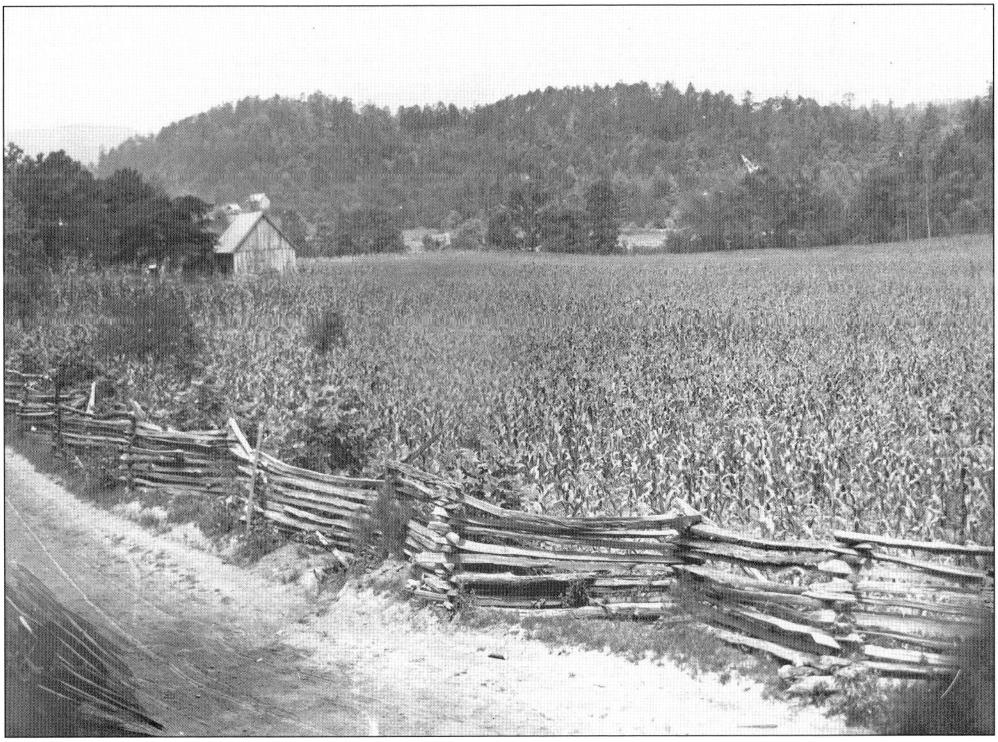

The first settlers in the Helen Valley were attracted by the rich bottom soil along the Chattahoochee River. Shown above is the Conley farm in the Helen Valley. In 1830, Henry Conley built a home on the site that would eventually become the Helen Station on the Gainesville & Northwestern Railroad. The cornfields are surrounded with high and strong split rail fencing to protect the crop against free ranging livestock, which dates this Martin collection photograph to the years before Georgia passed a fence law.

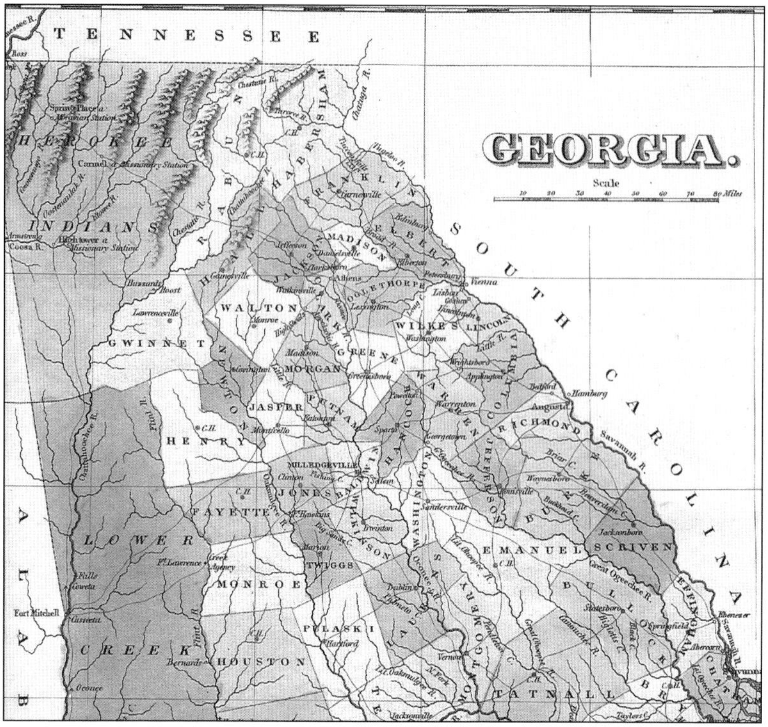

In the early 1800s, the State of Georgia began to distribute land through a lottery system. Surveyed lots varied in size. The lottery encouraged small farmers to migrate into the state. Maps of that time show the western progress of the border as the Creek and Cherokee leaders ceded land to the state. Land was surveyed into 202.5-acre lots.

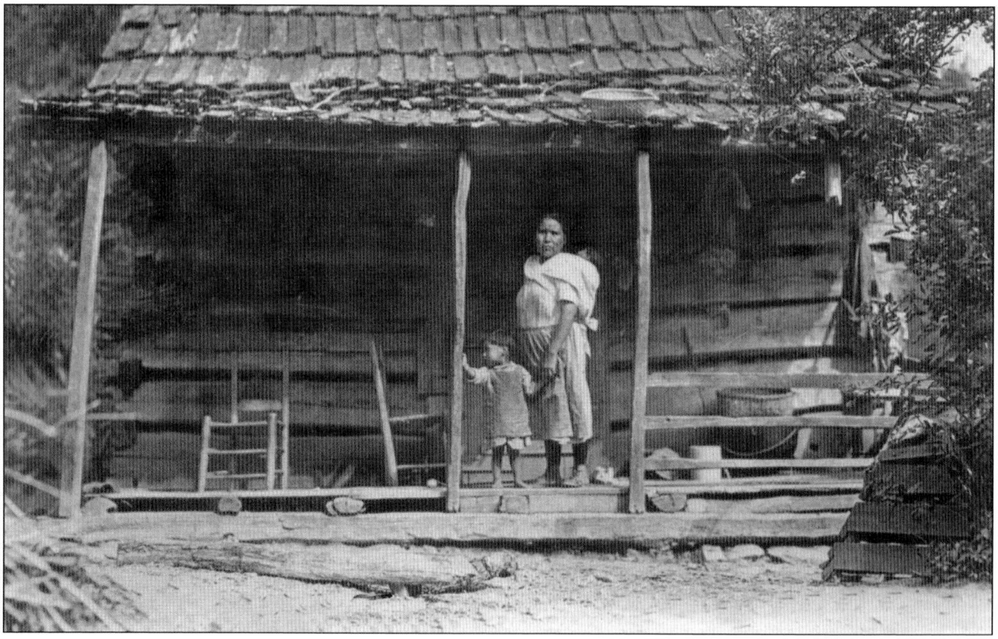

Before European American settlers arrived, native groups inhabited the area as far back as the Paleo-Indian period, which began about 10,000 BC. When European settlements first began, around 1820, most Cherokee communities had already been pushed to western parts of Georgia. When gold was discovered in 1828 and Andrew Jackson was elected president, western lands were annexed into Georgia, and laws criminalizing native resistance to property seizure were enacted. The Cherokee people were forced to leave all of North Georgia.

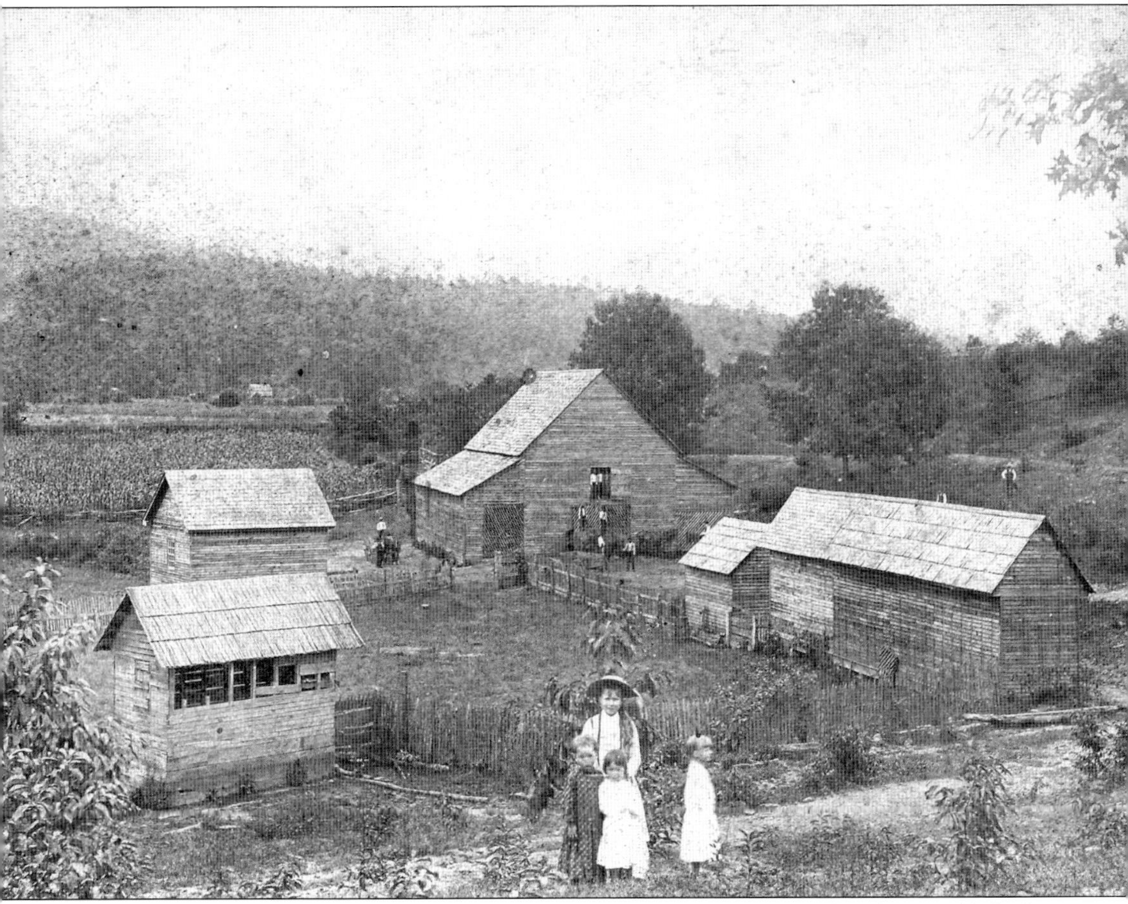

When the first land lottery winners settled the area around Nacoochee and Helen, they established farms. This c. 1855 view, facing north toward the Sautee Valley, shows the outbuildings and barnyard of the Williams-Johnston house and the agricultural heart of a wealthy valley farm. The roofs have different shingle styles: the placement of long shingles in vertical rows was a German convention. Most buildings in the valleys used alternating, overlapping, English-style shingle roofs. The Williams-Johnston house faced the Unicoi Turnpike (now Georgia Highway 17), a toll road operated by a private company. Opened around 1819, the road crossed through Cherokee territory and served as a trade route from the upper Savannah River watershed to eastern Tennessee.

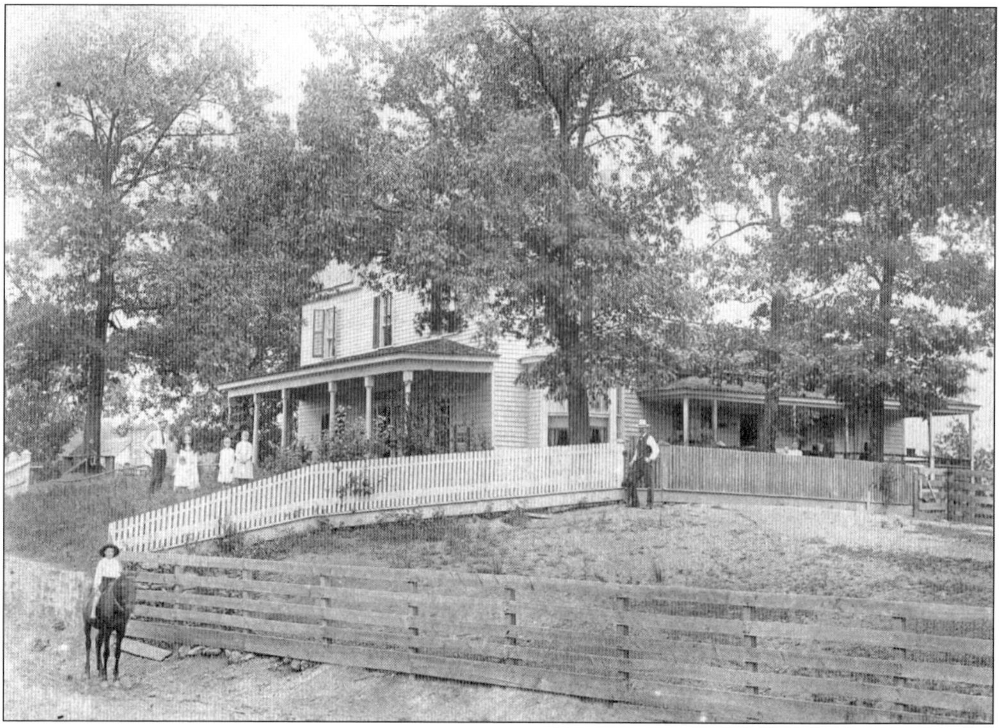

The Williams-Johnston house is seen above. The earliest settlers in the Helen and Nacoochee Valleys came in via the Unicoi Turnpike. These settlers were Georgia land-lottery winners from western North Carolina. The turnpike, initially established to facilitate trade, became the pipeline for new settlement into the region.

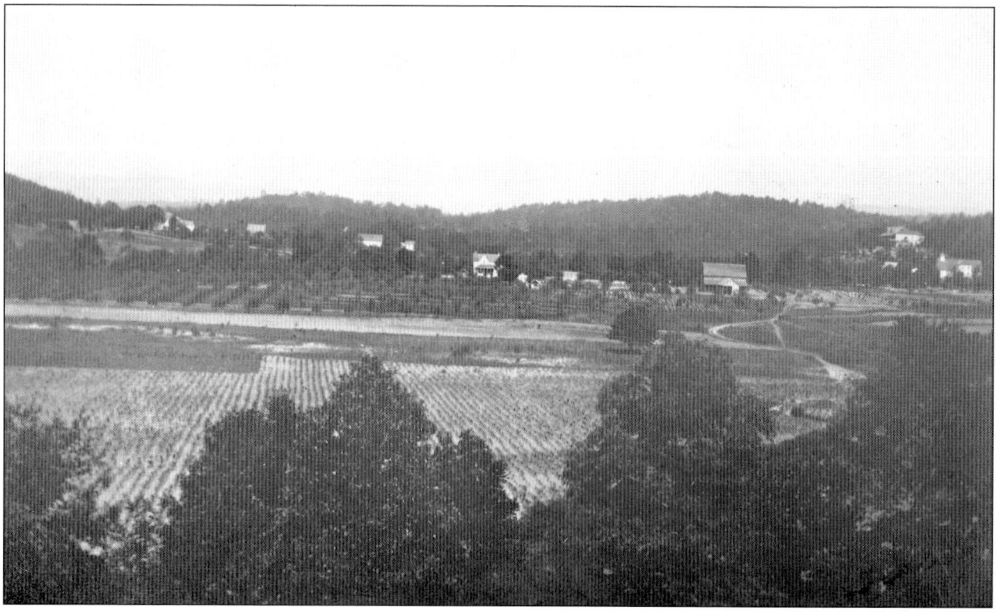

This image shows the densely settled north rim of the Nacoochee Valley with houses and farm structures lining the Unicoi Turnpike. Row crops of corn cover the rich bottomland along the Chattahoochee River.

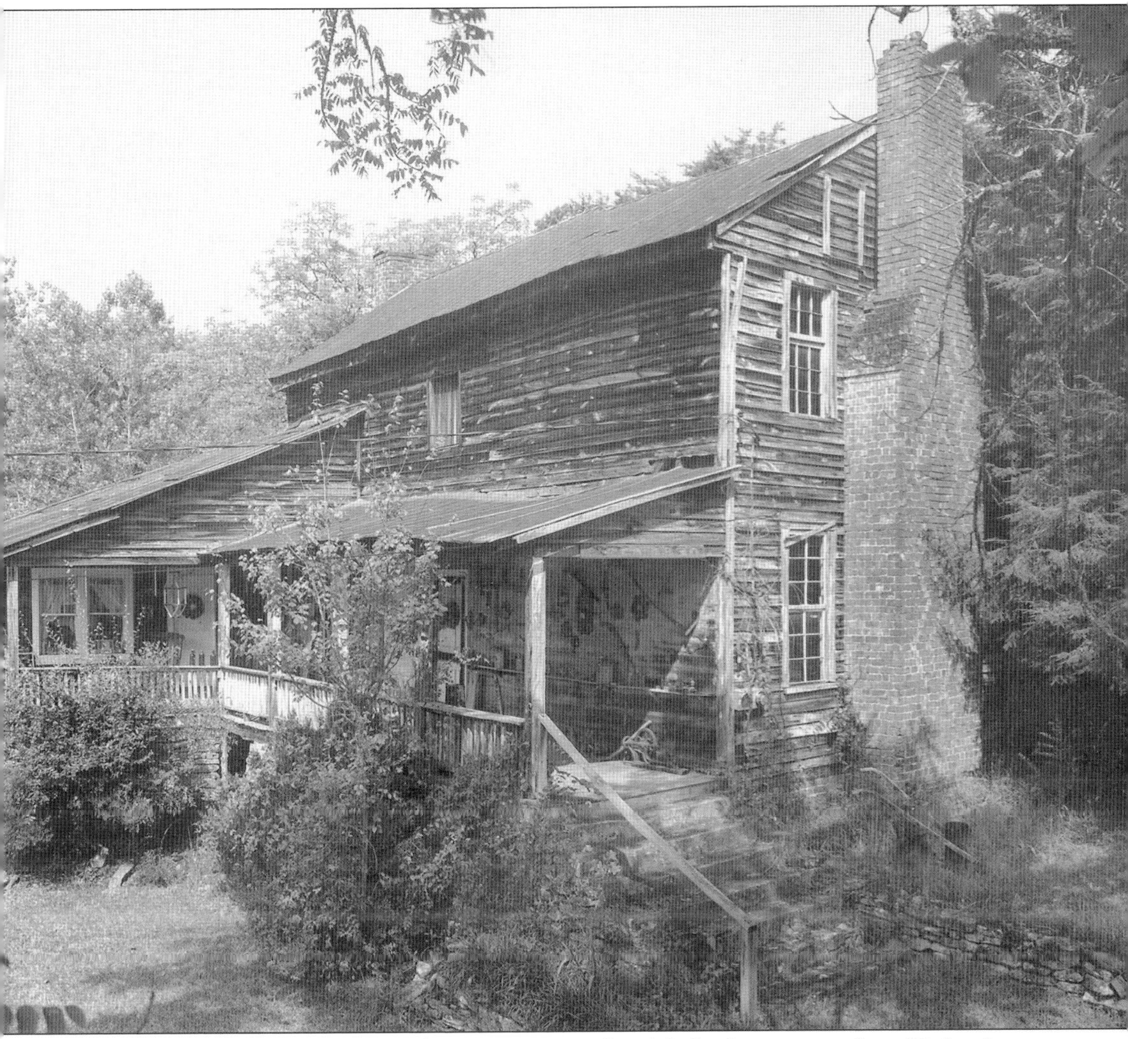

One of the earliest settlers in Nacoochee was circuit-riding Methodist minister Jesse Richardson, who built this home about 1830 near Dukes Creek in the Nacoochee Valley. The plantation house was built with sash-sawn lumber and has more in common with Piedmont farmhouses than the hewn log homes of the mountains. Known today as the Richardson-Lumsden house, it is one of the oldest houses in White County.

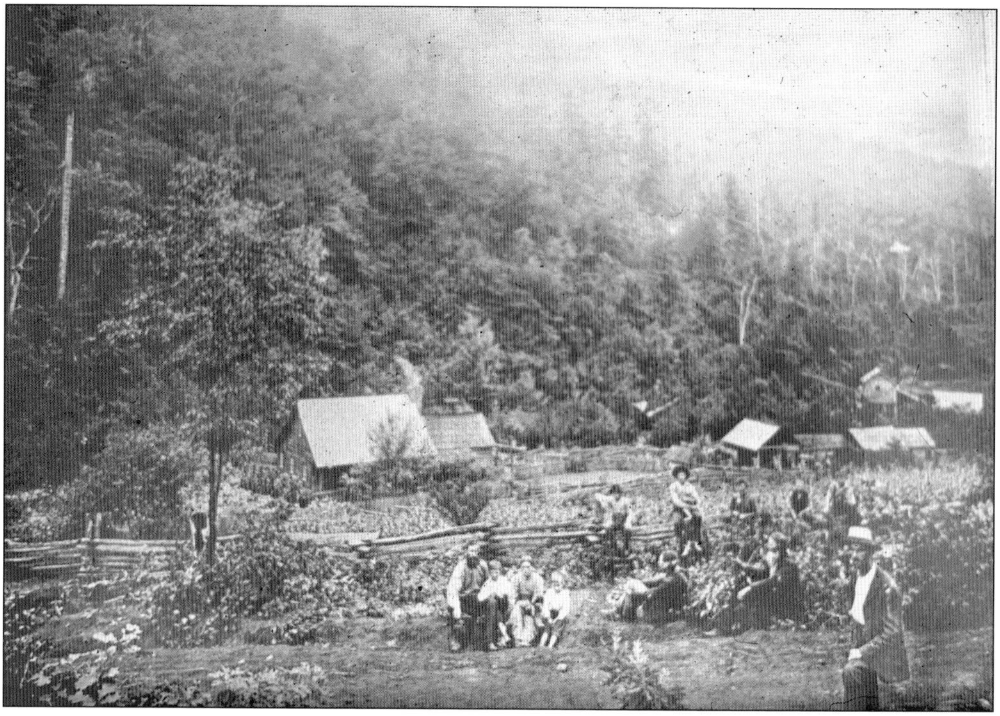

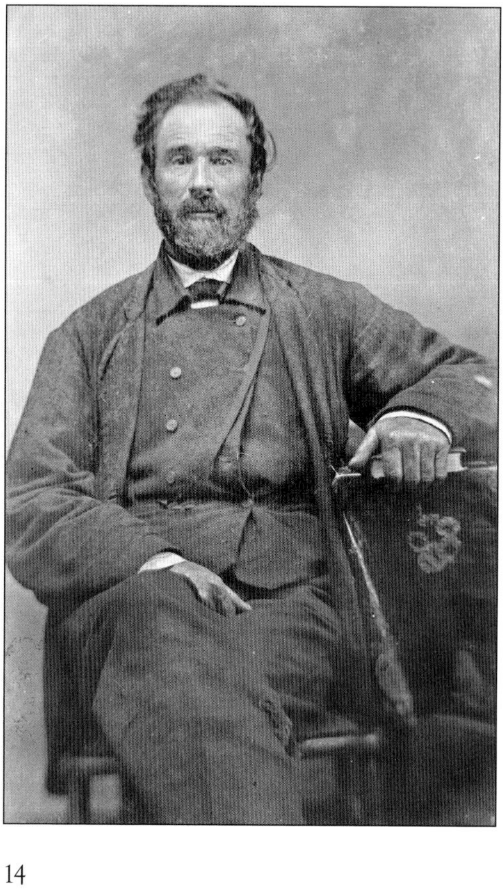

Settlers established homesteads along and around the Unicoi Turnpike. In 1822, family names like Pitner, England, Bell, Conley, Brown, Williams, Trammel, Richardson, Abernathy, Stovall, Coker, Mauldin, Sosebee, and Littlejohn were common in the area. These families, among others, were in a group of 61 families who migrated into Georgia from Burke and Rutherford Counties in North Carolina.

E.P. Williams, son of some of the first settlers in the Nacoochee Valley, was a wealthy landowner and slaveholder. Williams was given the contract for constructing the White County Courthouse in 1857, when the county was formed from Habersham County. His slaves made the brick and built the courthouse, which is preserved today in the Cleveland, Georgia, square.

Gold was discovered in Dukes Creek in 1828, and by 1830, hundreds of miners had come into the valleys. This image shows an early water-powered stamp mill on Dukes Creek. Using the power of the falling water, the overshot wheel turned a wooden camshaft that raised the heavy iron stamps then dropped them onto ore-bearing rock. The crushed ore was then washed to recover embedded gold.

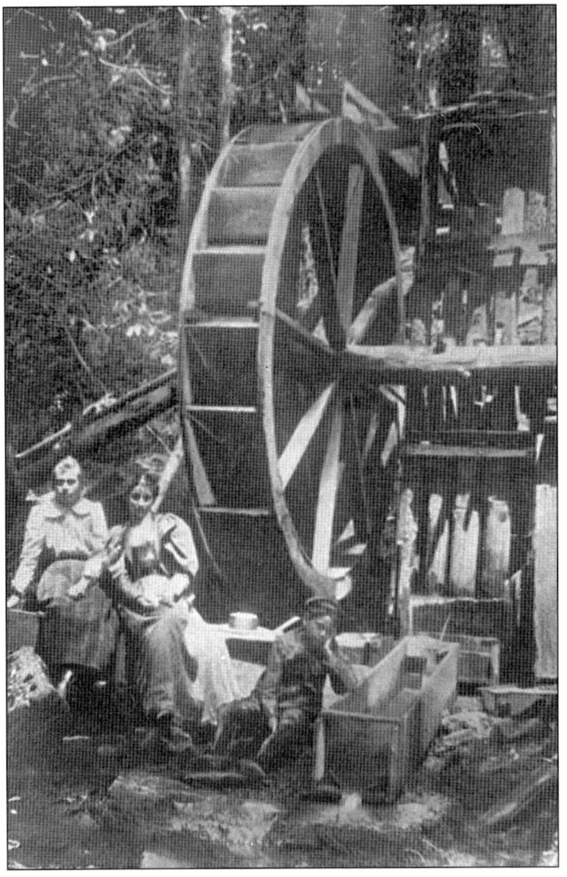

Hoping to find his fortune in the newly discovered gold region, John Humphries purchased land in the lower Helen Valley from early settler Richard England in 1830. After some initial success with his placer mining efforts, Humphries switched over to hardrock mining. But the operation proved costly and lasted only a few years. By 1850, most of the easily accessed surface gold was gone, and mining in the Helen area slowed. Richer discoveries around Dahlonega, Georgia, and California drew gold-mining operations elsewhere. Shortly after the Civil War, there was a resurgence in mining.

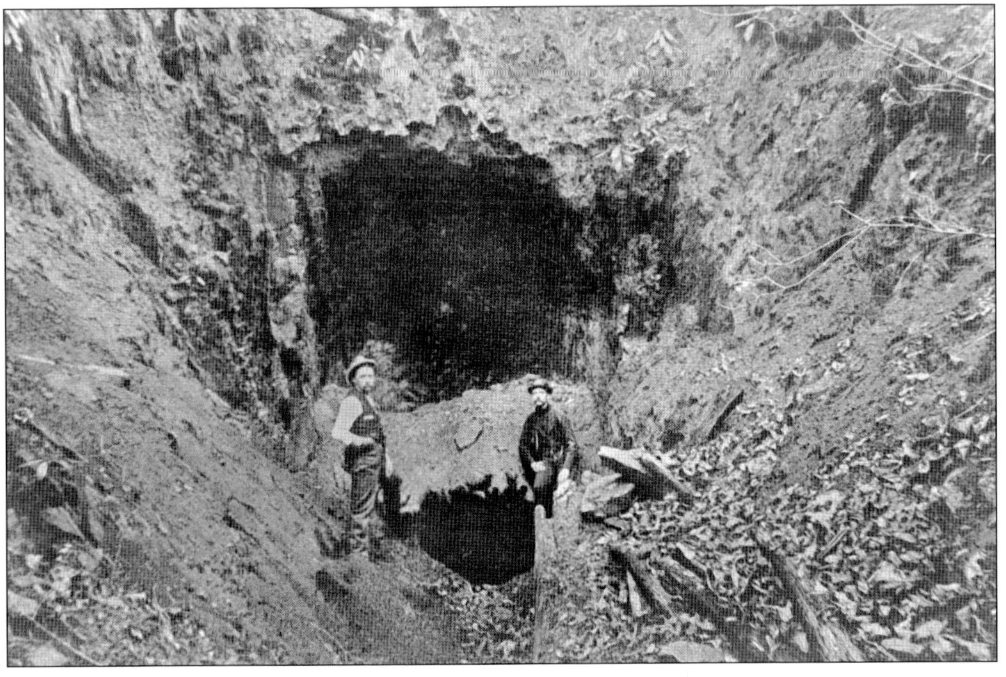

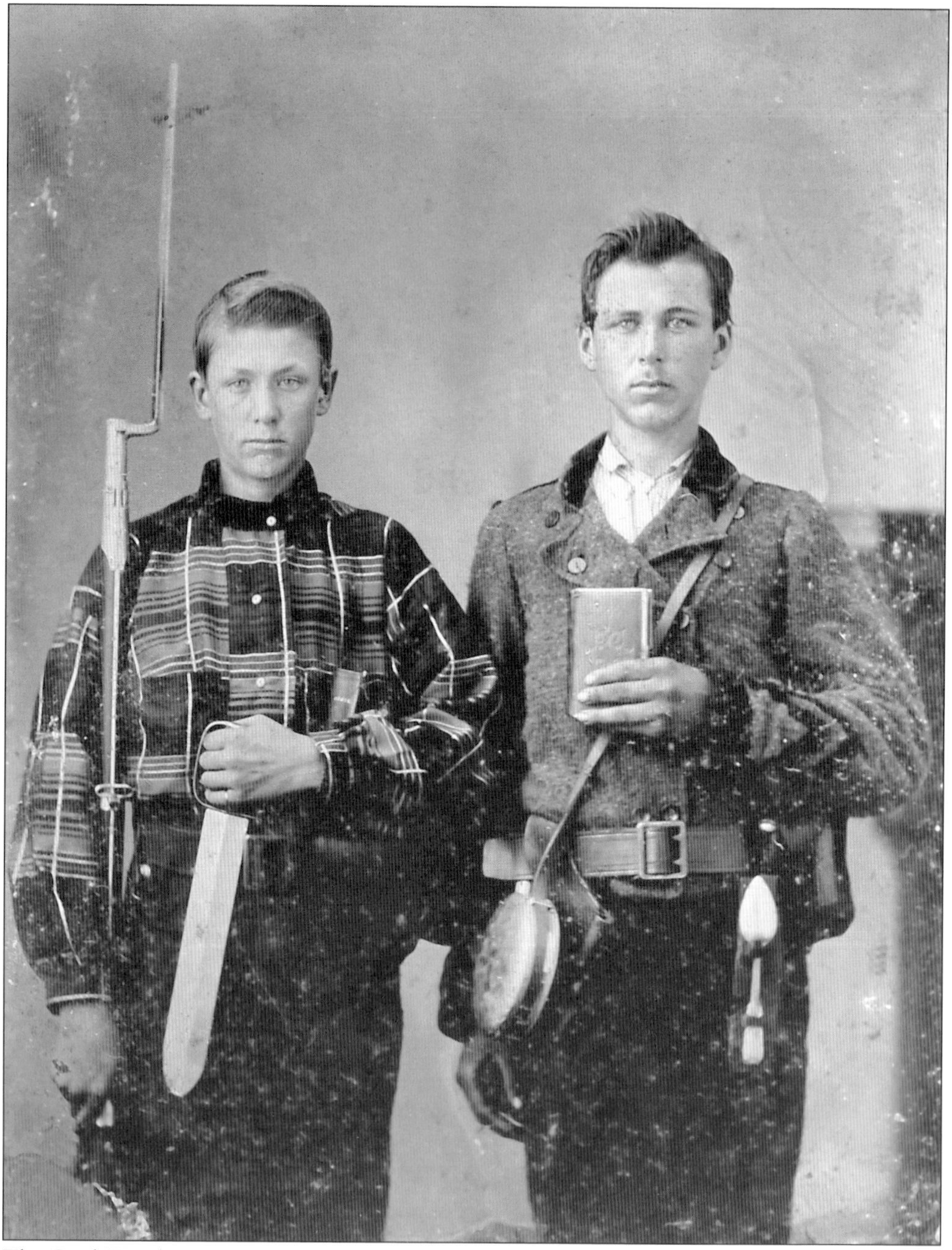

The Civil War drew many young men from farms and mining camps in northeast Georgia. This photograph of Jesse (left) and John (right) Lumsden, still attired as civilians, was taken the day before they left White County to enlist. The family operated an iron mine in the Mossy Creek area of the county until Jesse departed. He was 16.

Capt. J.H. Nichols built a home he called West End, which is now known as the Nichols-Hardman farm. Nichols was a wealthy Civil War veteran who bought several thousand acres in the Helen vicinity and Nacoochee Valley. Nichols's property extended up Smith Creek, and he is credited with discovering the high falls on the creek. He named the falls after his daughter Anna Ruby.

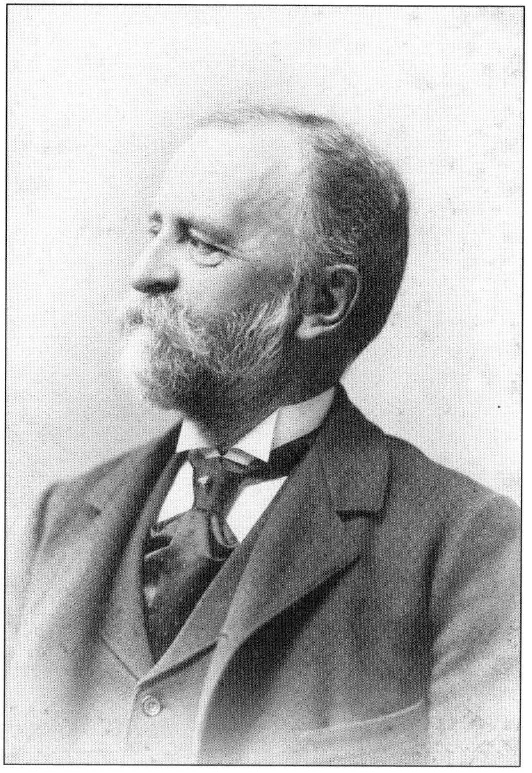

Known as West End, this fine Italianate-style farmhouse was built by Capt. J.H. Nichols. After the Civil War, Nichols, along with his wife and daughter, moved from Georgia's antebellum capital, Milledgeville, to the Nacoochee Valley. Nichols arrived a war-weary veteran seeking respite for his family after having suffered during Sherman's march to the sea. West End is now called the Nichols-Hardman house and is scheduled to become a state-operated historic site.

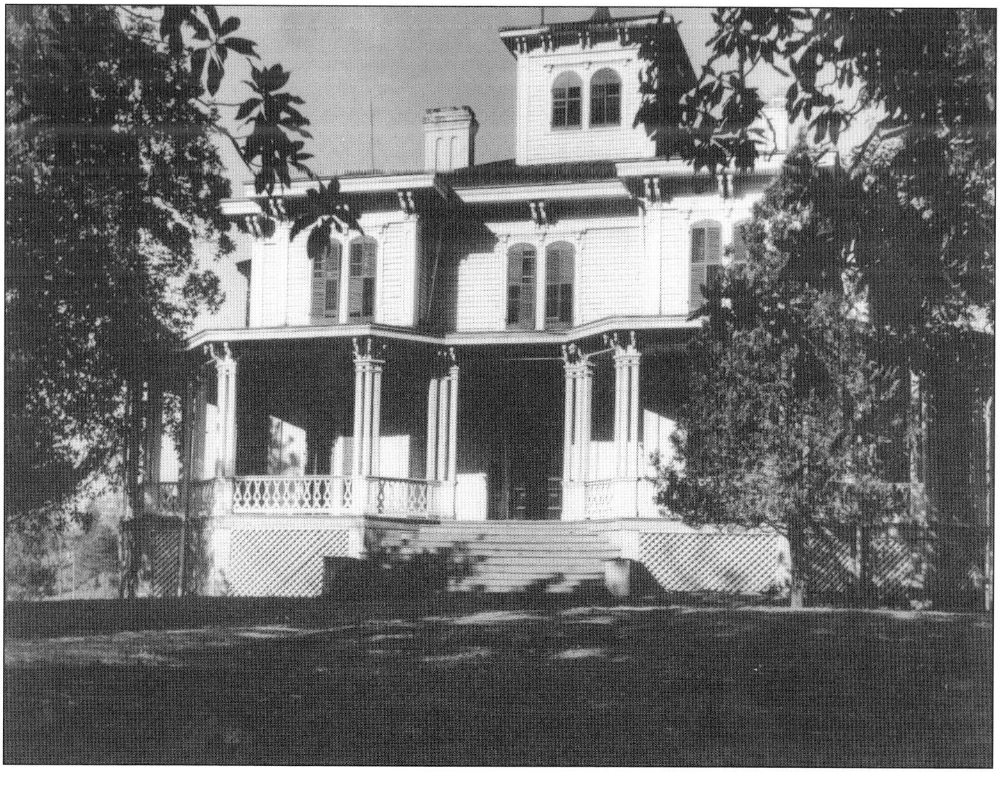

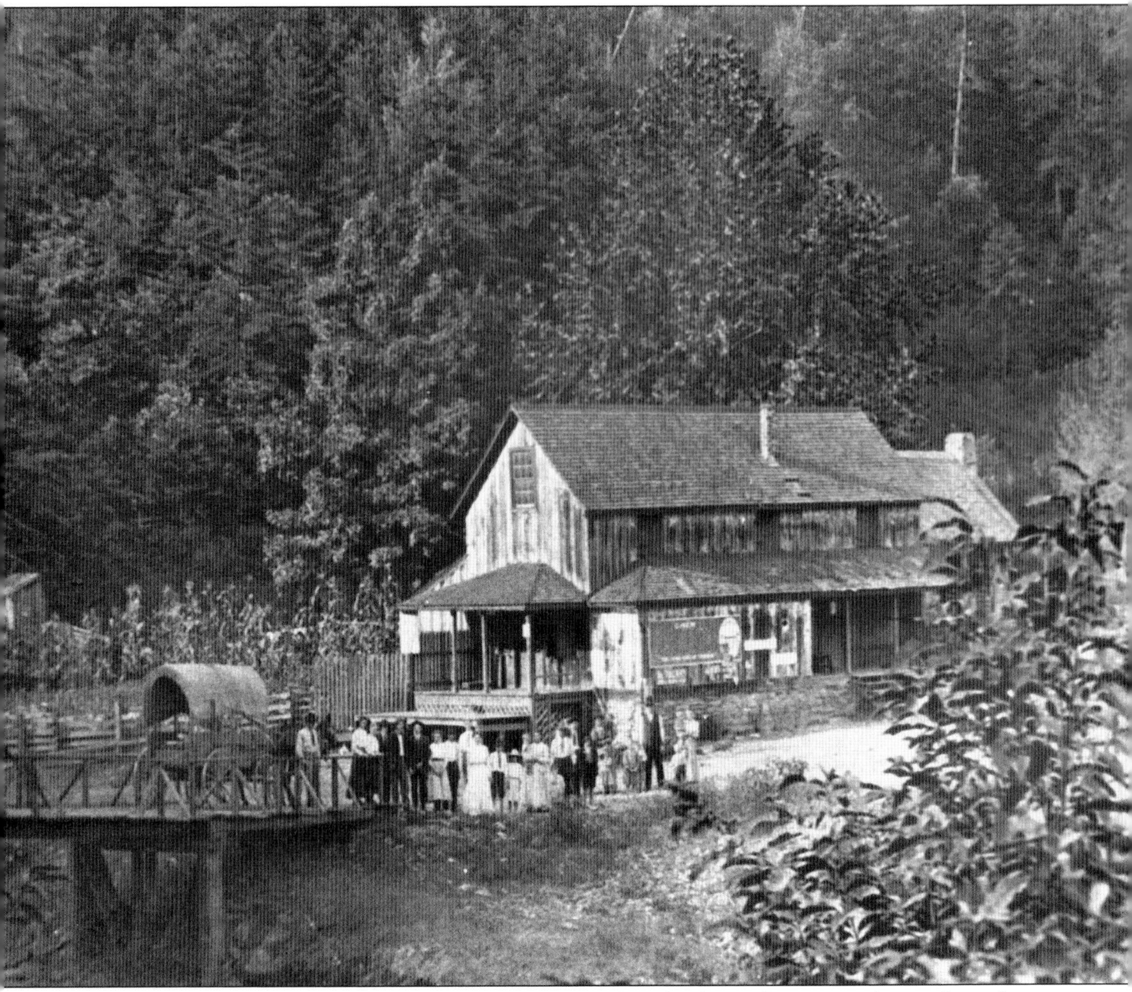

Roberts's Store, pictured above, originally owned by Charles Roberts, was located on the upper end of what is now Robertstown. Roberts, a well-to-do Englishman, acquired considerable acreage around 1890, and Robertstown was named for him. With the old Unicoi Road underused and in disrepair, Roberts constructed a new road, bypassing Unicoi Gap by way of Indian Grave Gap, and was granted permission by the general assembly to charge a toll. Roberts also engaged in gold mining and owned a winery and greenhouses.

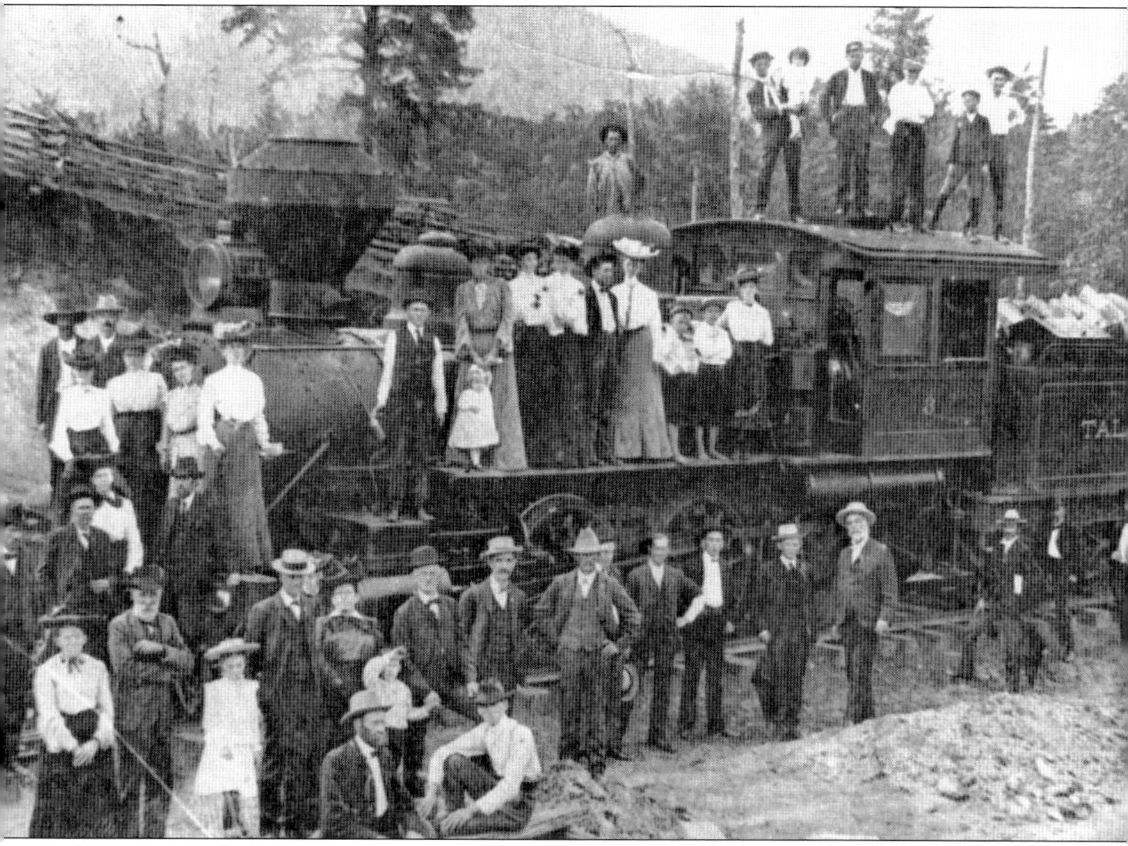

In 1856, the North Eastern Railroad was chartered by the State of Georgia to link the towns of Athens and Clayton. The Civil War delayed construction until 1871, but by 1882, the line to Tallulah Falls was complete. By 1904, the line reached Clayton. Eventually, the line between Cornelia and Clayton became the Tallulah Falls Railway Company. Providing passenger rail service to northeast Georgia, the Tallulah Falls Railway predated the Gainesville & Northwestern that served Helen by more than 25 years, but the Tallulah line was a vital link to the area for those who later would bring development to the Helen Valley.

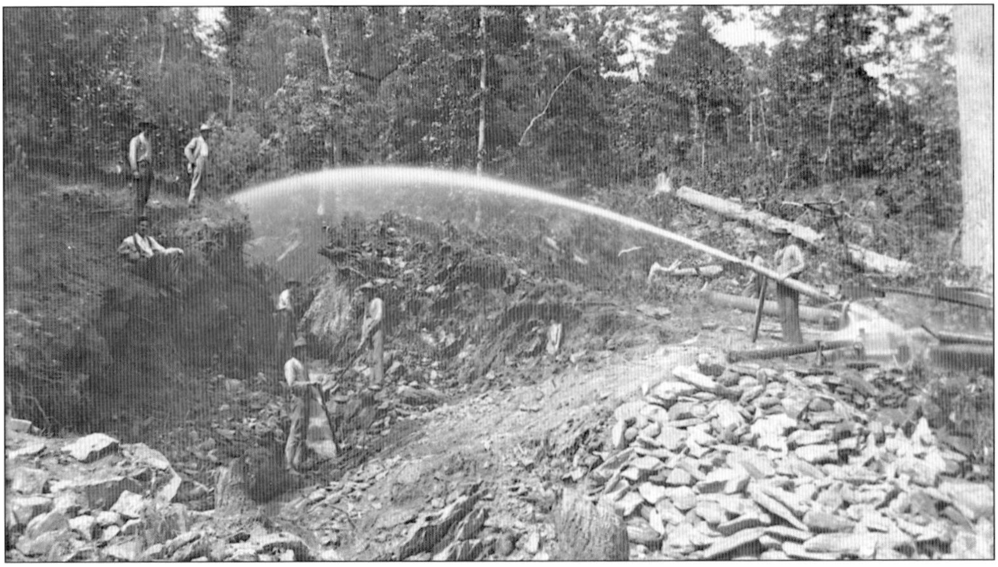

In the 1850s, J.R. Dean had built a water diversion system to aid in his gold-mining operations. Beginning at the base of Dukes Creek Falls and following the ridges into Helen, Dean built a series of ditches and flumes to power pressurized water cannons that were used to expose the gold-rich ore. About 1878, John Martin rebuilt and added to the Hamby Ditch. Water cannons like Little Giant, shown here, washed away entire hillsides to expose the ore.

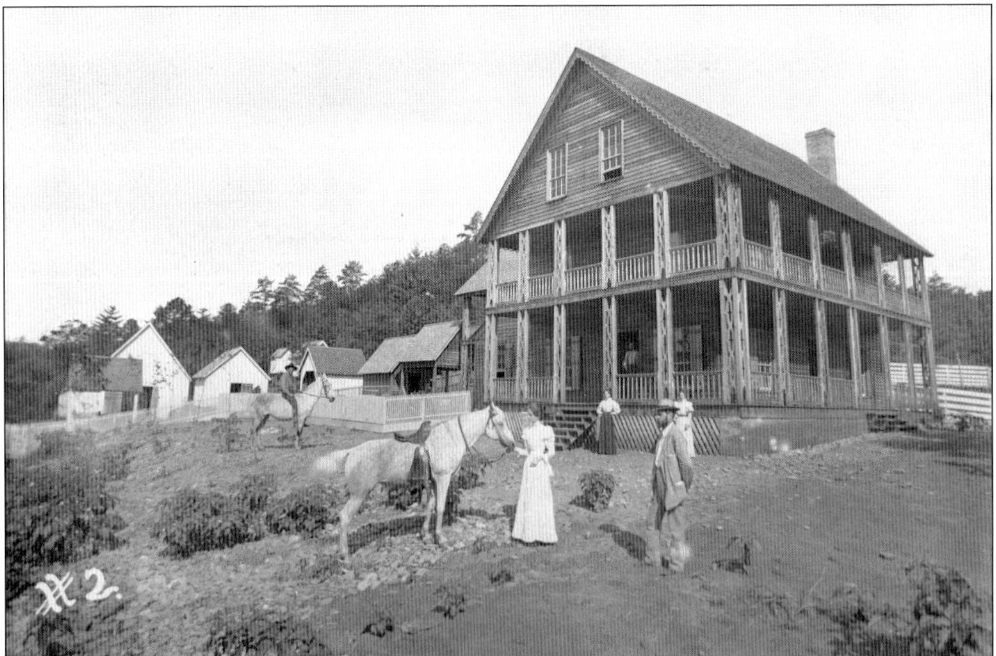

In 1876, Scottish-born John Martin acquired large land holdings in northern White County and began gold-mining operations. He built this home at the western end of the Nacoochee Valley. Using this structure as both his home and headquarters, Martin managed his vast holdings and operations for about 25 years. The structure stands to this day and operates as Nacoochee Antiques in Nacoochee Village.

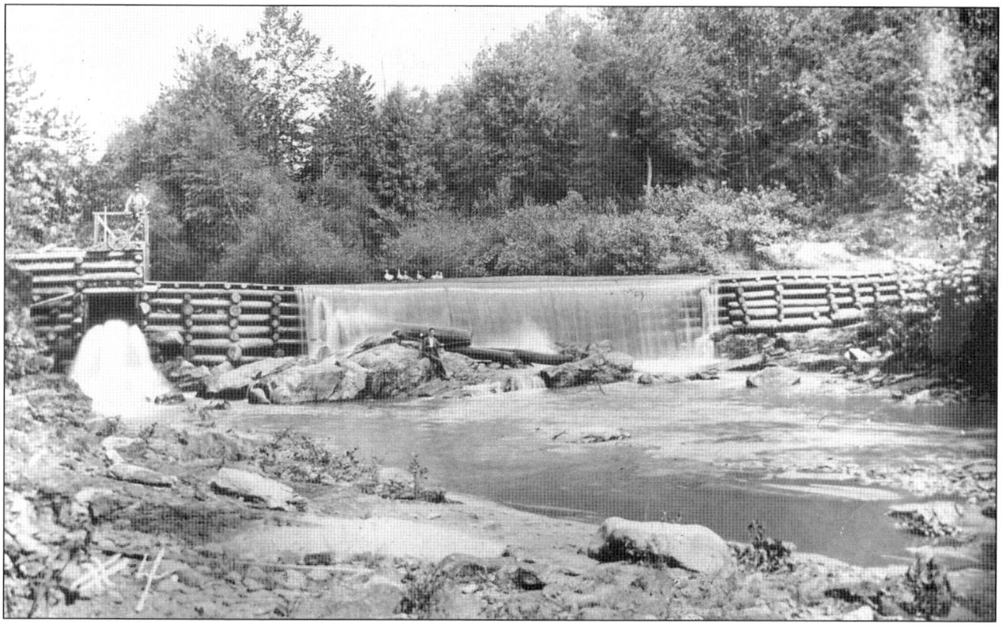

Nora Mill has been operated as a gristmill and sawmill since it was originally constructed by early pioneer Daniel Brown in 1824. The mill was purchased by John Martin in 1876 and then sold to Dr. Lamartine G. Hardman in 1902. Hardman renamed the mill in memory of his sister Nora. The mill is still in operation. The 100-foot wood raceway feeds water to the turbine that turns the 1,500-pound French burr millstone.

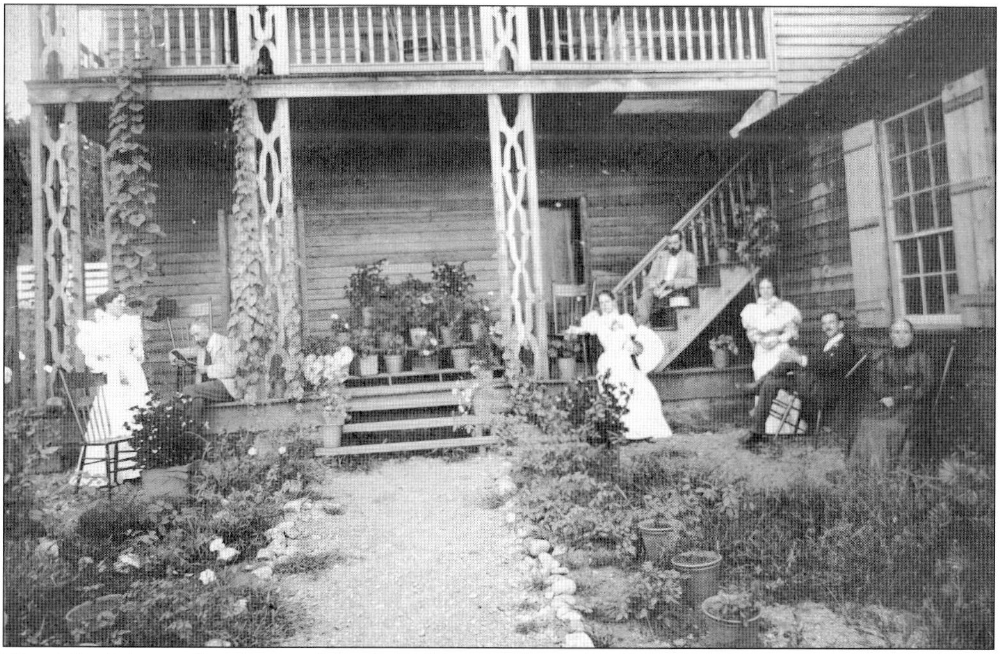

The John Martin family posed for this photograph on the back porch of their Victorian home. Martin's property holdings and gold-mining concerns made him a wealthy man. The women of the family wore fashionable dresses and enjoyed considerable leisure time, judging by the flowers and formal dooryard garden.

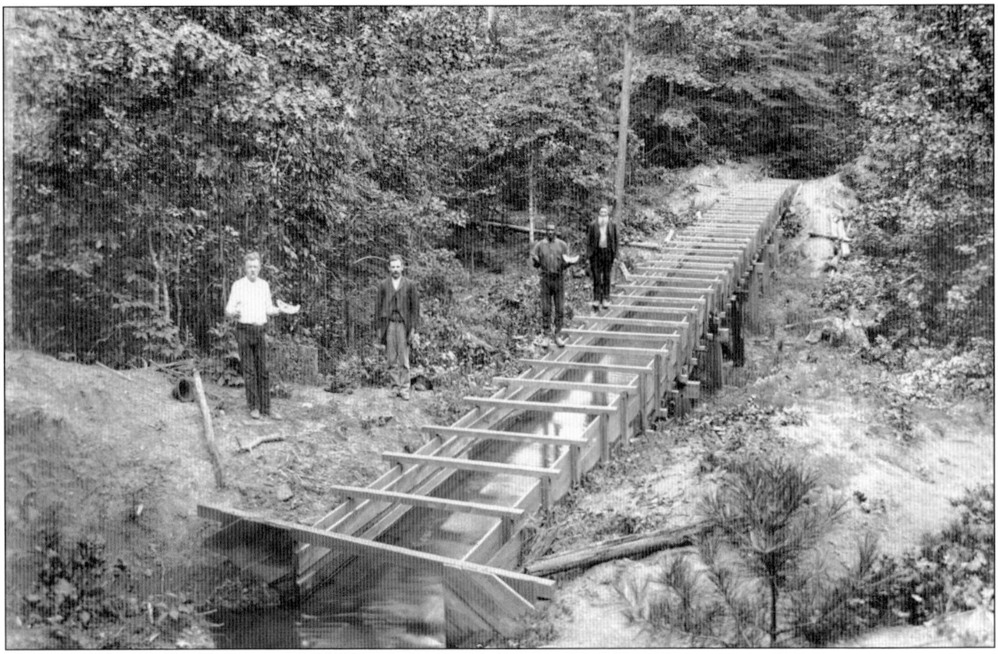

John Martin is said to have spent $50,000 reviving and enlarging Hamby Ditch. At its peak around 1885, the ditch ran for over eight miles, from the base of Dukes Creek Falls to the Helen Valley. In some sections, the ditch was simply a dug-out trough. In other areas, wood flumes were built to span gaps and hollows along the route.

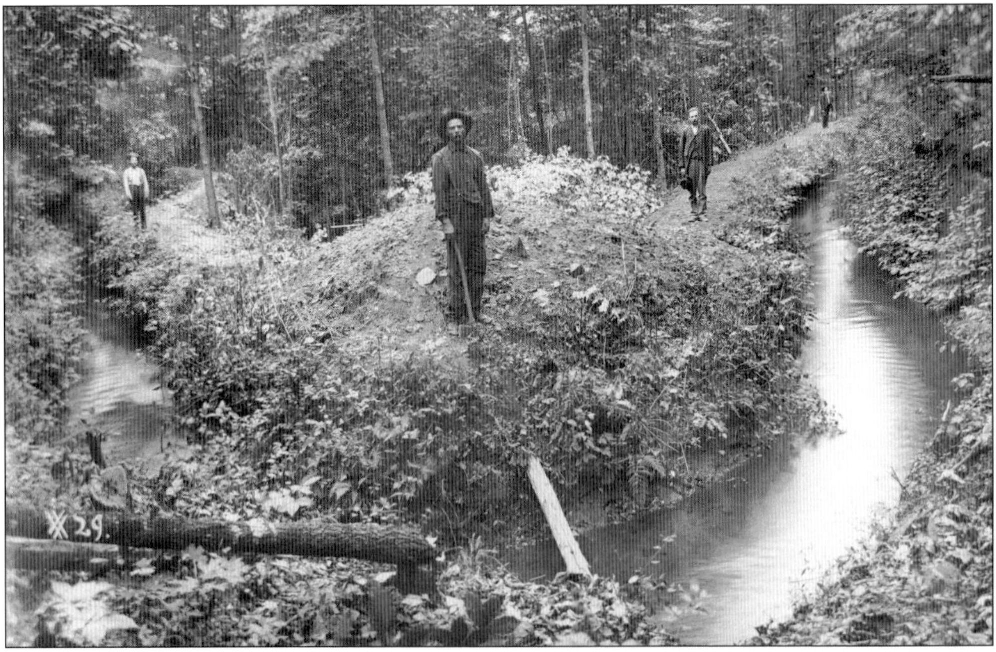

The Hamby Ditch required constant maintenance and upkeep. Workers had to walk along the route and clear fallen trees and remove debris to keep the water flowing. Double bit axes and crosscut handsaws were the tools of the trade for the ditch walkers. Undoubtedly, beyond fallen trees, other obstacles they encountered included mud slides, floods, snakes, and bears.

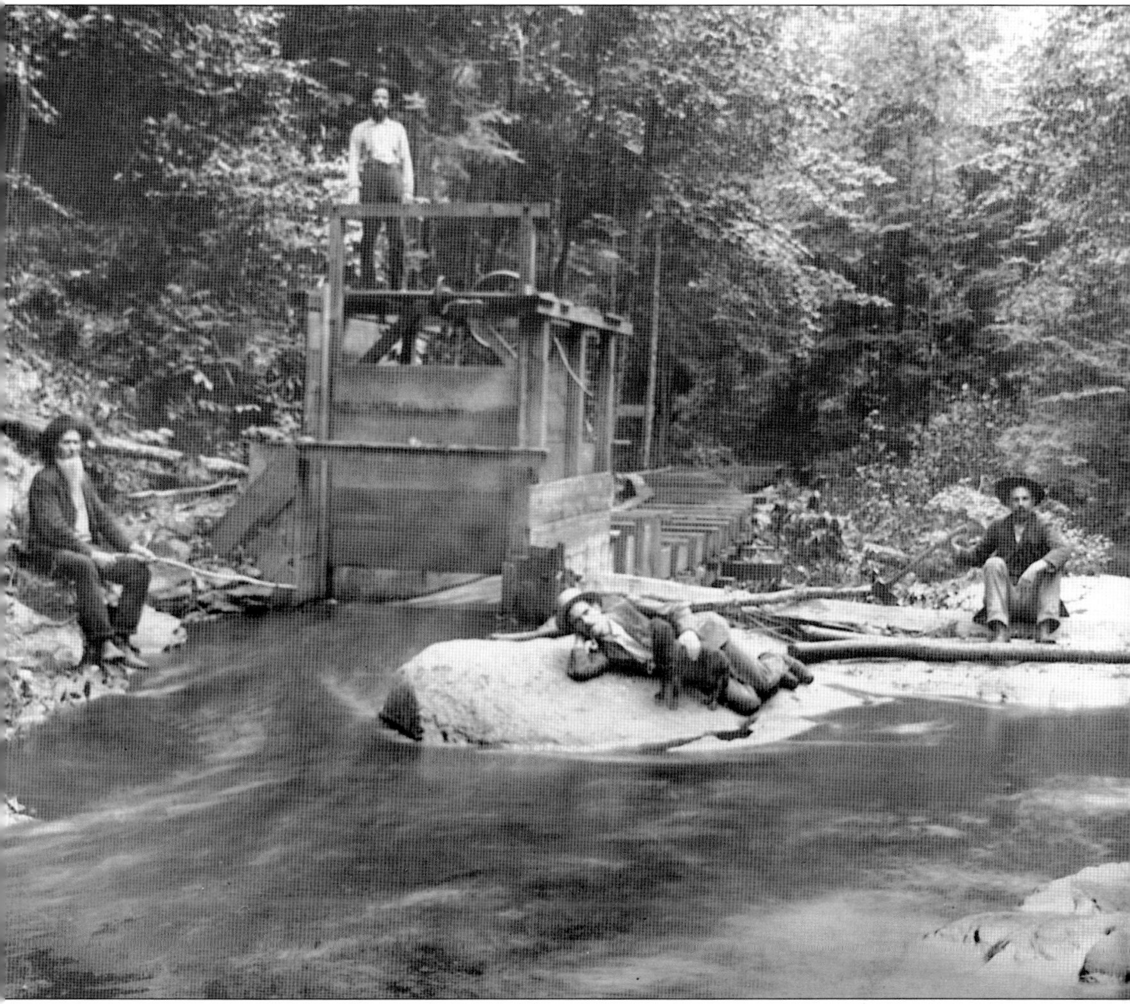

About 1895, John Martin commissioned a photographer to document his gold-mining operations. His remarkable collection of images is a true window into what it must have been like to live and work during that era. This image of the inlet of the Hamby Ditch, just below Dukes Creek Falls, depicts what more than likely was a rare occurrence: creek-side rest and relaxation. Today, visitors to Helen can walk to the falls just off the Richard B. Russell Scenic Highway.

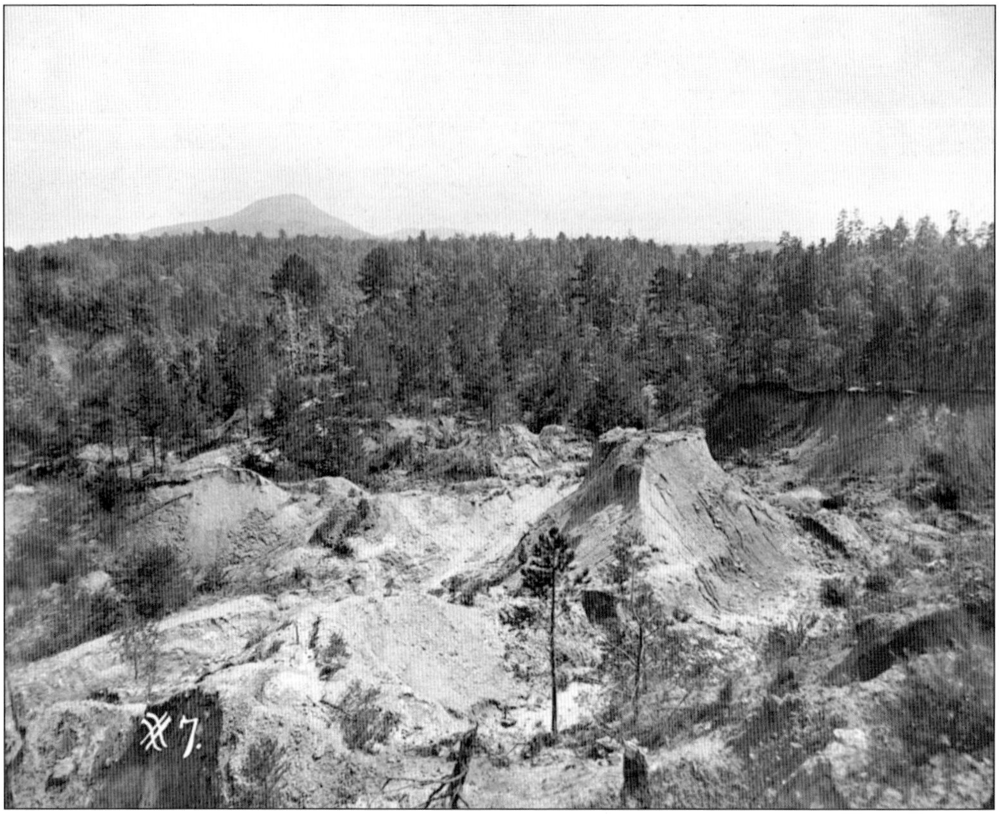

The use of high-pressure water cannons to wash away topsoil and expose ore-bearing rock was destructive to fragile mountain topography. Early filmmakers used these old mining landscapes as settings for westerns. Over time, the plant life has recovered, but evidence of hydraulic mining can still be seen in the Helen vicinity today.

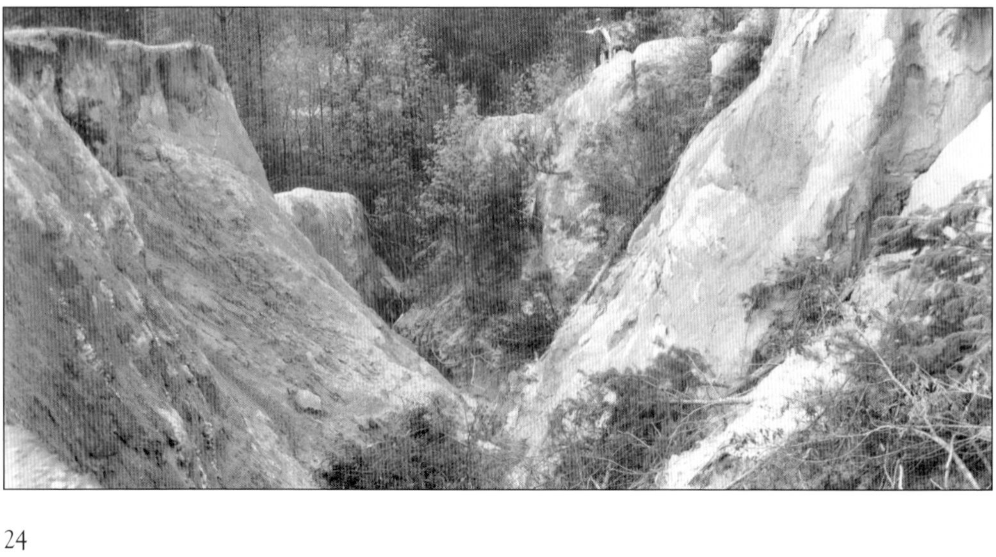

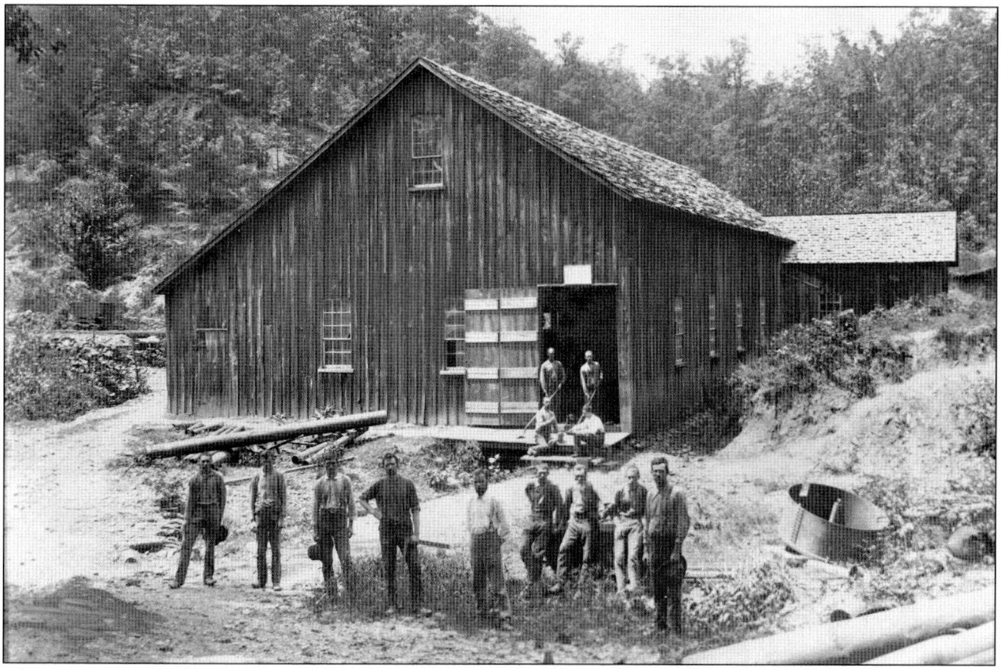

This stamp mill received ore from the Reynolds vein through a sluice. The cart at the left corner of the building brought the ore from the sluice to the mill. Stamp mills were used to crush the ore-bearing rock. This was the first step in extracting the gold from the ore.

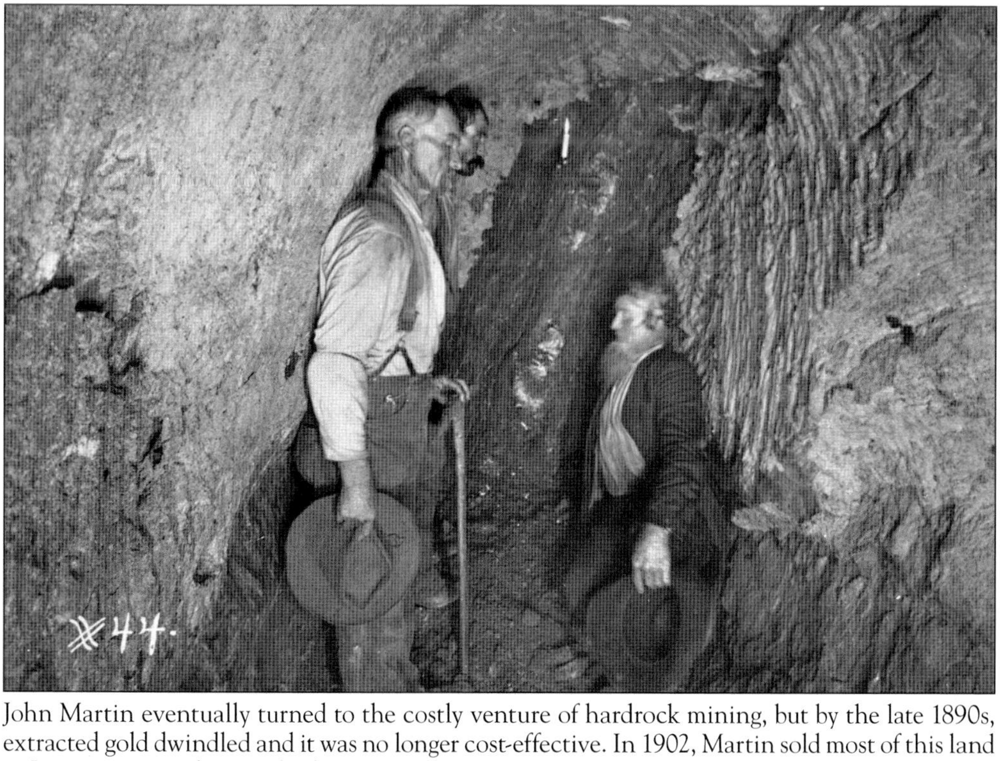

John Martin eventually turned to the costly venture of hardrock mining, but by the late 1890s, extracted gold dwindled and it was no longer cost-effective. In 1902, Martin sold most of this land to Lamartine Hardman, who later served as governor of Georgia from 1927 to 1931.

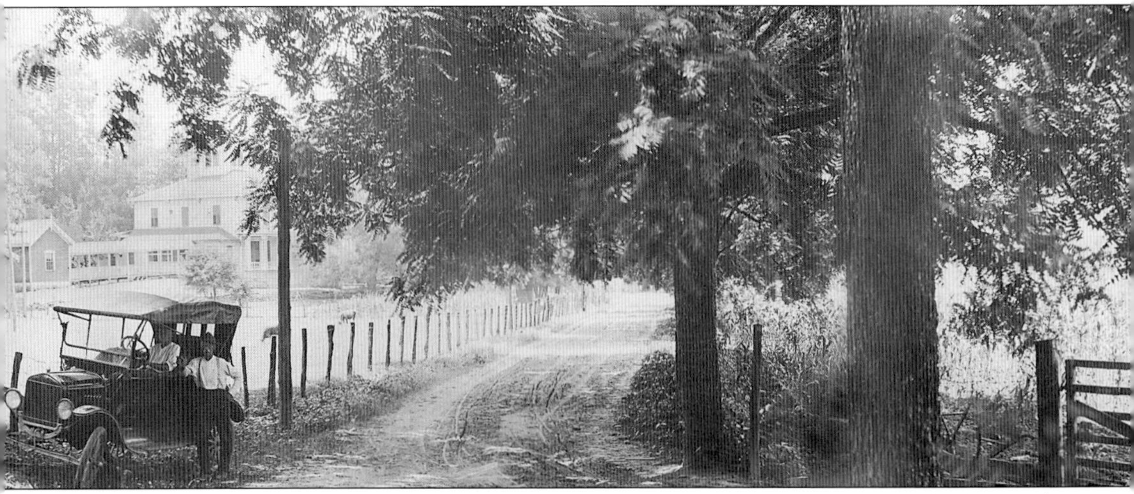

In this early-20th-century view of the Unicoi Turnpike, an automobile has stopped by the Hardman farm. What was first tread upon at least 12,000 years ago by ancient food-foraging wildlife—then became for centuries a native footpath and realm, then for 100 years guided the way of countless settlers starting a new civilization, and then led miners to fortune or ruin—has mellowed here to an unassuming, sun-dappled country road. The Helen and Nacoochee Valleys were close-knit communities, with most inhabitants related to the original settlers from the 1830s. Few of the residents at that time could have imagined the changes about to occur.

Two

A New Century 1900–1932

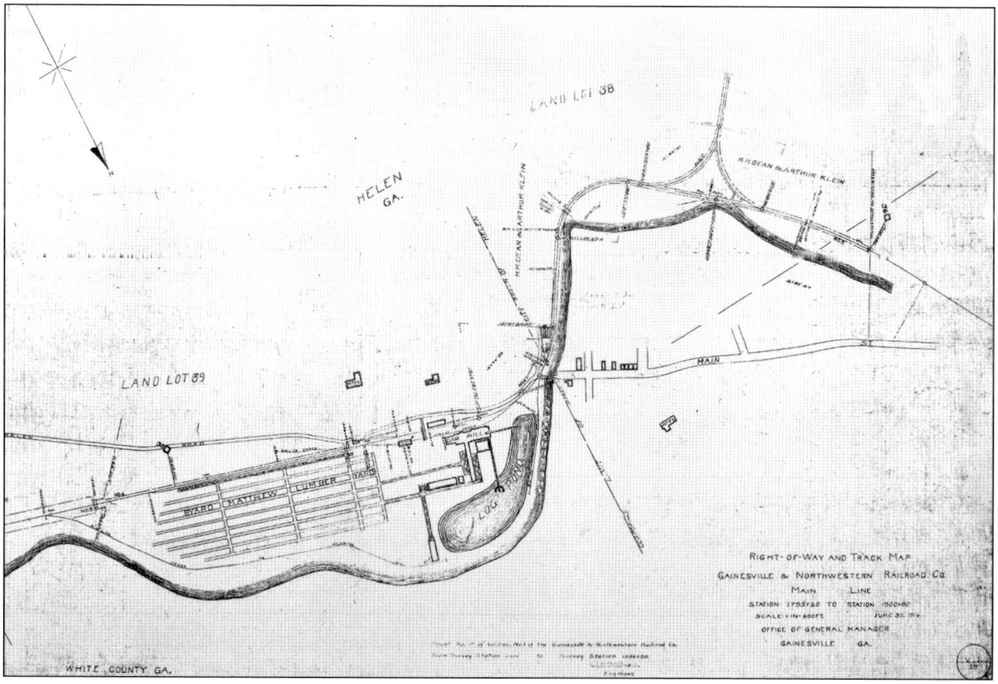

The new century had huge changes in store for Helen. While not yet named, the Helen Valley was settled and well inhabited. Some residents were descendants from the original land lottery winners, others were kin to the miners drawn to the area by two recent gold rushes. But development of the area was not fully realized until the arrival of what was to have the biggest impact on the area since the Cherokee Nation was forced out in the 1830s: the huge industrial complex called the Byrd-Matthews Lumber Company.

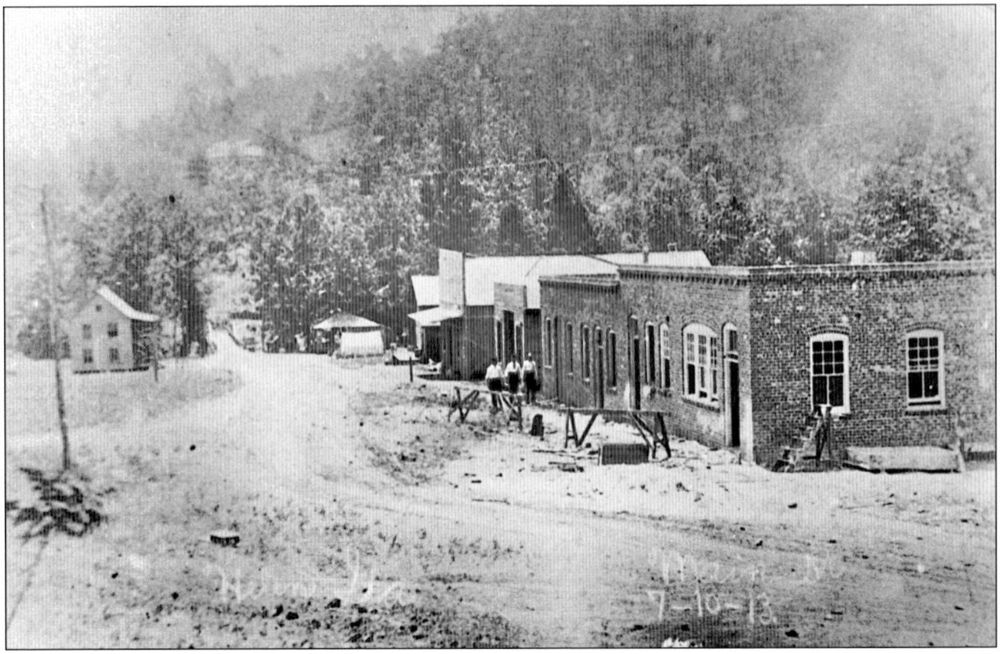

Dated July 7, 1913, this is one of the earliest photographs of downtown Helen. John Mitchell, more than even the Byrd-Matthews Company, was pivotal in developing both Helen and Robertstown. Mitchell developed and offered lots for sale in both townships; Byrd-Matthews concentrated on their sawmill and railroad operations.

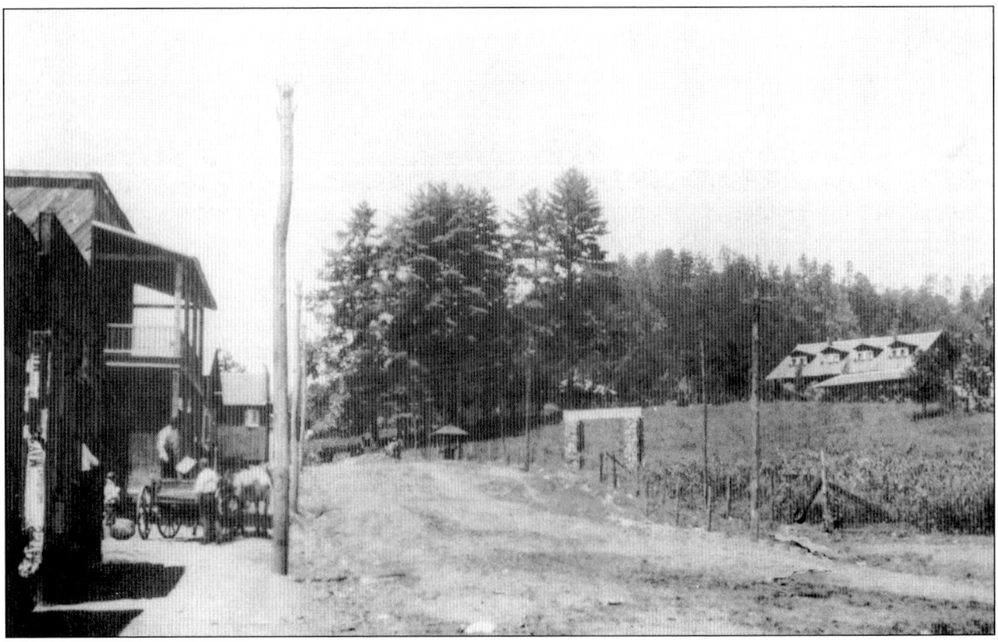

John Mitchell had built the Mitchell Mountain Ranch Hotel on a hilltop across the river from the Byrd-Matthews mill. Access to Mitchell's property from the mill site was initially by a ford across the Chattahoochee River, just past the mill. A steel bridge was added by 1914.

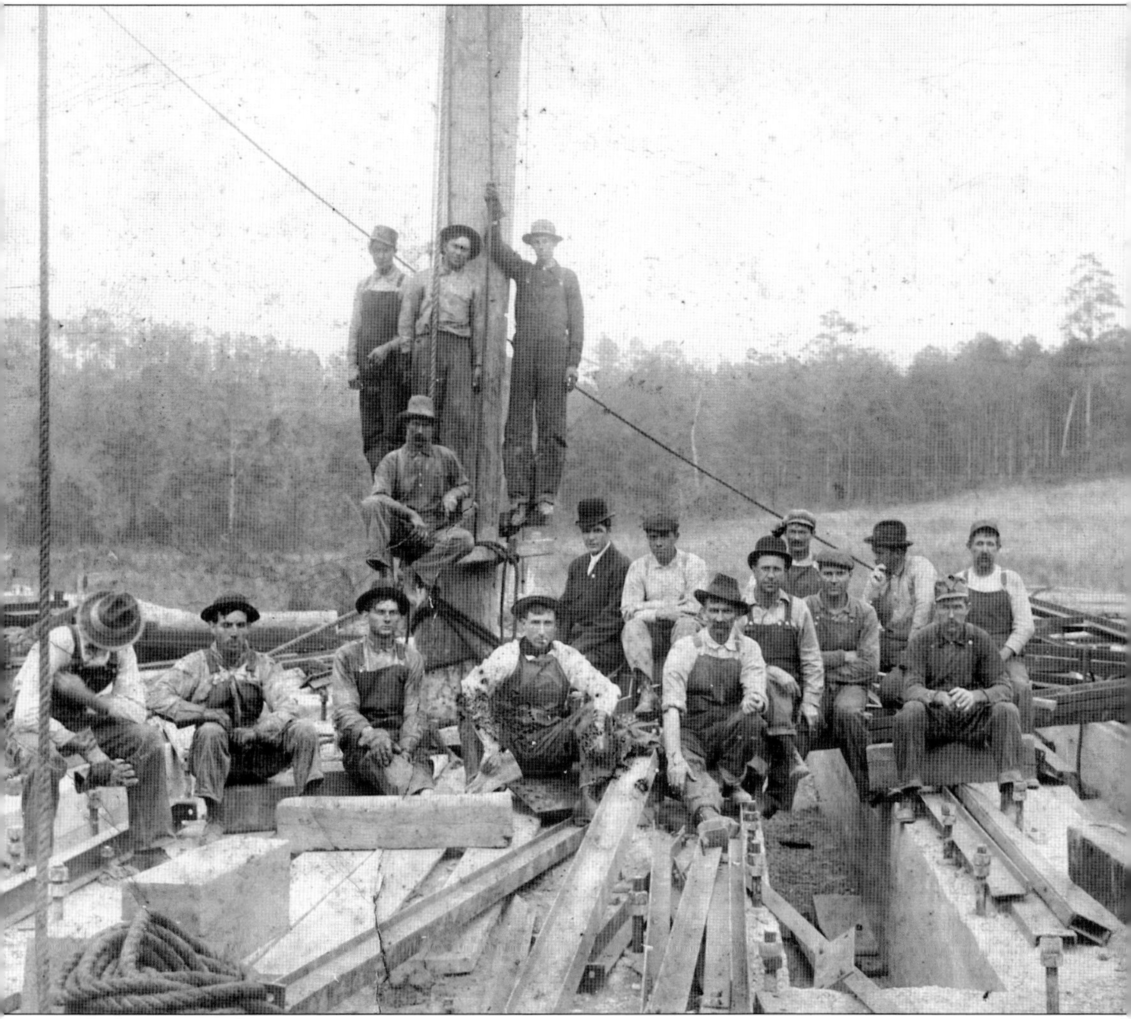

Around 1913, during the construction of the sawmill, workers pose at the Byrd-Matthews Lumber Company. The lumber company employed 150 workers to cut, transport, and process timber into finished lumber. Mill hands appear to have worked in overalls, while timbermen wore trousers with suspenders. Overalls may have been too restrictive in cutting operations using an axe and saw. An integral part of the Byrd-Matthews mill was their subsidiary company, the Gainesville & Northwestern Railroad, a 35-mile line that provided both freight and passenger service from Gainesville to Helen and Robertstown.

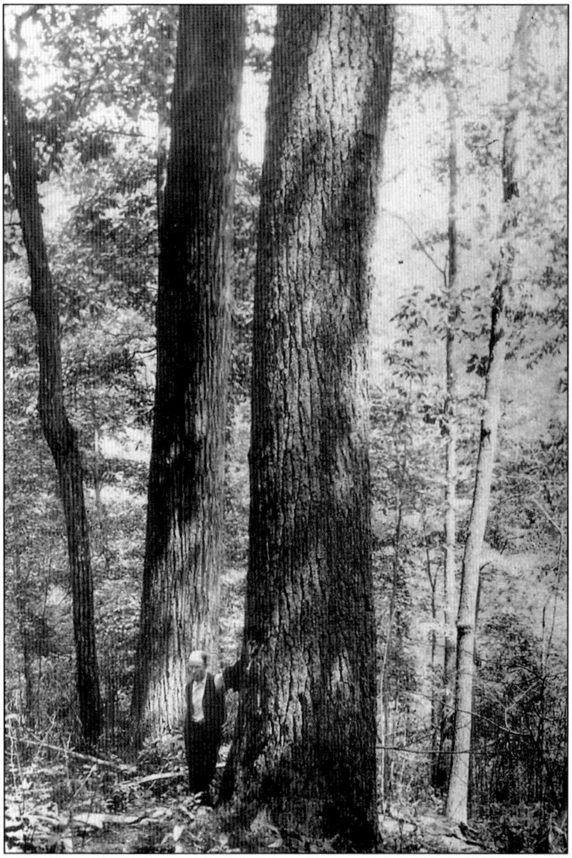

Giving scale in this image is the size of the virgin timber harvested from the Helen area. Stands of white, yellow, and forest pine as well as high-quality poplar, oak, and chestnut were harvested from the Helen Valley to above Anna Ruby Falls, Blood Mountain, and Wild Cat Creek in Rabun County. Lumber was offered in widths to 48 inches, and beams were cut 24 inches by 24 inches by 20 feet.

As shown in this c. 1913 image, the boiler and smokestacks for the powerhouse were brought in for assembly. The boiler and powerhouse provided electricity not only for the mill, but also for the town of Helen. When the power plant began shutting down in the evening, the lights in Helen would dim around 9:30 p.m., and by 10:00 p.m., all power was off.

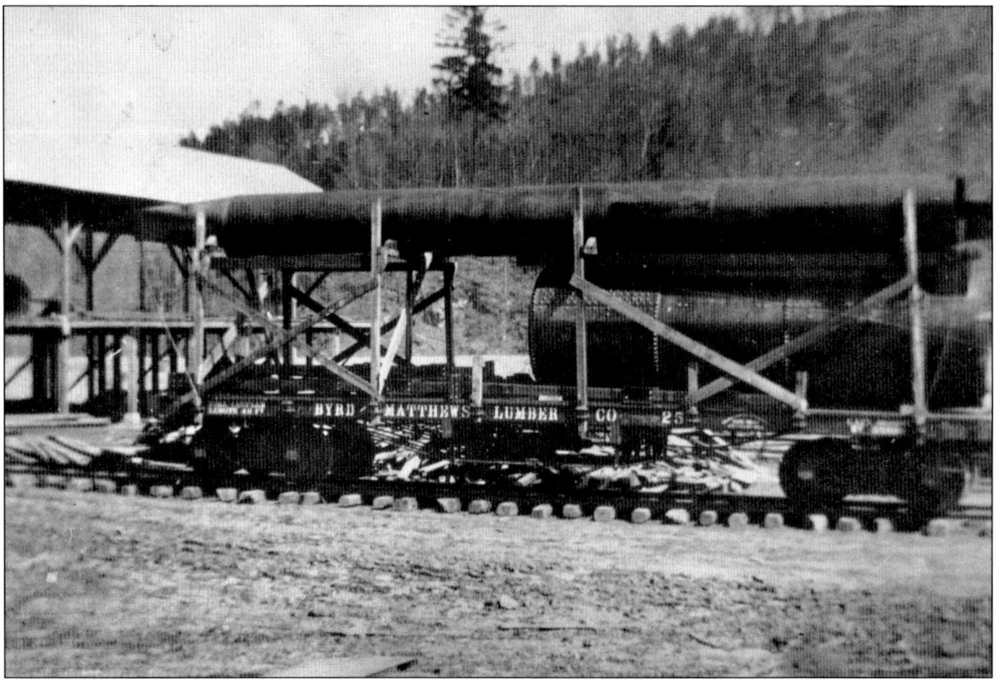

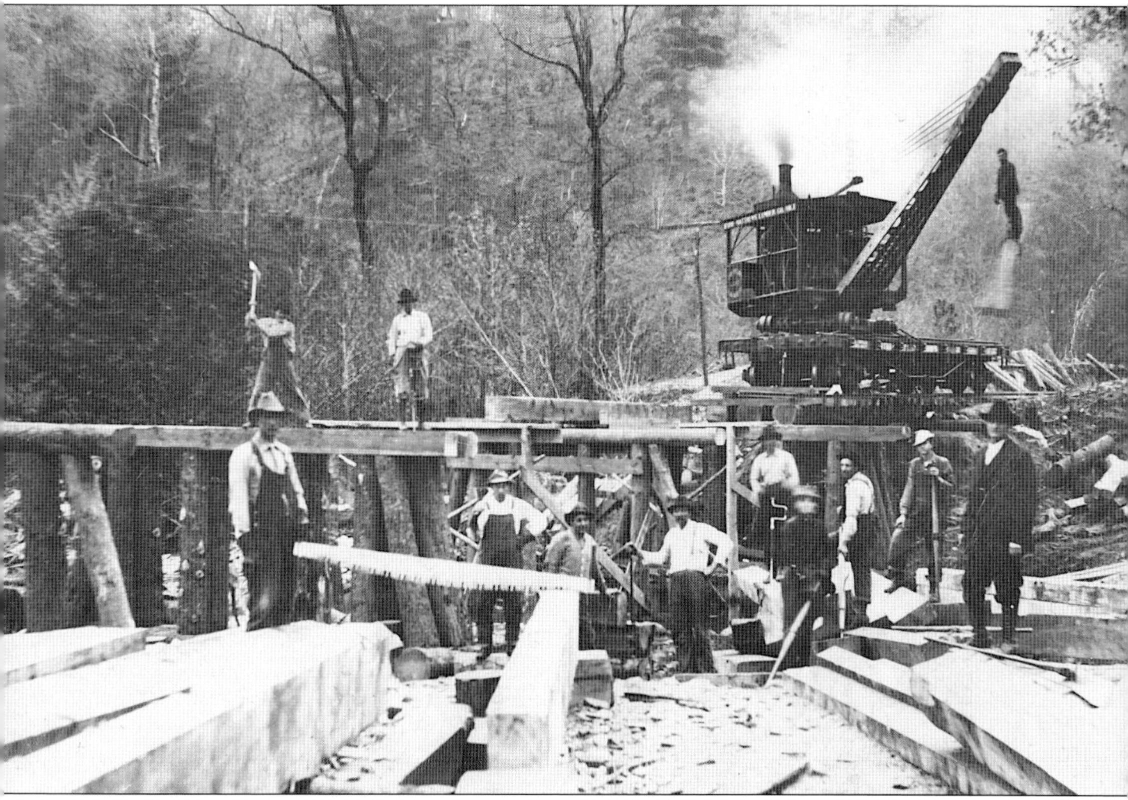

Low pile trestles were constructed over rivers and streams. This steam crane is lettered for the Byrd-Matthews Lumber Company. The trestles were sturdy, but the weight of the iron train cars carrying full loads of logs or cut lumber made every crossing a risky, low-speed operation.

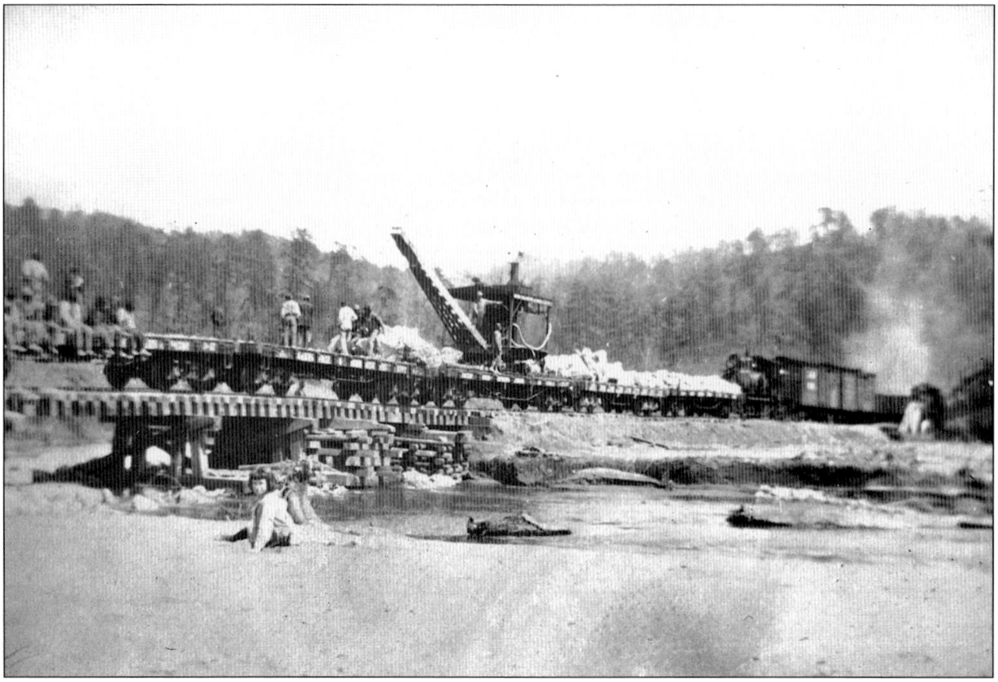

A train of flatcars and boxcars crosses a low pile trestle near the mill. Steam cranes were used in standard-gauge track construction. The young child in the foreground enjoys the spectacle presented by the railroad workers that bright afternoon.

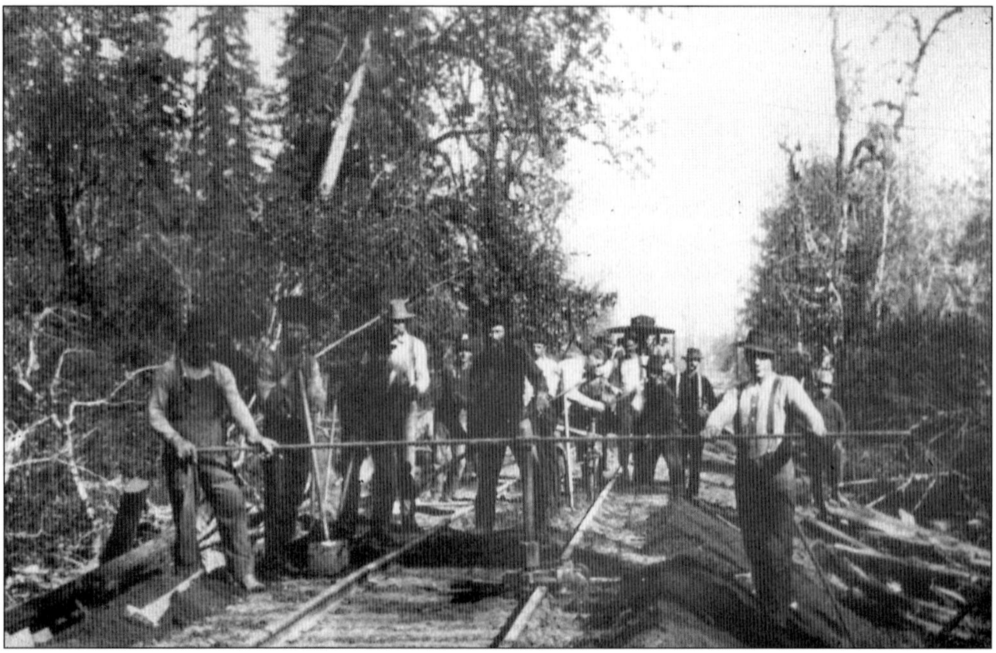

The construction crew on the Gainesville & Northwestern Railroad lay track along the 35-mile stretch between Gainesville and Robertstown. The railroad was a wholly owned subsidiary of the Byrd-Matthews Lumber Company, and while the company never showed a profit on paper, the railroad served the mill well by shipping out finished lumber.

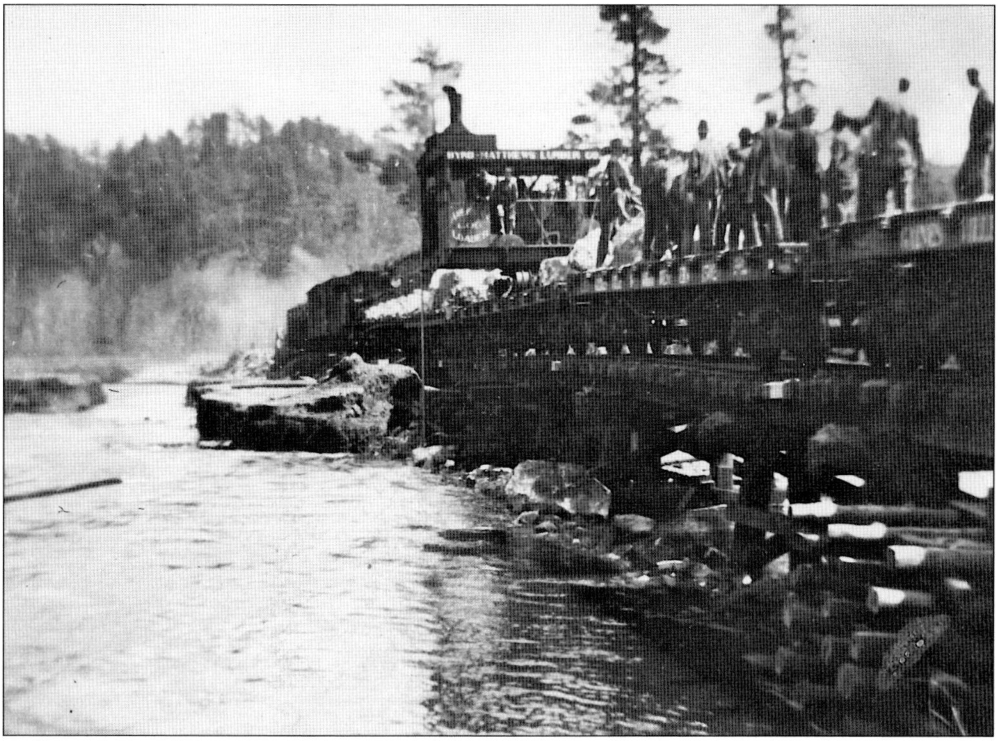

A construction railcar is equipped with a steam crane to lower boulders around a low pile trestle to increase stability. Note that the flatcar is lettered for the Gainesville, either the Midland or Northwestern lines. There were at least four similar trestle crossings between Nacoochee Valley and Helen.

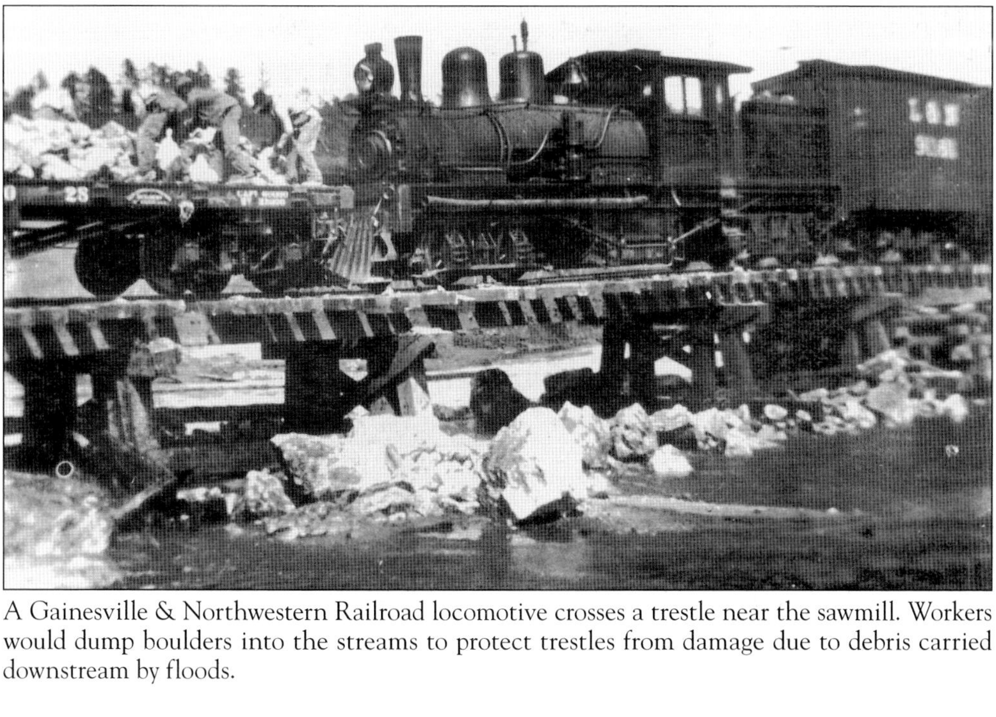

A Gainesville & Northwestern Railroad locomotive crosses a trestle near the sawmill. Workers would dump boulders into the streams to protect trestles from damage due to debris carried downstream by floods.

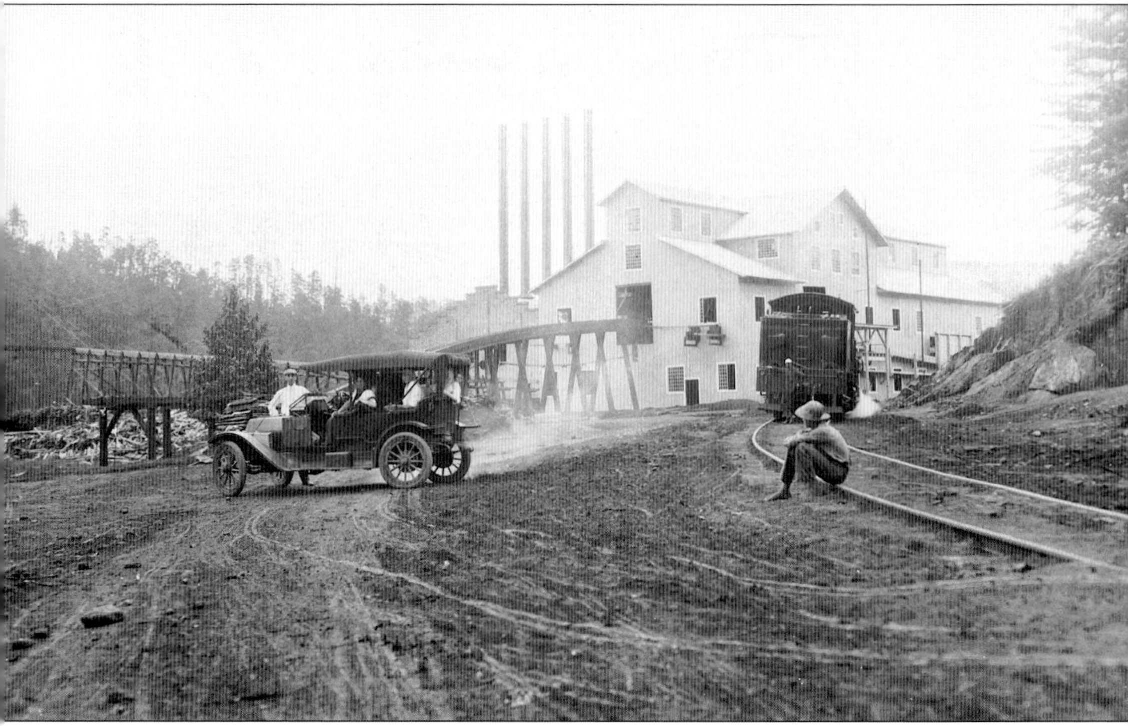

A.R. Byrd and C.D. Matthews of Missouri formed the Byrd-Matthews Lumber Company to harvest lumber on 36,000 acres of land Byrd owned in White, Towns, Union, and Habersham Counties in North Georgia. The company began with a $400,000 loan from Matthews and would eventually become one of the largest band sawmills in the East. The Gainesville & Northwestern Railroad was a subsidiary. Along with the mill came the town of Helen. The image shown here is an early view of the north end of the mill. The log pond is on the left. The main line of the railroad is on the right, curving south toward Nacoochee. Posing are, from left to right, Wilbur Linton, Lent "Speedy" Burke, Hubert Allen, Nora Allen, Fran Allen, and Roscow Palmer on the tracks.

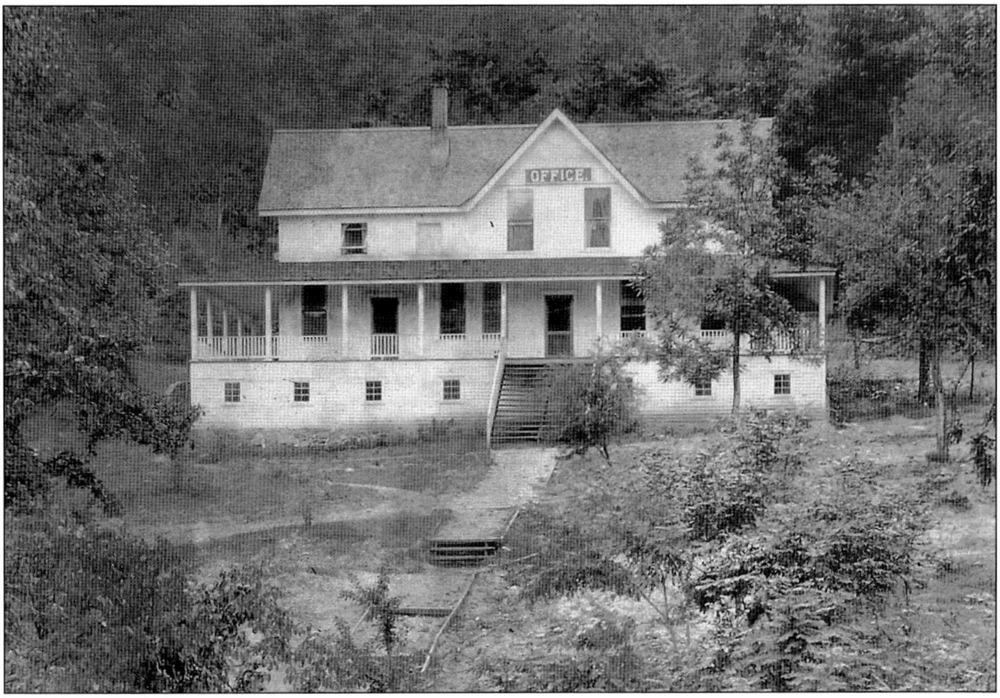

The Byrd-Matthews Lumber Company office in Helen was built west of the mill above the Gainesville & Northwestern Railroad tracks. Secluded by more than 75 years of tree growth, the house remains standing today, just above Main Street, as a private residence. At one time, close to 10 structures associated with the sawmill dotted the hillside over the mill site. The Marshall Hotel, which was lost to fire before 1917, was also located on this hillside.

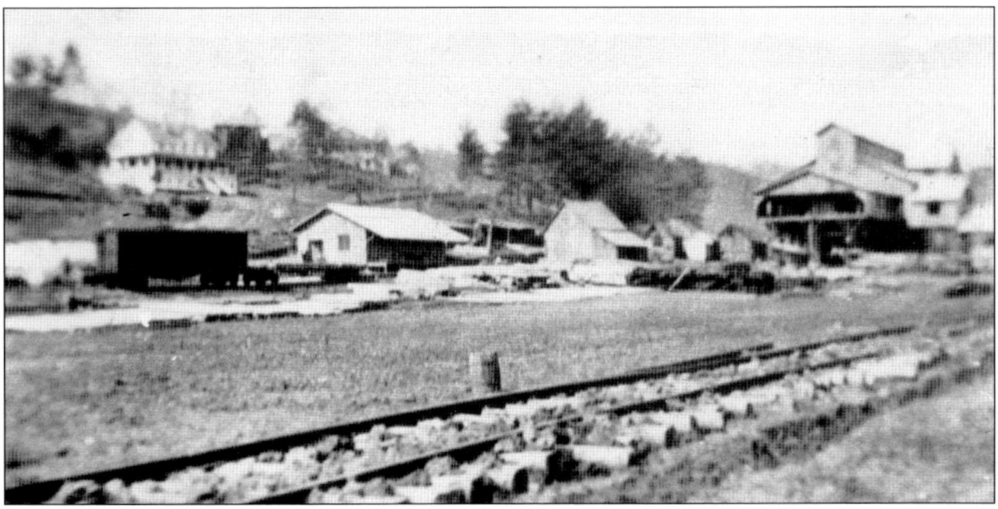

This view of the Byrd-Matthews mill is from the rarely photographed southeast side of the mill yard, facing northwest. The white building above the railroad car on the left is the mill office. The Marshall Hotel was located to the left of the office, out of view.

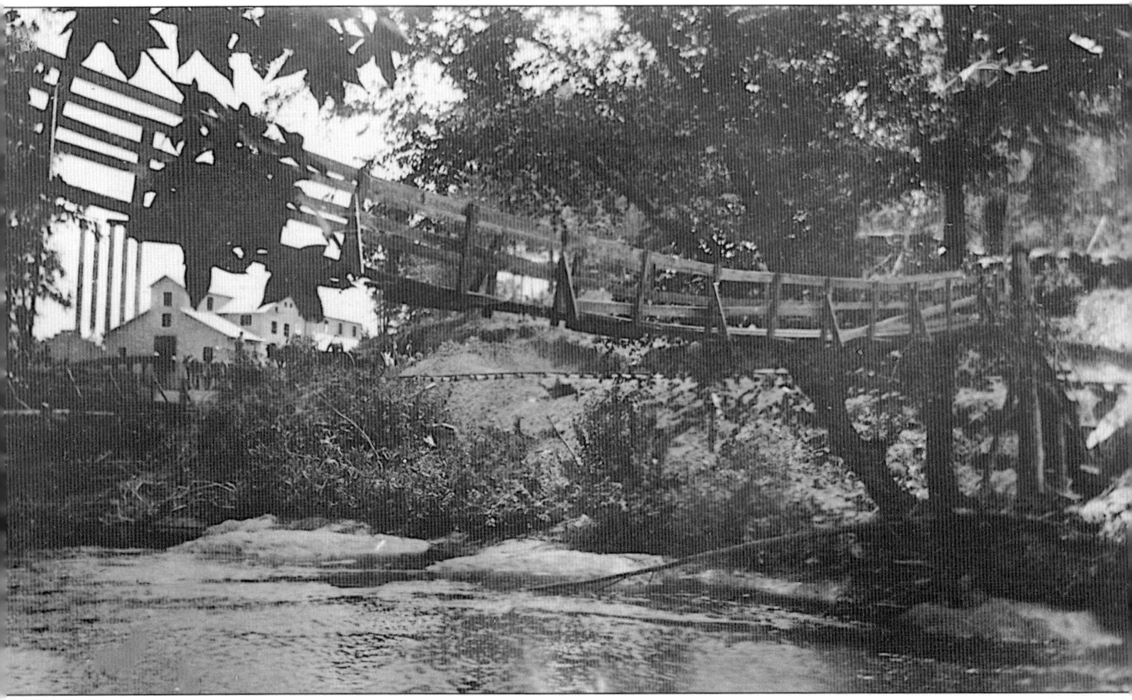

By 1914, an iron vehicle bridge and wood footbridge crossed the Chattahoochee River near the Helen Depot. Before the iron bridge was completed, vehicles had to ford the river. The iron bridge was installed to provide access to John Mitchell's property and the Mitchell Mountain Ranch Hotel. The train tracks were located on the west side of the river, following the bend of the river, but on the other side of the river from Main Street. The building in the background is the Byrd-Matthews mill. The Helen train depot was eventually built past the end of the footbridge, across the railroad tracks. Paul's Steak House Restaurant was constructed in 1963 on the approximate site of the Helen depot.

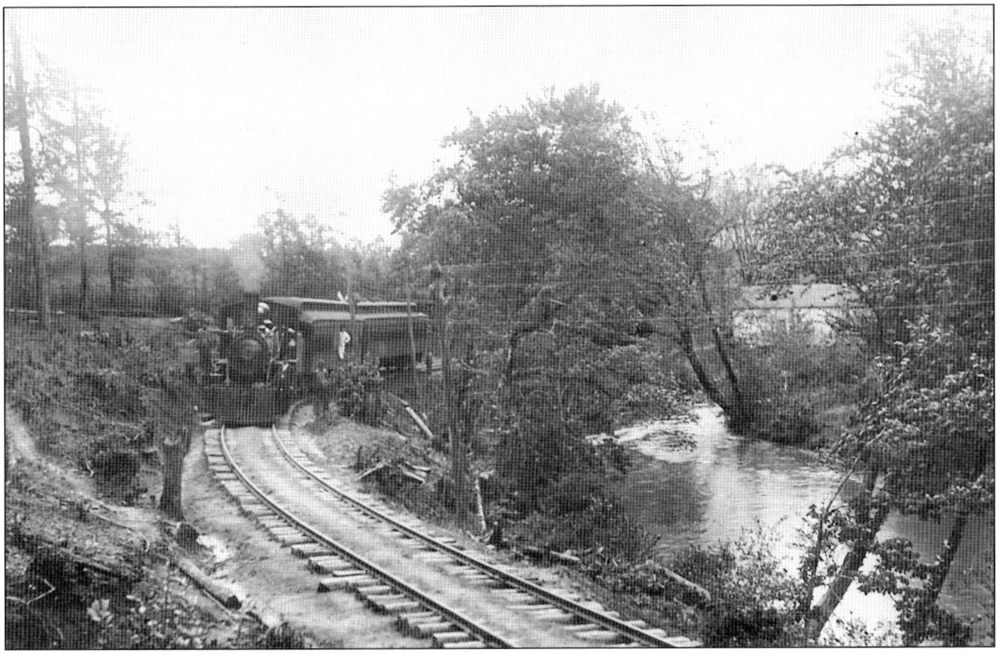

The Gainesville & Northwestern 203 pulls two coaches north toward the Helen Valley. In the background is the covered vehicle bridge crossing the Chattahoochee River near the Nacoochee Station. The railroad followed the river on the opposite side of the road, which today is called Georgia Highway 17/75. Nora Mill is located on the right, across the Chattahoochee River, out of view.

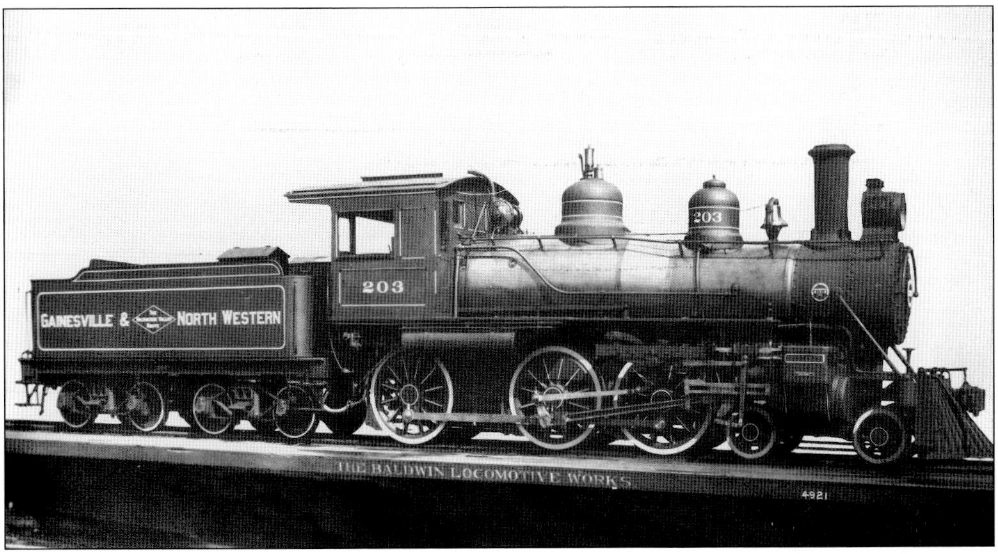

Photographed by manufacturer Baldwin Locomotive Works, the Gainesville & Northwestern Railroad 203 was the only new locomotive ordered by the owners. The tender (coal car) is lettered with the railroad herald, "The Nacoochee Valley Route."

GAINESVILLE & NORTHWESTERN RAILROAD COMPANY

Change in schedule, through passenger and freight service to Helen and Robertstown. Effective Sunday April 27th, 1913.

Sunday Only	Daily Except Sunday		STATIONS		Daily Except Sunday	Sunday Only
P. M.	P. M.				A. M.	A. M.
2 40	2 10	Leave	Gainesville	Arrive	11 00	11 00
2 50	2 20	"	New Holland Jct.	"	10 45	10 45
3 10	2 40	"	Clark	"	10 25	10 25
3 30	3 00	"	Dewberry	"	10 05	10 05
3 45	3 20	"	Brookton	"	9 50	9 50
3 55	3 40	"	Clermont	"	9 30	9 40
4 10	3 50	"	County Line	"	9 10	9 25
4 35	4 15	"	Meldean	"	8 50	9 05
4 55	4 45	"	Cleveland	"	8 30	8 45
5 15	5 05	"	Asbestos	"	8 05	8 25
5 35	5 30	"	Nacoochee	"	7 40	8 05
5 45	5 45	"	Helen	"	7 25	7 55
5 55	5 55	Arrive	North Helen	Leave	7 15	7 45

In this 1913 Gainesville & Northwestern Railroad timetable, Robertstown is labeled as North Helen. Although later dissolved, Robertstown was incorporated as a township about the same time as was Helen and, at one point, had as many residents as Helen.

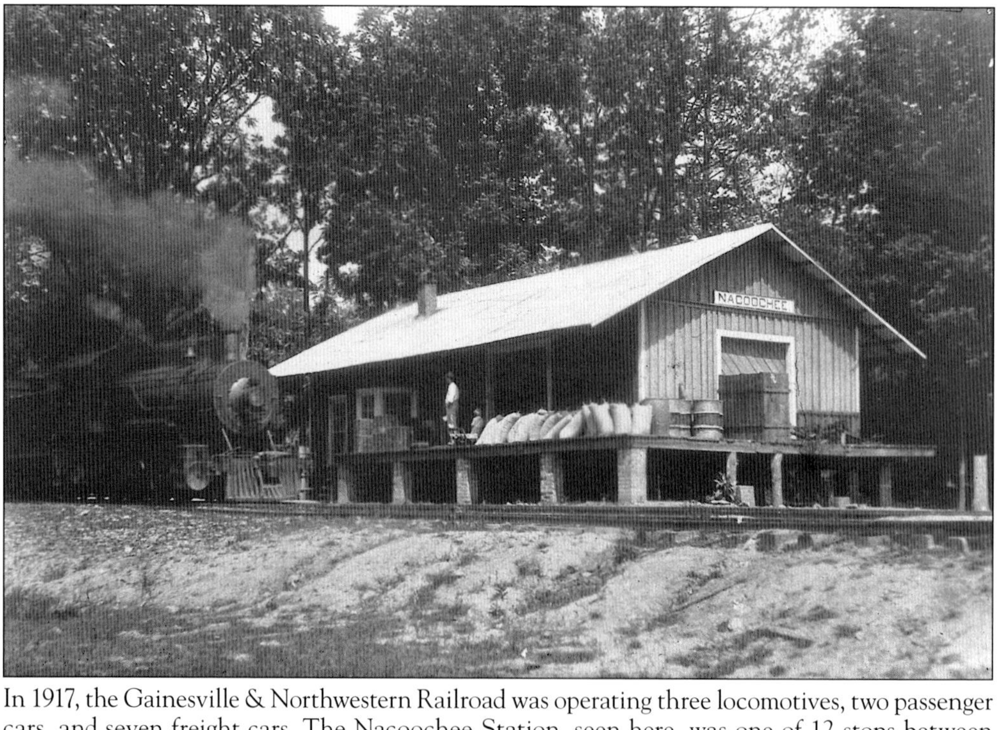

In 1917, the Gainesville & Northwestern Railroad was operating three locomotives, two passenger cars, and seven freight cars. The Nacoochee Station, seen here, was one of 12 stops between Gainesville and Robertstown.

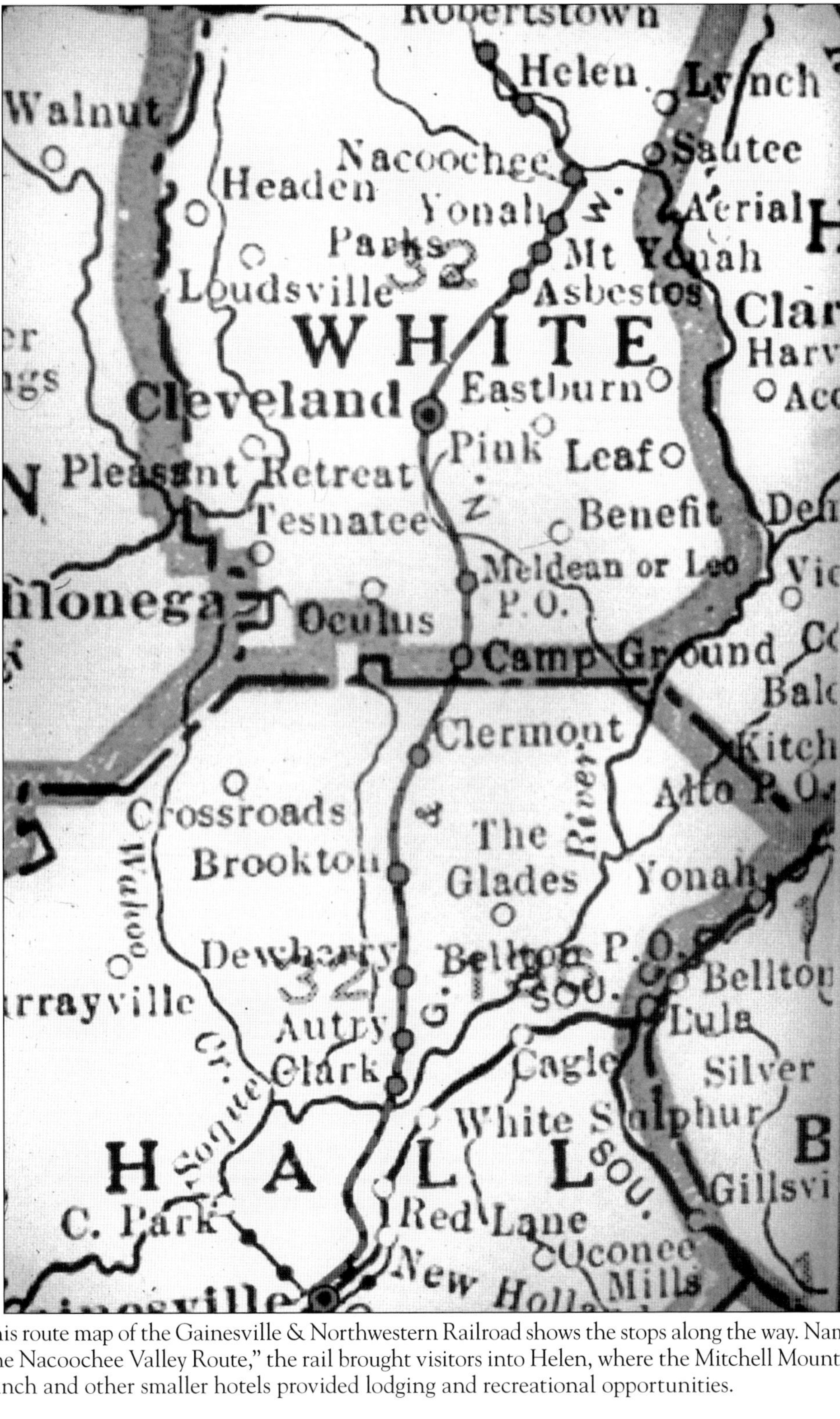

This route map of the Gainesville & Northwestern Railroad shows the stops along the way. Named "the Nacoochee Valley Route," the rail brought visitors into Helen, where the Mitchell Mountain Ranch and other smaller hotels provided lodging and recreational opportunities.

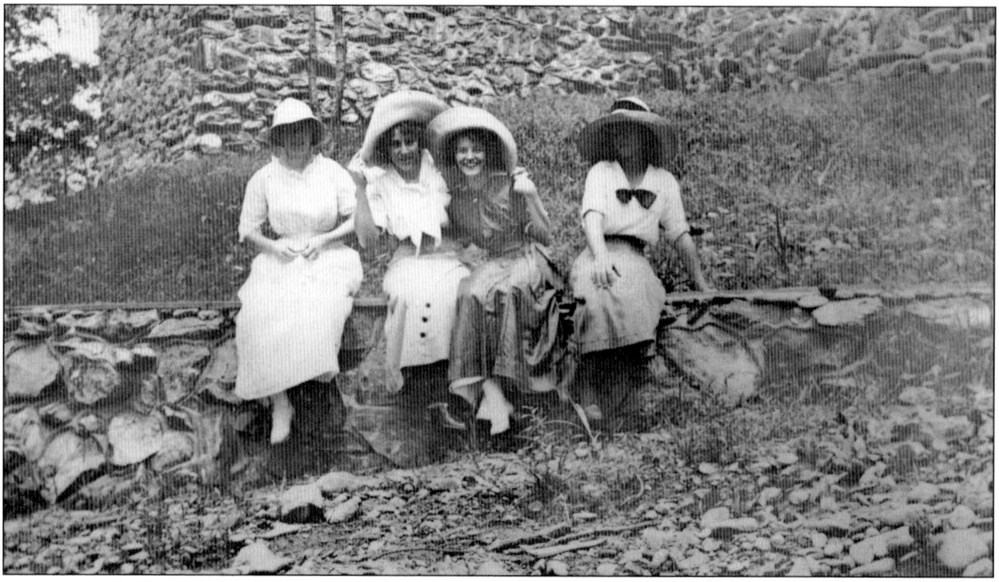

Along the hill of the southern rim of the Helen Valley, the Byrd-Matthews Lumber Company built an office, the Marshall Hotel, and a number of houses for workers and managers. Nearby, four women pose on a retaining wall in front of an unidentified structure. The wall and the ruins of the rock foundation survive today, but the forest is reclaiming most of this section of the lumber town.

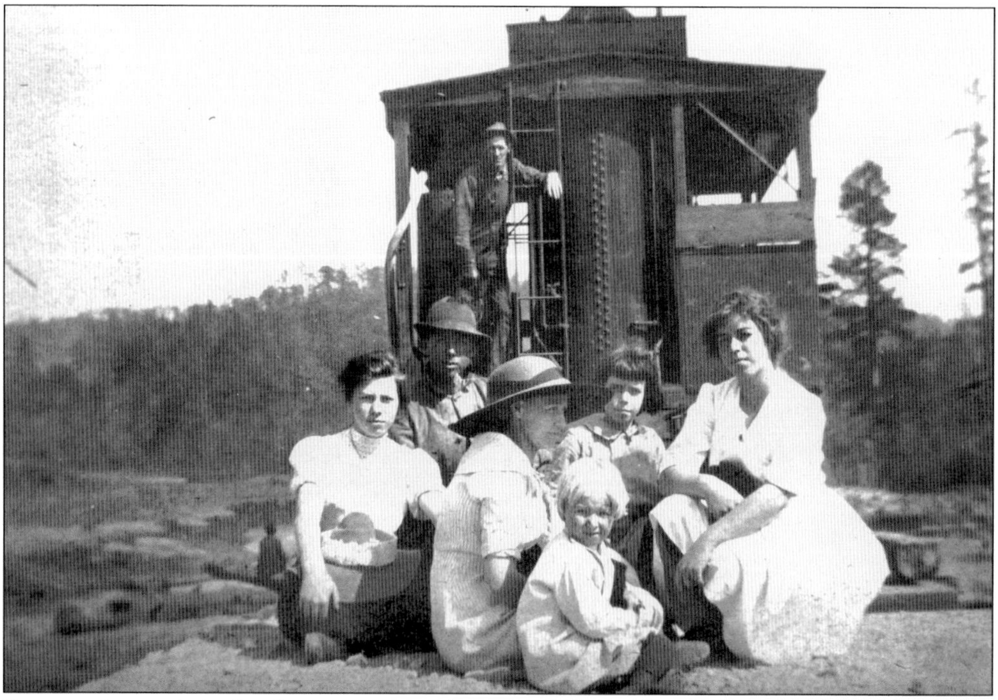

Because the area's lumber business was such a large industrial enterprise, it became something of an attraction. Here, friends visiting a local Nacoochee family have made a trip to see the mill and are posing just to the rear of a steam-powered loader. The loader operator appears willing to pose for the camera as well.

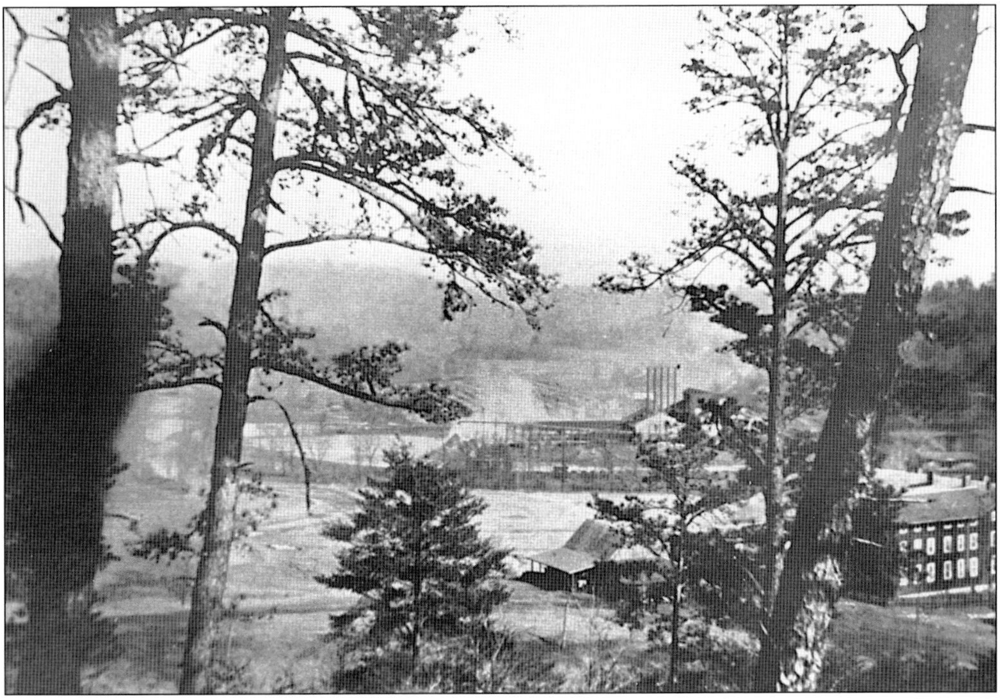

This c. 1922 view facing south over the Helen Valley shows the back of the Mountain Ranch Hotel, outbuildings, and the sawmill. The 27-room wing added to the hotel in 1921 is clearly visible.

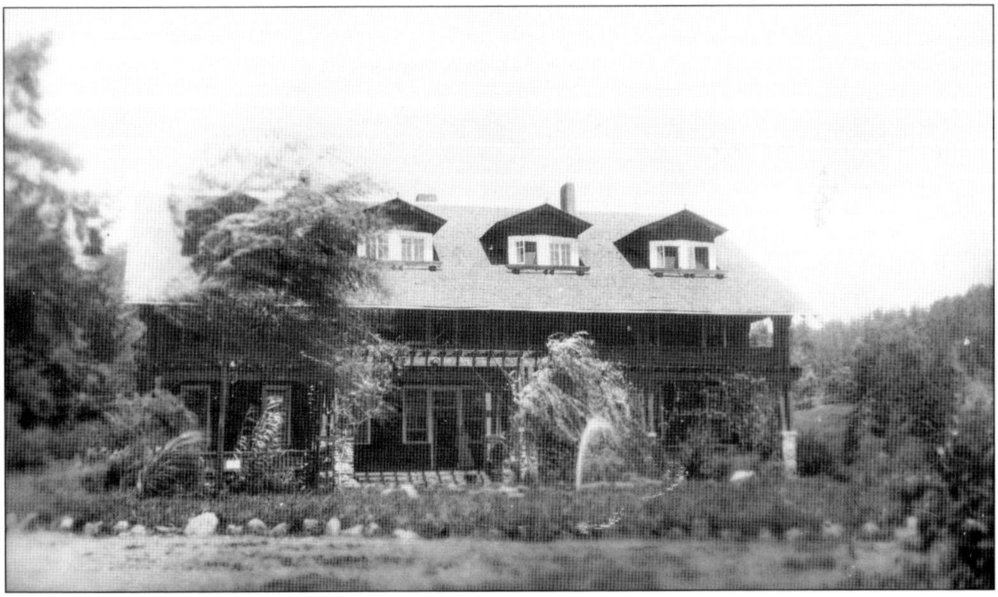

John Mitchell was associated with the Byrd-Matthews mill operation by way of the Byrd Cattle Company. Mitchell managed Byrd's Texas cattle operations from St. Louis, but he also purchased large tracts of land at the same time Byrd-Matthews was acquiring land around Helen. Mitchell, more than anyone else, was responsible for establishing Helen as a township. His Mitchell Mountain Ranch Hotel was one of the first buildings in Helen to have running water and electricity.

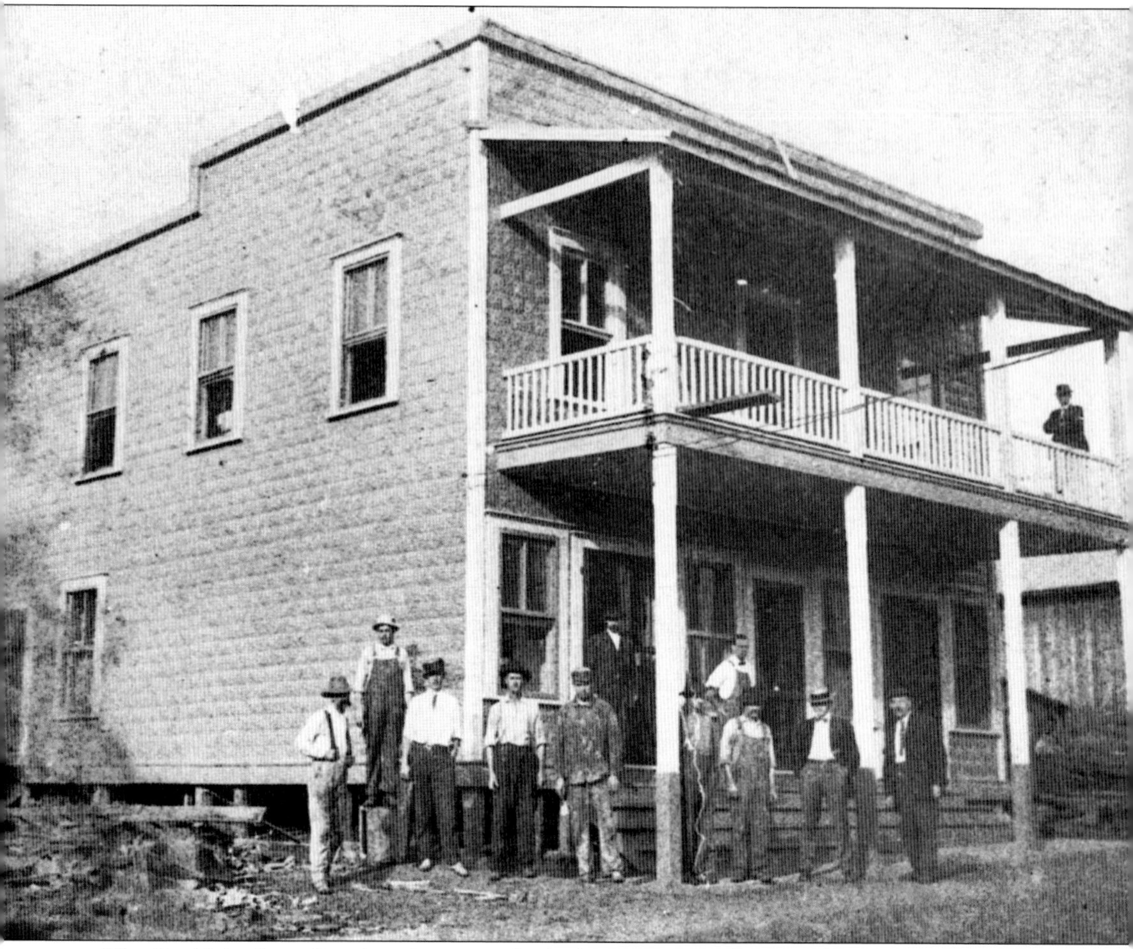

The Byrd-Matthews Lumber Company built the Commercial Hotel during the construction of the Helen sawmill complex. The hotel was used to house timbermen when they came down from the mountains on weekends. Nicknamed "woodhicks," the timbermen were known to work hard and play hard. Many left the woods to fight in World War I, and the resulting labor shortage, along with demands for higher wages by workers who remained, contributed to the precarious financial position of the Byrd-Matthews Lumber Company.

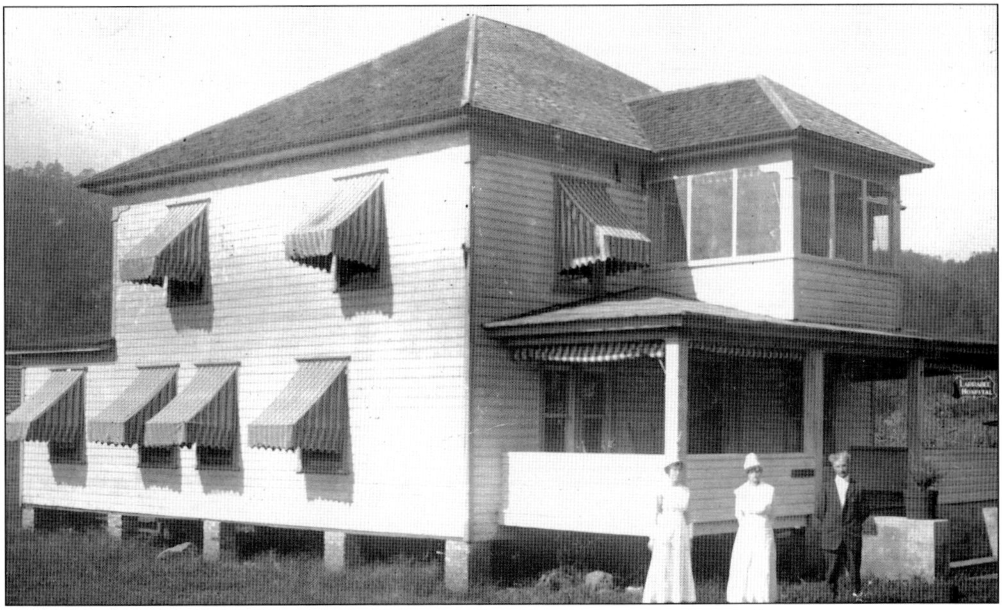

The Byrd-Matthews Lumber Company built the Larabee Clinic, shown here, primarily to make medical resources available to the mill workers and timbermen. The mill also built a water-treatment facility, sewage system, and telephone network for the mill community. Shown from left to right are aide Sevilla Wright, Nurse Zeeme, and physician Charles Larabee.

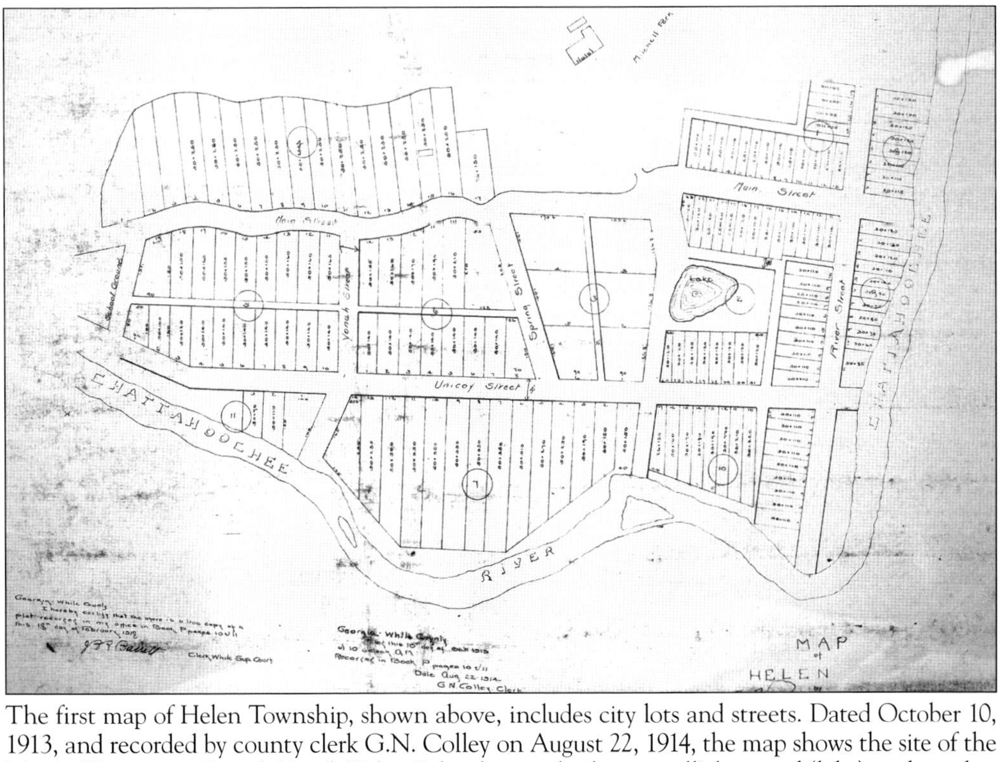

The first map of Helen Township, shown above, includes city lots and streets. Dated October 10, 1913, and recorded by county clerk G.N. Colley on August 22, 1914, the map shows the site of the Mitchell Mountain Ranch Hotel, Helen School grounds, the sawmill's log pond (lake), and another lake between what are now Dye and River Streets. Note that Unicoi Street is spelled "Unicoy."

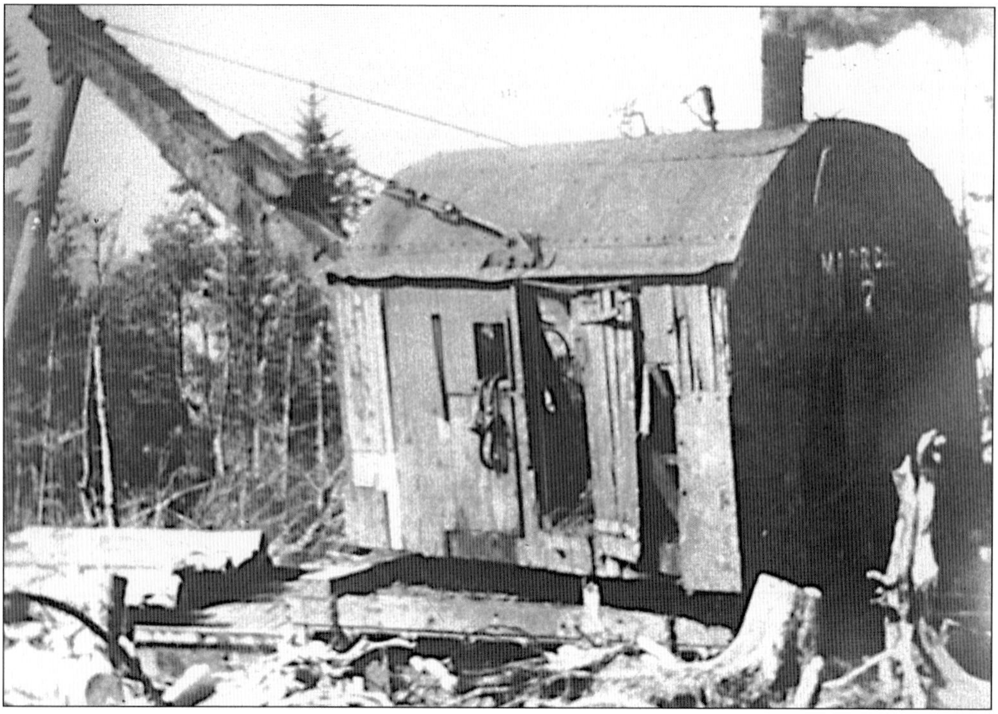

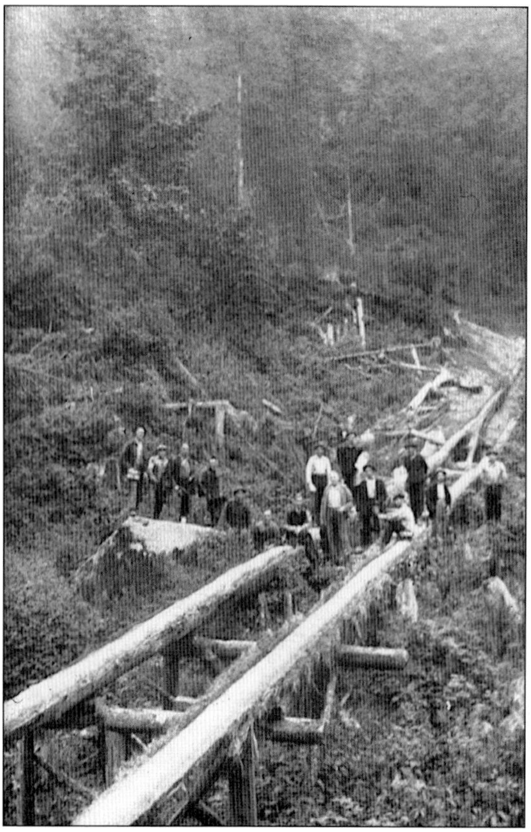

Barnhart log loaders were used to transport logs out of the woods. The loaders themselves were mounted on flatcars and had wheels, and as they loaded logs in front of them on the same flatcar, they could move in reverse until the car was fully loaded with logs. When the loader reached the back of its flatcar, it would move itself backwards to the next empty flatcar behind it, by means of steel wheel channels that were placed between the train's flatcars, connecting them. This process was repeated to the end of the train, thus saving having to move the cars to the logs for loading.

The speed with which mill could produce lumber kept crews busy building roadbeds and laying rail farther into the woods. Timber, roughly hewn from nearby trees, was left untreated since the rails were temporary.

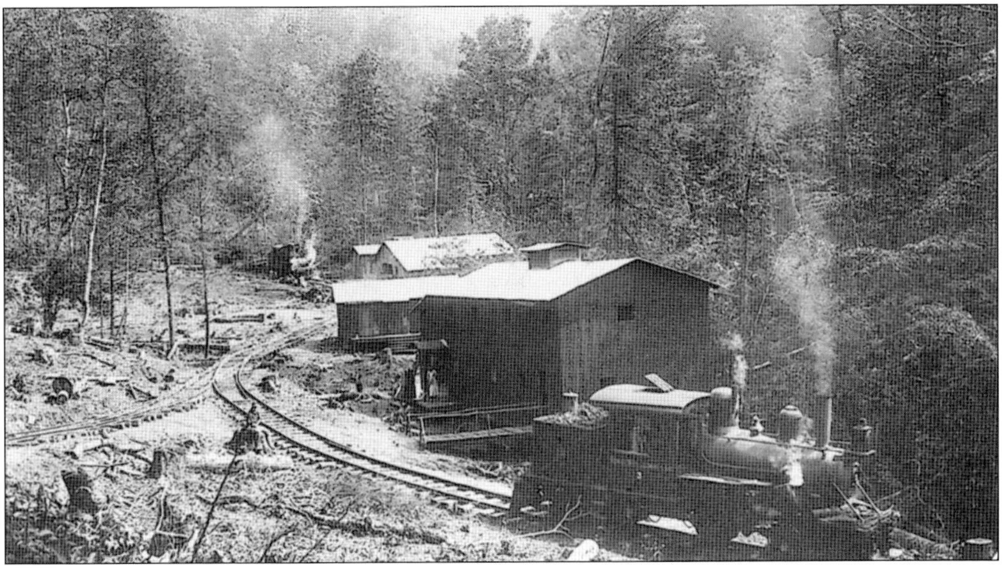

Shown above is a Morse Brothers Land and Lumber Company logging camp. Often bunkhouses were moved on the log cars. Camps like this one provided onsite housing for the timbermen during the week. On weekends, the timbermen traveled on log buggies back into Helen, where they "let off steam." The narrow-gauge Climax Railroad locomotive is readied to take on logs destined for the sawmill.

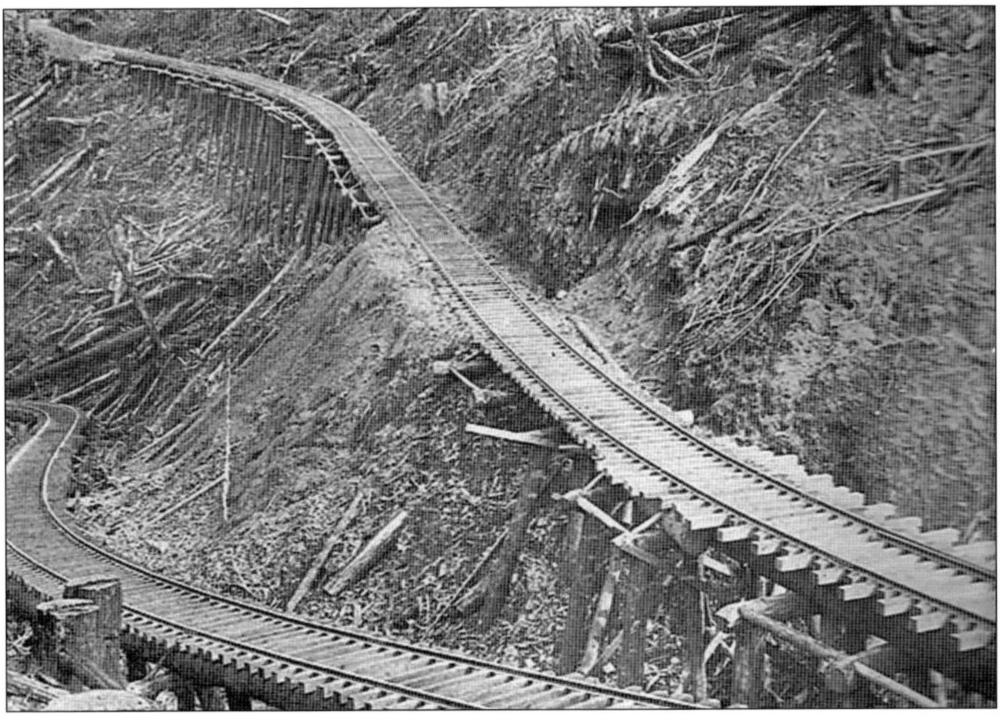

In the mountains, logging railroads used numerous switchbacks to minimize steep grades and gain elevation gradually. Grading work and bridge construction standards were designed to be temporary; after timber from an area was completely harvested, the temporary rails, wood, and other materials were disassembled, transported to the next site, and reused.

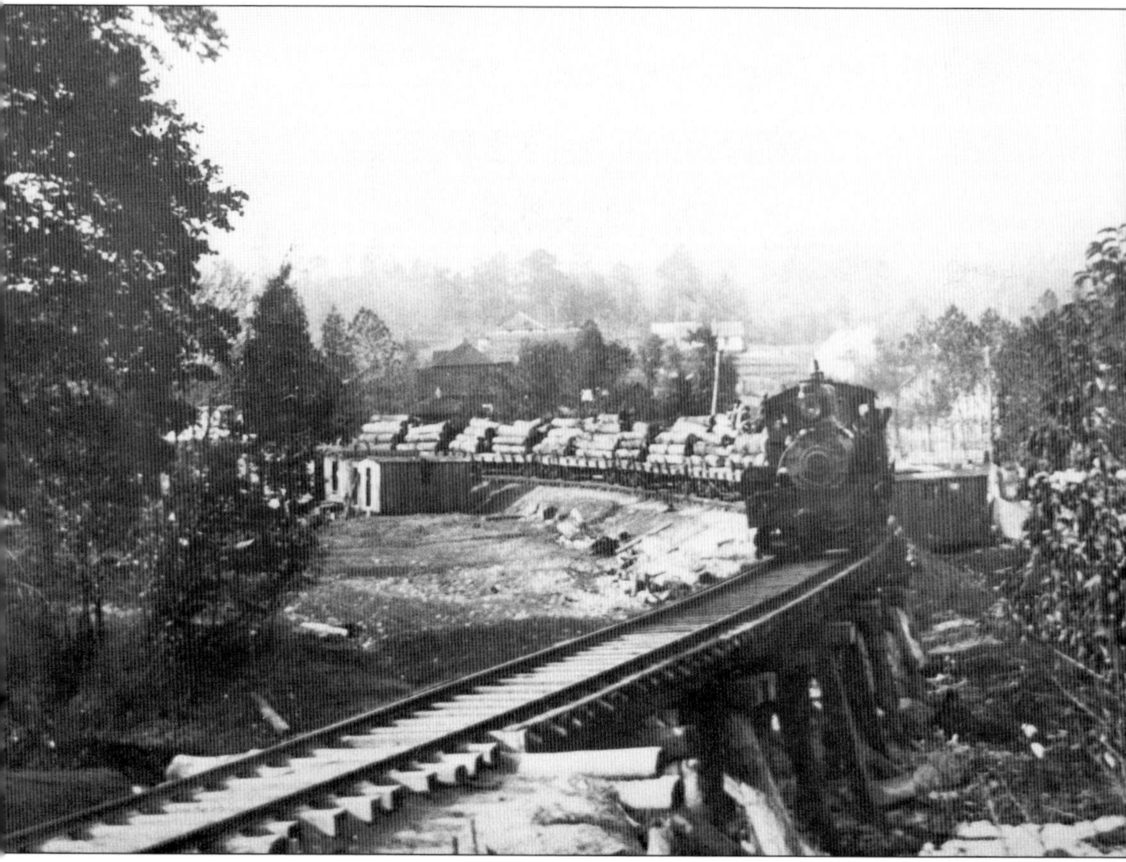

In this c. 1916 photograph, a load of logs bound for Helen passes through Robertstown and crosses Smith Creek on standard-gauge tracks laid by the Byrd-Matthews Lumber Company. The load is pulled by a Shay geared locomotive owned by the company.

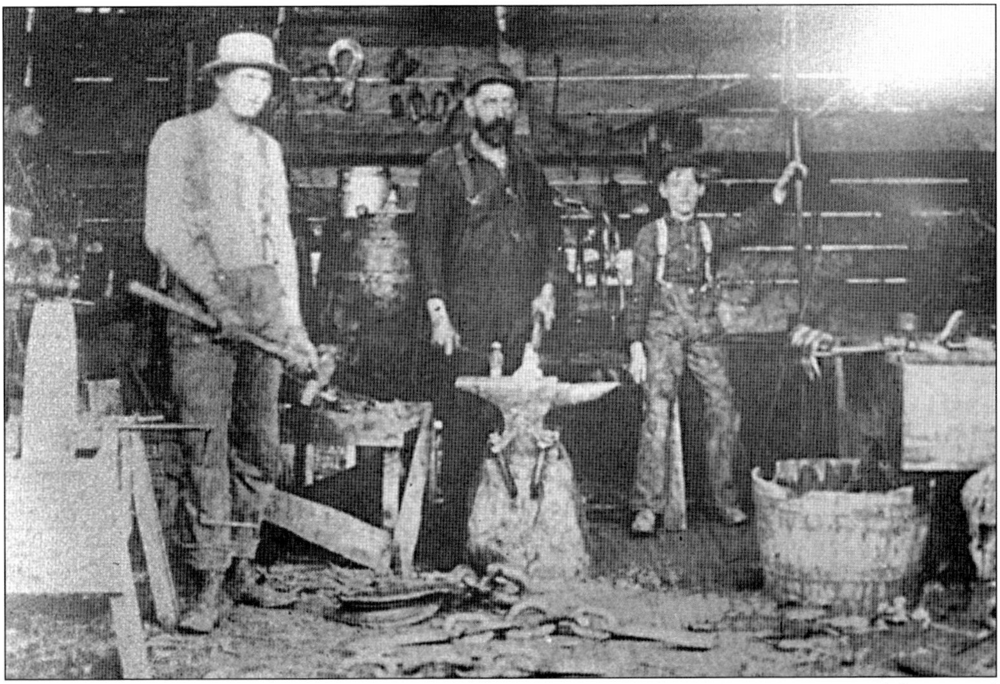

The blacksmith of the Byrd-Matthews Lumber Company mill repaired logging gear and sharpened tools. From left to right are the striker with the large sledgehammer, the master, and a young apprentice pulling the bellows at the forge.

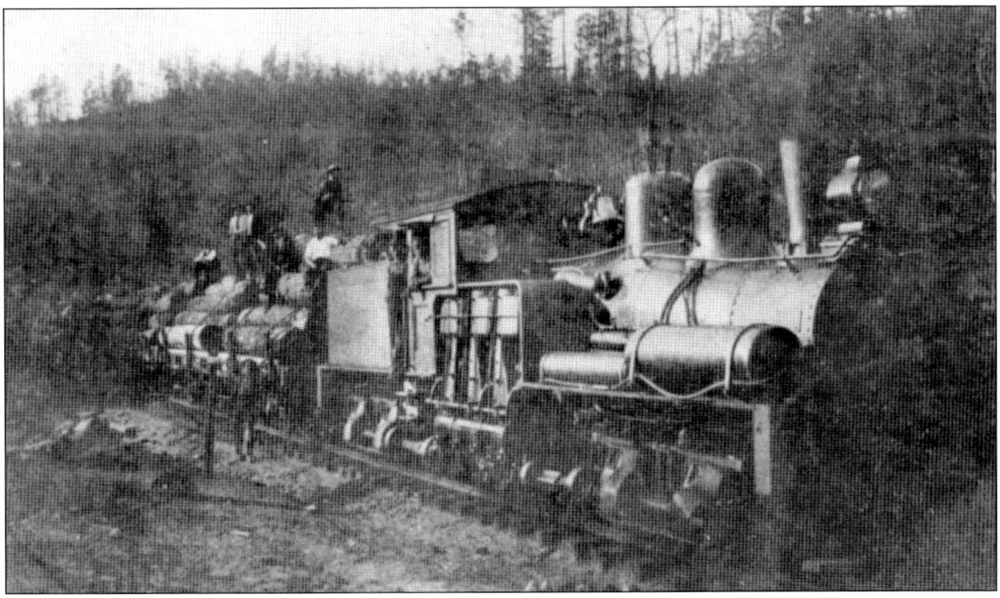

The Byrd-Matthews Lumber Company began timber operations with standard-gauge Shay locomotives. Ideally suited for logging, the Shay transferred power to the wheels with a crankshaft, line shafts, universal joints, and bevel gears at each wheel on the right side of the locomotive, shown here. The weight of the boiler and the tender was concentrated over the small wheels (called trucks) of the Shay, giving it tremendous pulling power. The small, four-wheel trucks were able to negotiate rough track and sharp curves.

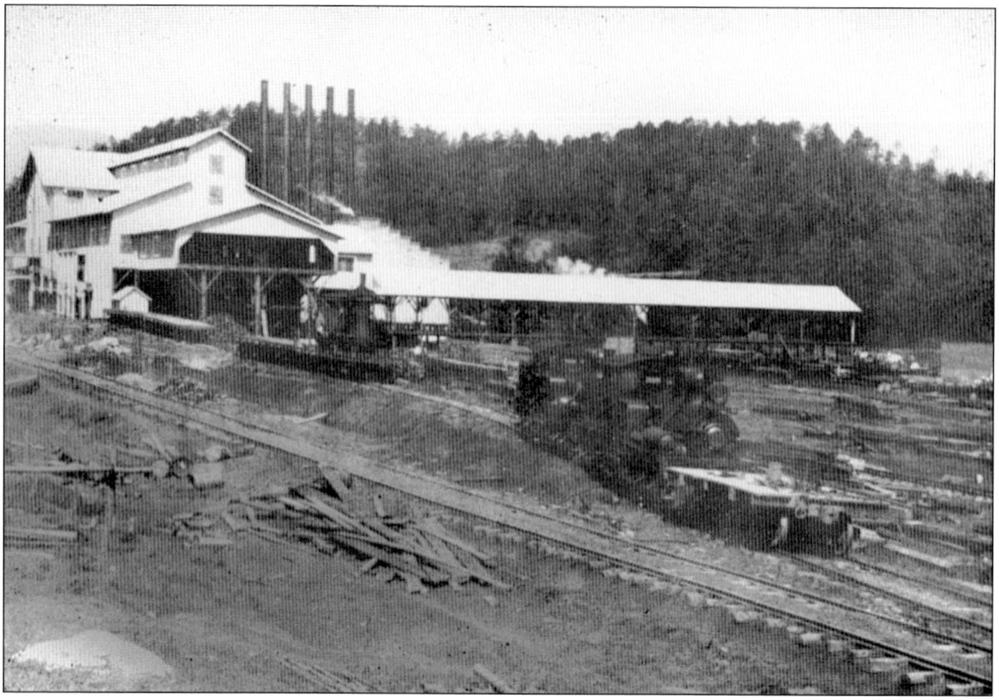

This view of the south side of the mill with sheds shows a Shay locomotive shifting the position (called shunting) of a flatcar in the yard. The mill is fully operational, but the mill yard is not yet loaded with lumber.

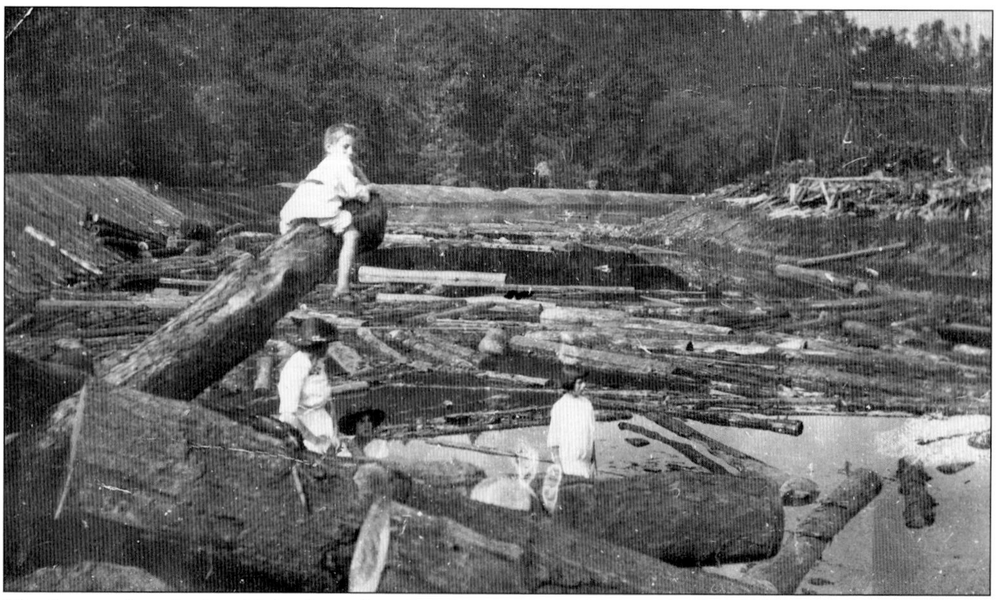

The log pond at the Byrd-Matthews Lumber Company mill functions as a makeshift playground for the children photographed above. Two mothers keep a watchful eye on the pair. The embankment to the left is the roadbed of the log unloading track; the mill is on the right, out of view. The Chattahoochee River curves around the log pond at the tree line.

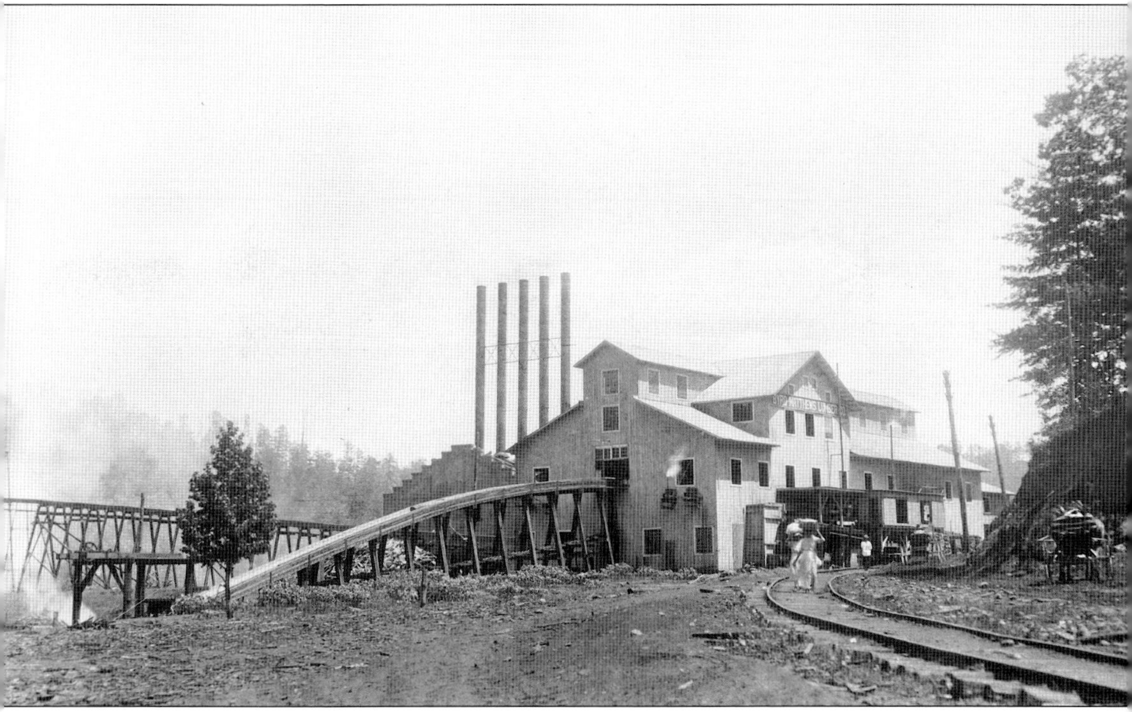

Shown here is the north end of the mill, with the log skip coming up from the log pond. Logs were dumped into the log pond for cleaning and preservation. When ready to be milled, the logs traveled up the skip and into the mill for sawing. The brick structure on the left is the powerhouse. Each smokestack served a 100-horsepower boiler. Four boilers were on line at any one time with a fifth rotated out for maintenance. Electric power, generated by the boilers, served various hotels and ancillary buildings. By 1917, the Byrd-Matthews operation in Helen had been sold to the Morse Brothers Land and Lumber Company, which had extensive timberland holdings that stretched from White, Union, and Rabun Counties in Georgia into eastern North Carolina.

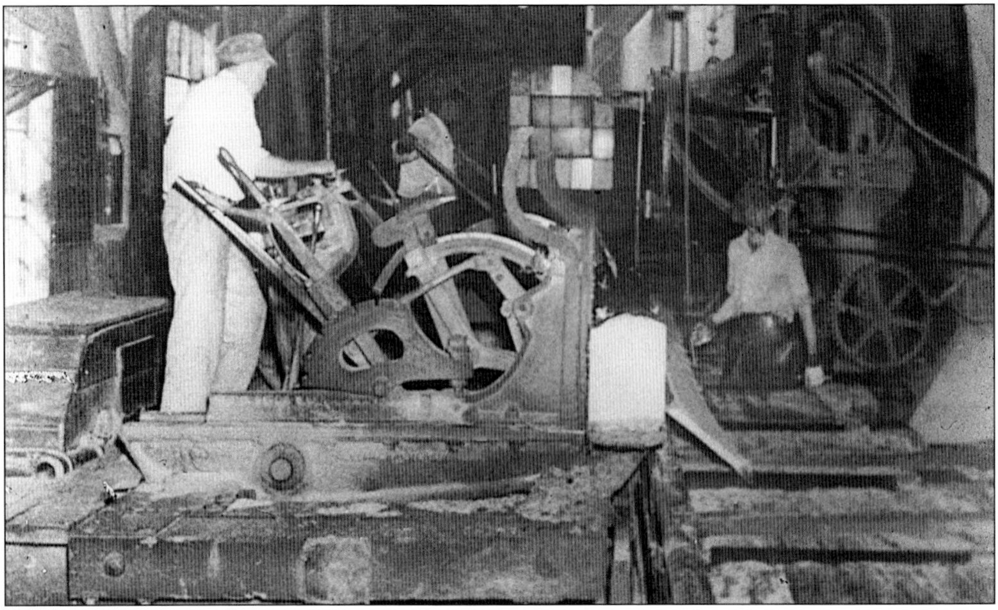

This interior view of a band sawmill shows the log carriage and the band saw, much like the setup that was at the Helen mill. Sawyers stood on the carriage operating the dog levers and rode along with the log being cut. The sawyer was the highest paid worker at the mill, earning $8 per day. The average labor wage was $1.50 per day.

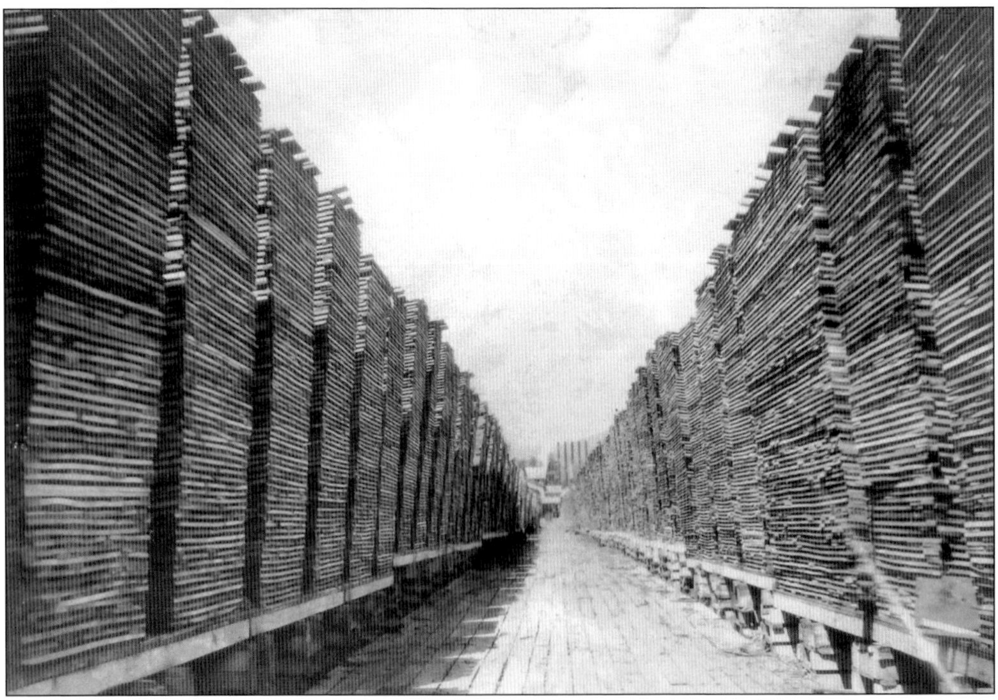

Beyond long rows of lumber drying in the sawmill yard are the five smokestacks from the powerhouse. Stacks of stickered lumber dried in the yard awaiting transport by train. The mill could produce 125,000 board feet of cut lumber per day. Used exclusively to measure lumber, a board foot equals the volume of a one foot length of board one foot wide and one inch thick.

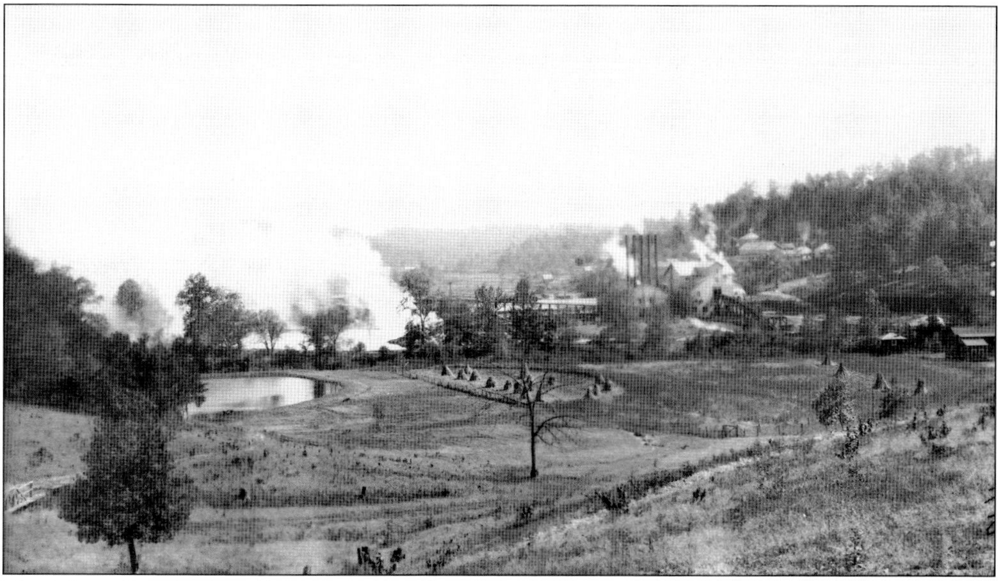

The Morse Brothers Land and Lumber Company mill is photographed from the hill behind the Mitchell Mountain Ranch Hotel around 1917. The millpond is at center left. Another smaller pond is in the foreground and is part of the Mitchell Ranch property. The field to the left of the haystacks is where the Helen baseball team would eventually compete on behalf of the Morse Brothers Land and Lumber Company.

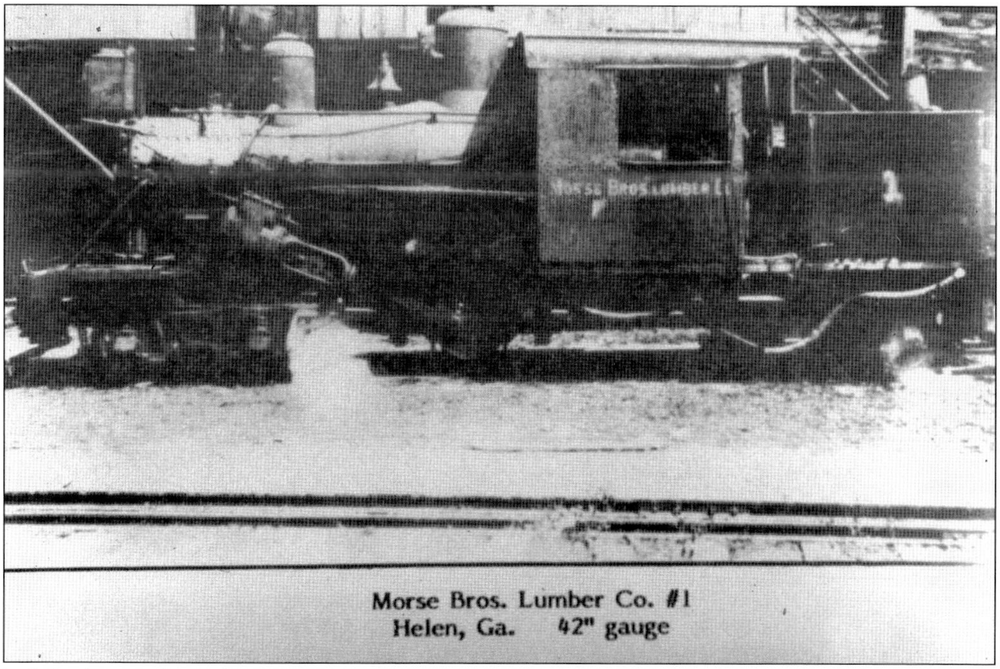

While the Byrd-Matthews Lumber Company relied on a standard-gauge Shay locomotive to haul logs out of the woods, the Morse Brothers Land and Lumber Company laid 42-inch narrow-gauge tracks into the mountains and added a third rail inside the standard-gauge tracks south to the Asbestos depot. The Morse Brothers Land and Lumber Company used Climax-built locomotives to pull log trains to the mill.

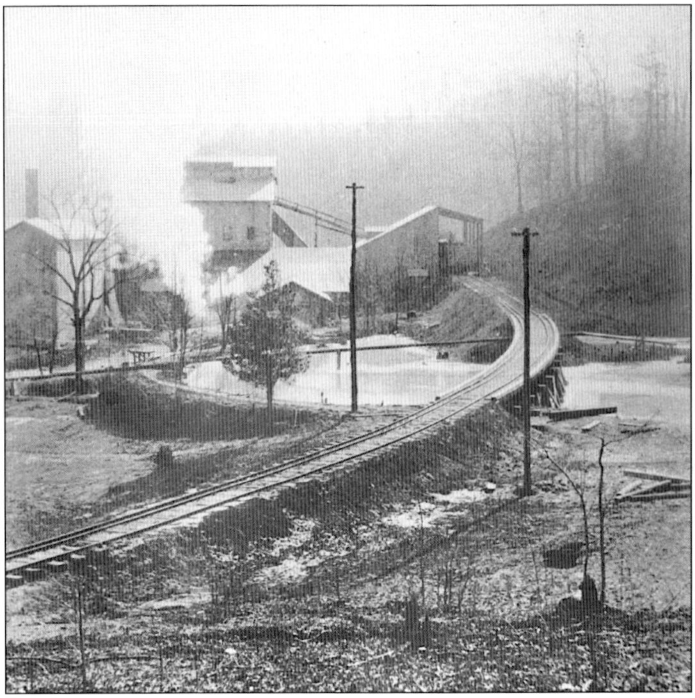

Located on the west side of the Chattahoochee River at the base of Hamby Mountain, the Smethport Extract Company utilized the proximity of the Gainesville & Northwestern Railroad lines. The company extracted tannin, a substance used to tan leather, from chestnut trees. The business operated for about five years. Most of the company's land holdings were sold and incorporated into the national forest.

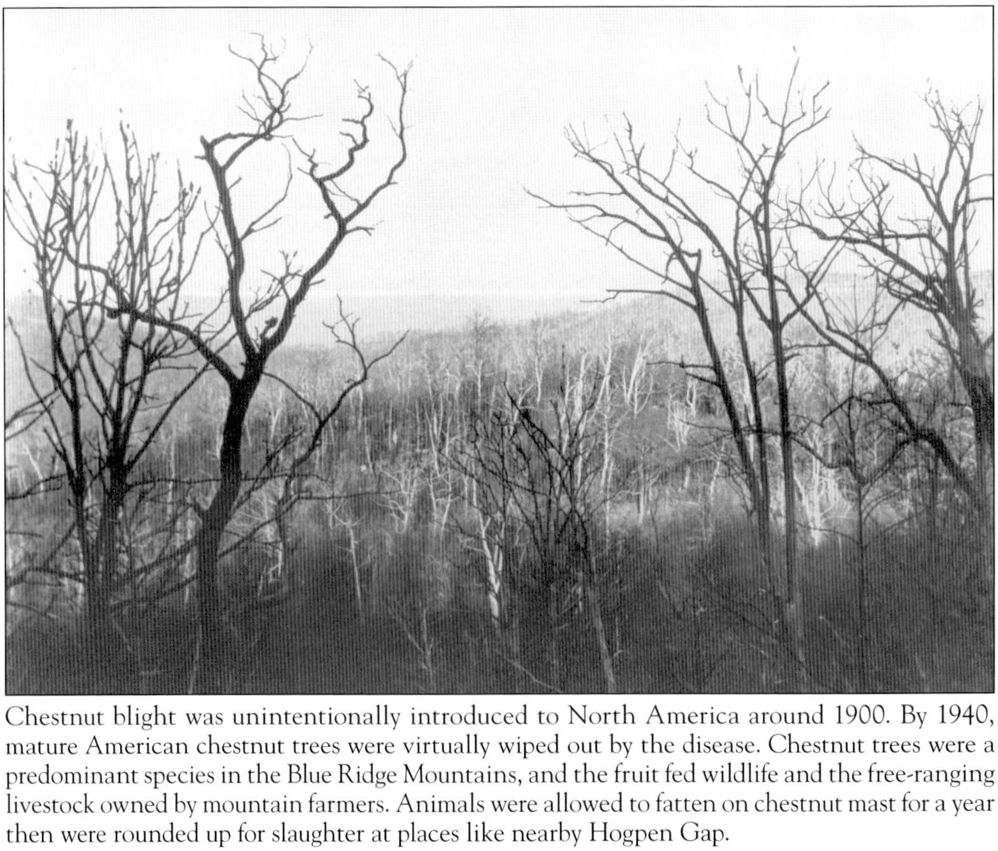

Chestnut blight was unintentionally introduced to North America around 1900. By 1940, mature American chestnut trees were virtually wiped out by the disease. Chestnut trees were a predominant species in the Blue Ridge Mountains, and the fruit fed wildlife and the free-ranging livestock owned by mountain farmers. Animals were allowed to fatten on chestnut mast for a year then were rounded up for slaughter at places like nearby Hogpen Gap.

Helen's first baseball team was associated with the Morse Brothers Land and Lumber Company sawmill. The team played in what then was an open field between the Chattahoochee River and the hill where the Mitchell Mountain Ranch Hotel stood. The team disbanded when the mill closed, then resumed briefly in the 1950s. Baseball Hall of Fame member Johnny Mize is said to have played for the mill team when he was a student at nearby Piedmont College.

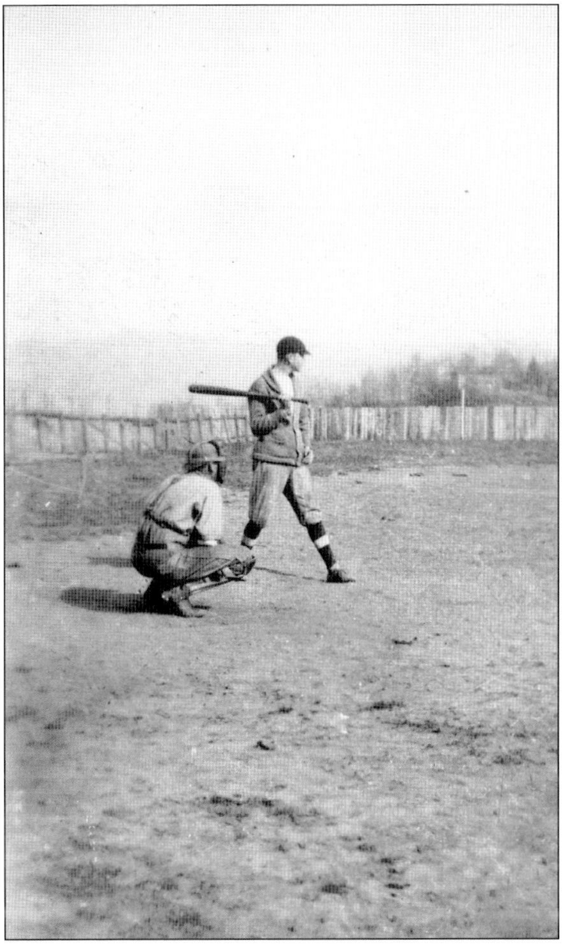

In the late 1800s, wildlife and game were plentiful in North Georgia. By the time the sawmill left Helen, the forest was devastated and wildlife was virtually wiped out as well. A North Georgia–born US Forest Service ranger, Arthur Woody, vowed he would repopulate the deer herds in North Georgia. Arthur spent the better part of 30 years fulfilling that pledge and in the process helped build the Chattahoochee National Forest.

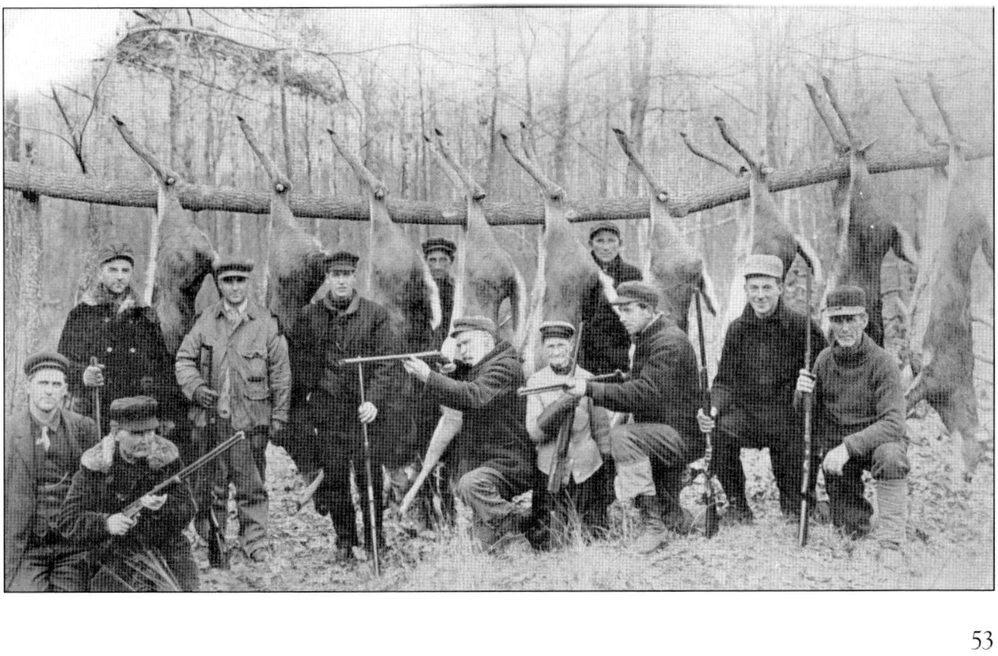

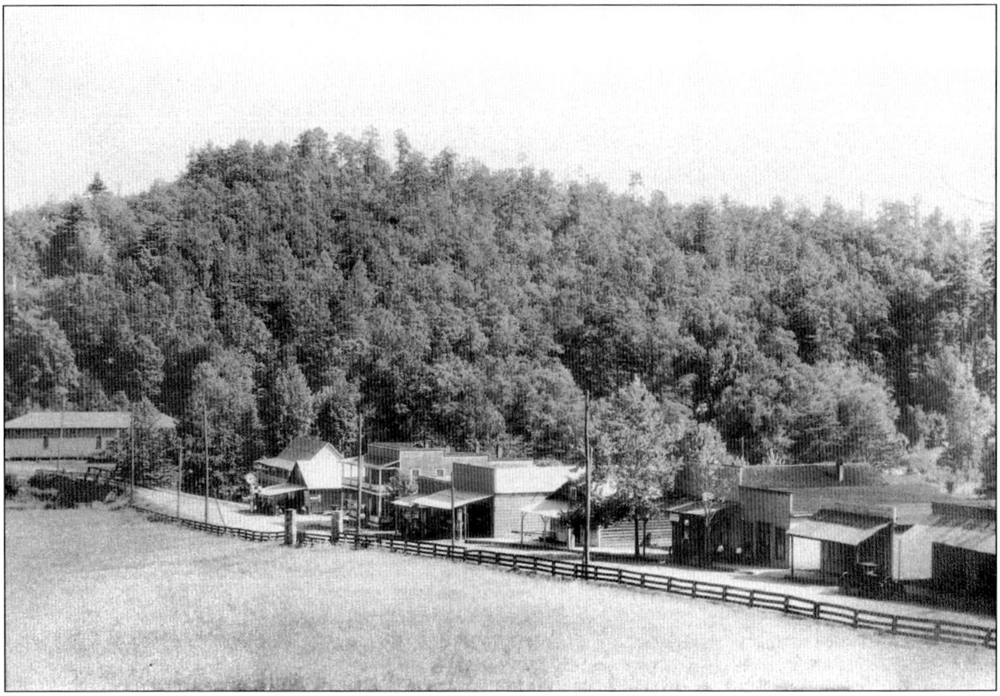

This 1928 image of downtown Helen was taken from the Mountain Ranch Hotel hill. The grassy field in the foreground is where cows grazed and the Helen baseball team played. The Helen train depot is on the far left, across the steel bridge. Some 40 years later, the depot site became the location of Paul's Steak House. The years ahead would be tough on small towns across the country, including Helen.

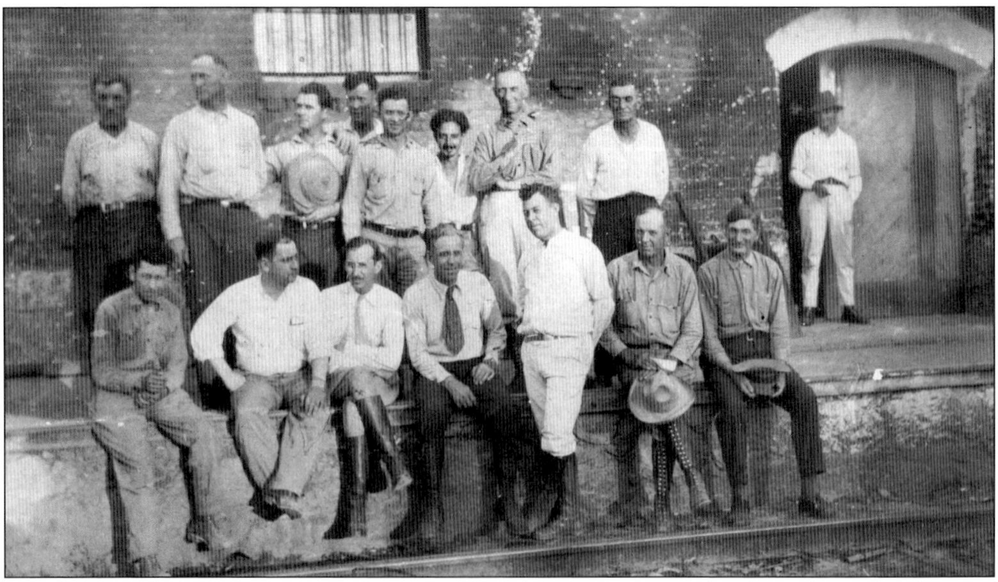

The Morse Brothers Land and Lumber Company sawed their last board on May 5, 1931. The sawmill was dismantled and shipped to Mexico. A group of the Helen workers followed along with the mill, but that venture did not last long. First damaged by a flood, then interrupted by a violent local uprising, the mill closed and workers left Mexico. Some workers later returned to Helen.

Three

QUIETER TIMES 1933–1969

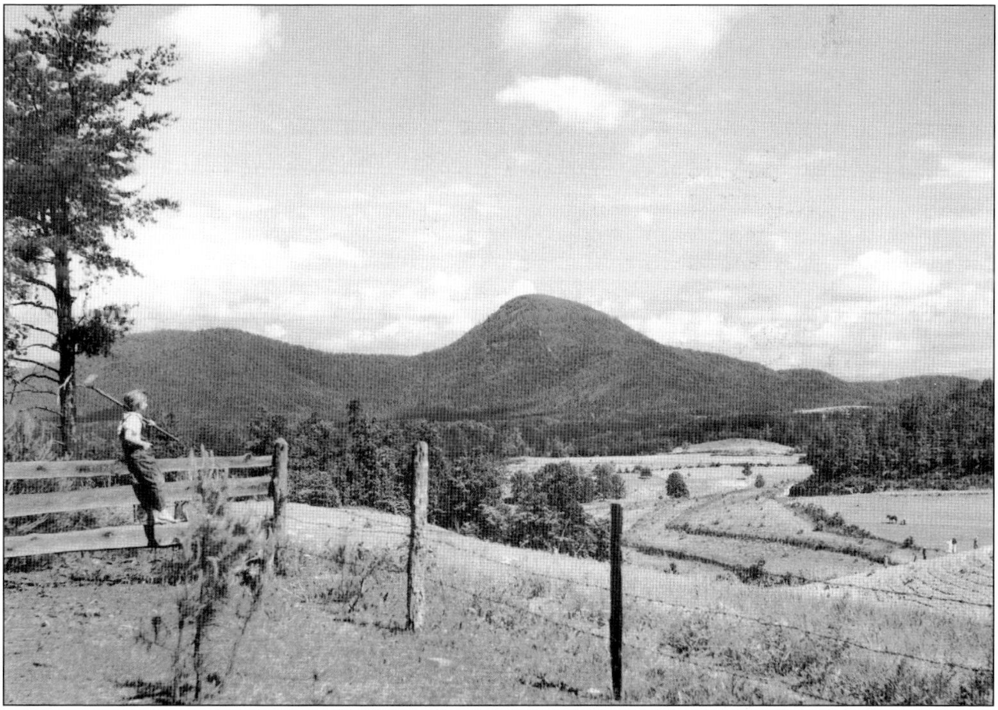

Yonah Mountain is said to stand watch over all of White County. From the Helen and Nacoochee Valleys to Mossy Creek and Town Creek to Leaf, Yonah's predominant profile is visible from almost every corner of the county. Yonah comes from the Cherokee word for "bear," and for years, fanciful tales have circulated about the mountain's history and mystical powers. It is said lovelorn natives leapt to their deaths rather than be separated. Other tales tell of invading Spanish explorers searching the caves of Yonah for Indian gold. Yonah, at the very least, captures the imagination and elicits passionate musings.

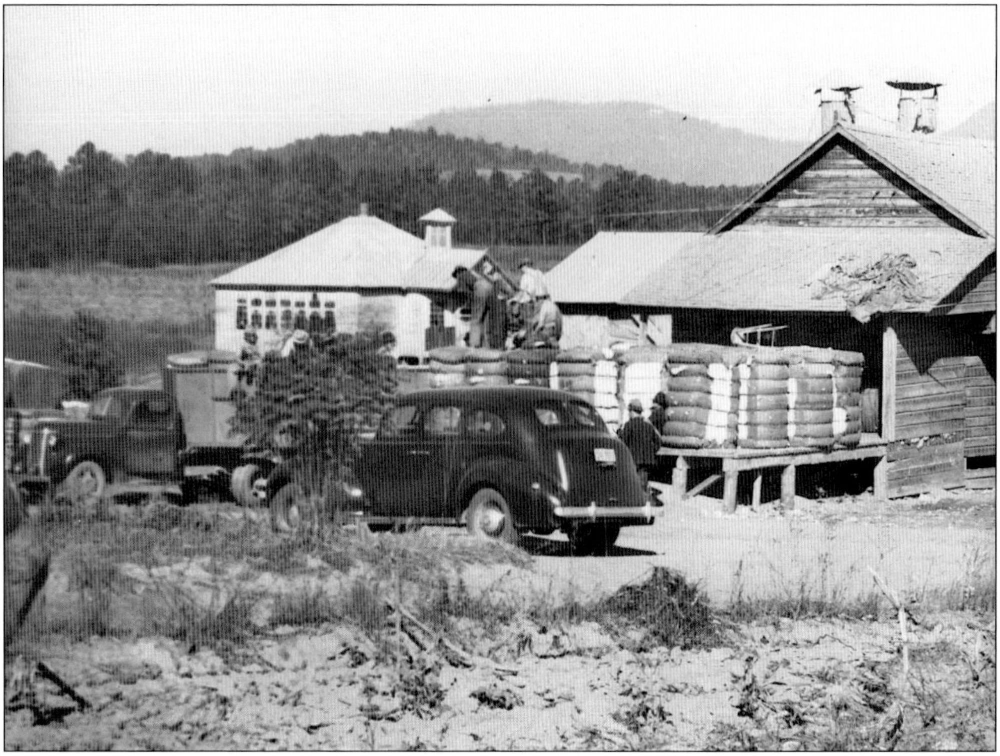

Photographed about 1936 in Leaf, just eight miles from Helen, the E.T. Irvin cotton gin processes a load of cotton bales destined for the sizeable cotton mill in Gainesville/New Holland. Although not on the scale as in southern Georgia, the "king of crops in Georgia" was also grown in White County. With the sawmill gone and the country stricken by the Depression, cotton cultivation was a welcome vocation for many.

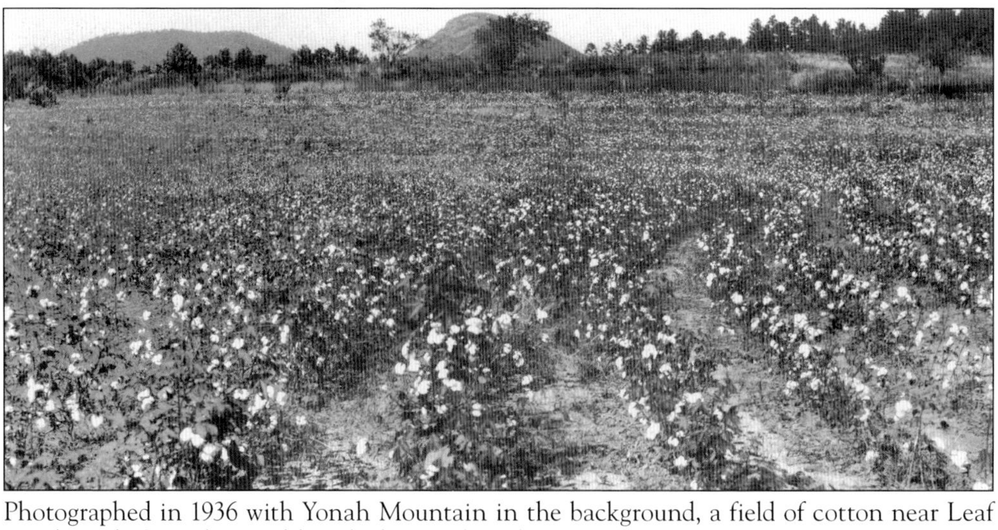

Photographed in 1936 with Yonah Mountain in the background, a field of cotton near Leaf stands ready for picking. Although the textile industry in the Southeast struggled through the Depression, it kept many people employed, and in nearby Gainesville, several large textile plants were in operation. By the 1950s, poultry replaced cotton as the local cash crop, creating job growth in emerging industries.

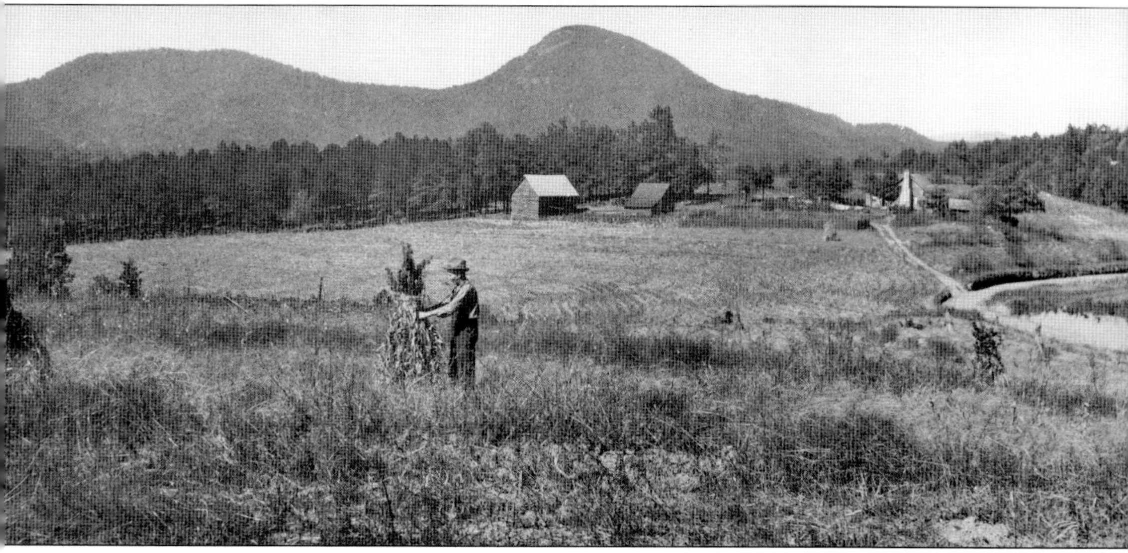

Before and during the Depression, most agriculture in and around Helen consisted of subsistence farming. Other than the sawmill in Helen, there were few industry-related job opportunities. Mountain families worked the land to feed themselves and their farm animals. A few enterprising farmers grew extra corn to sell or convert to a spirituous commodity, but most farmed honestly and tirelessly to bring food to their table.

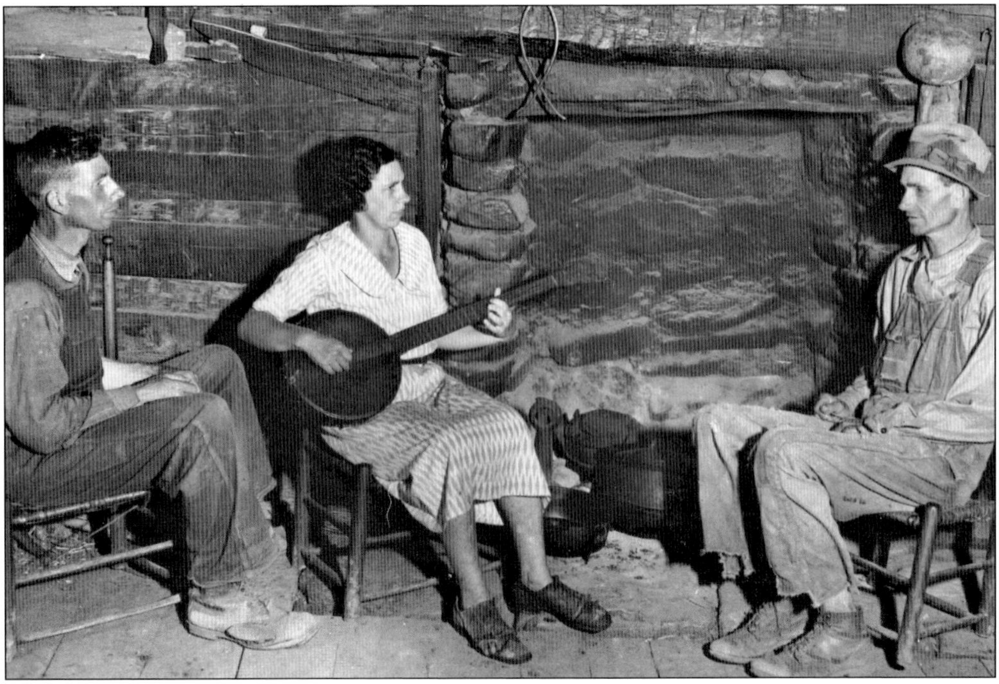

Mountain families survived the Depression by hard work and flinty self-reliance. Some subsistence farmers also made pottery, operated grain mills, panned for gold, or distilled corn whiskey to raise cash. When time allowed, entertainment might include playing music, singing, or just relaxing by the fire, as suggested by this c. 1936 image.

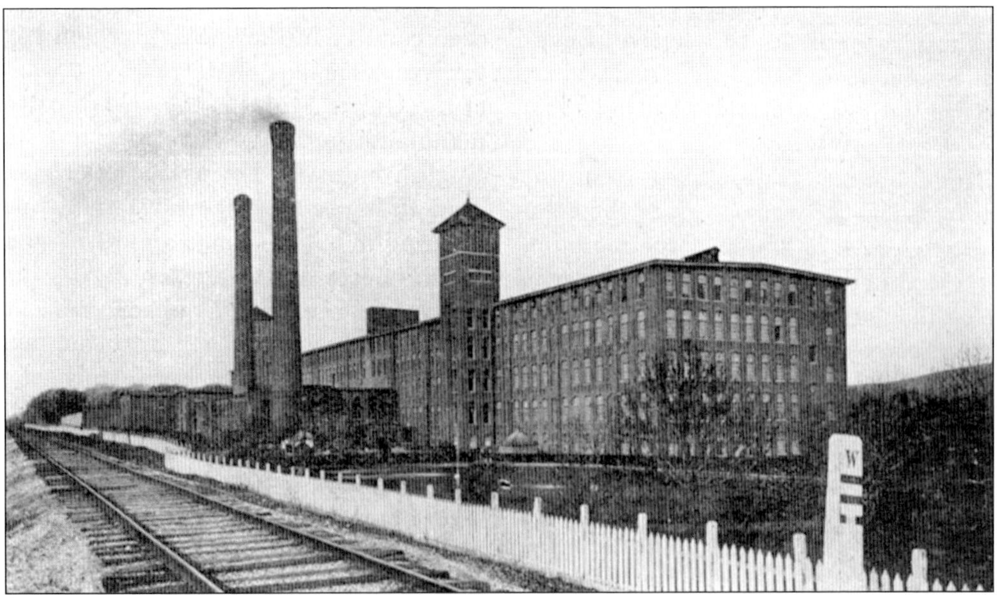

Most Depression-era jobs were in urban centers beyond the reach of Helen and Nacoochee. Many local residents moved to cities such as Gainesville, Toccoa, Atlanta, or Greenville to work in textile mills. The mill in New Holland, near Gainesville, was preferred because it was close enough for weekend visits with family.

In 1933, the federal government raised the price of gold by 70 percent, renewing interest in the feasibility of gold mining in the Helen area. In this 1936 image, Bill Hudson poses with a five-and-a-half-ounce gold nugget he found on Dukes Creek in May 1936. One of the last of the Nacoochee miners, Hudson restored Hamby Ditch and mined gold until the mid-1940s.

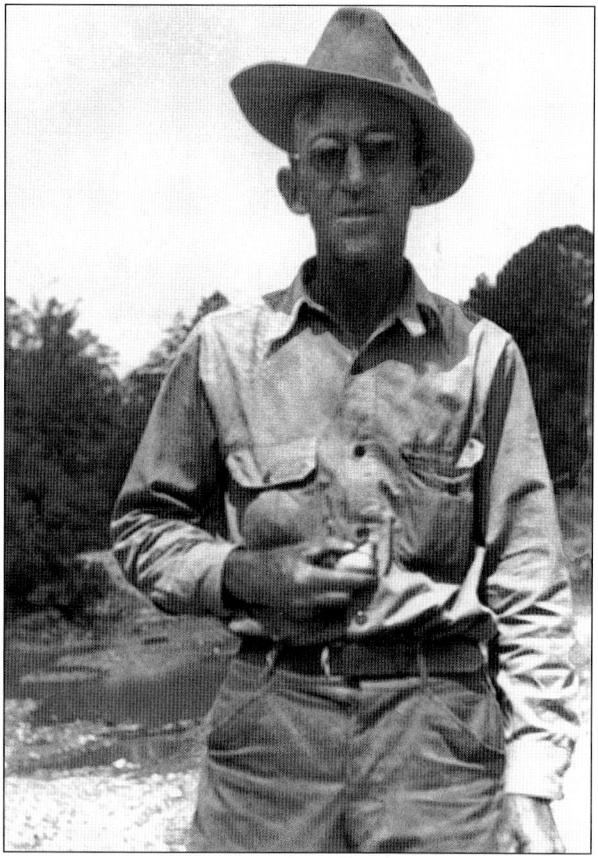

The Franco-American Company operated a hardrock mining operation on Little Hamby Mountain at the north end of Helen for a brief period in the 1930s. Even with new power tools like the jackhammer, tunneling into hard rock was backbreaking work. Despite the higher price of gold, labor was too expensive, and the operation only lasted a few years.

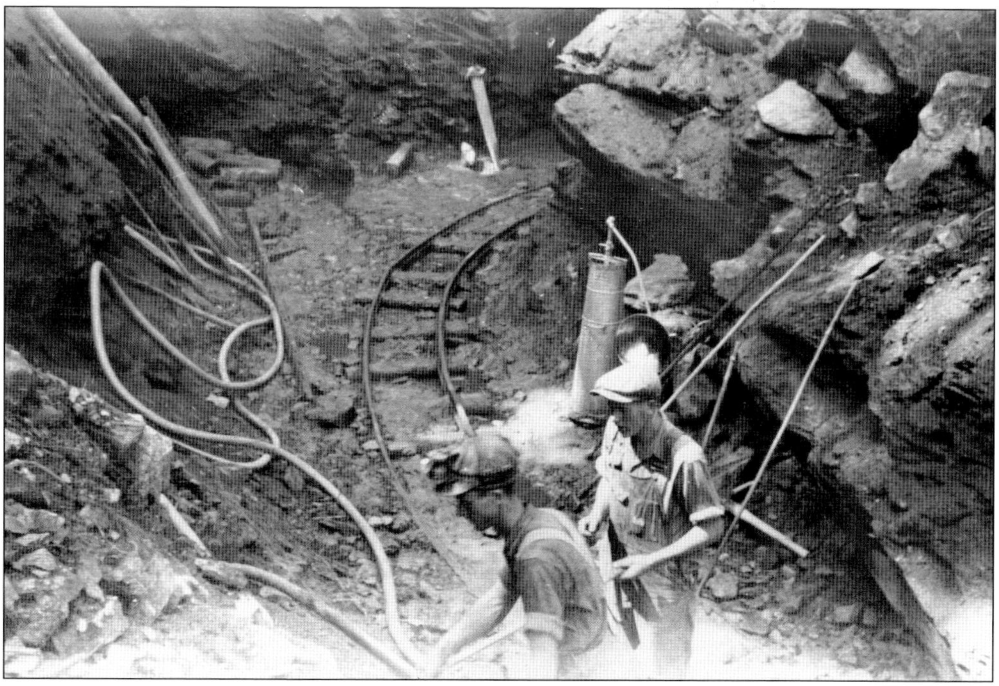

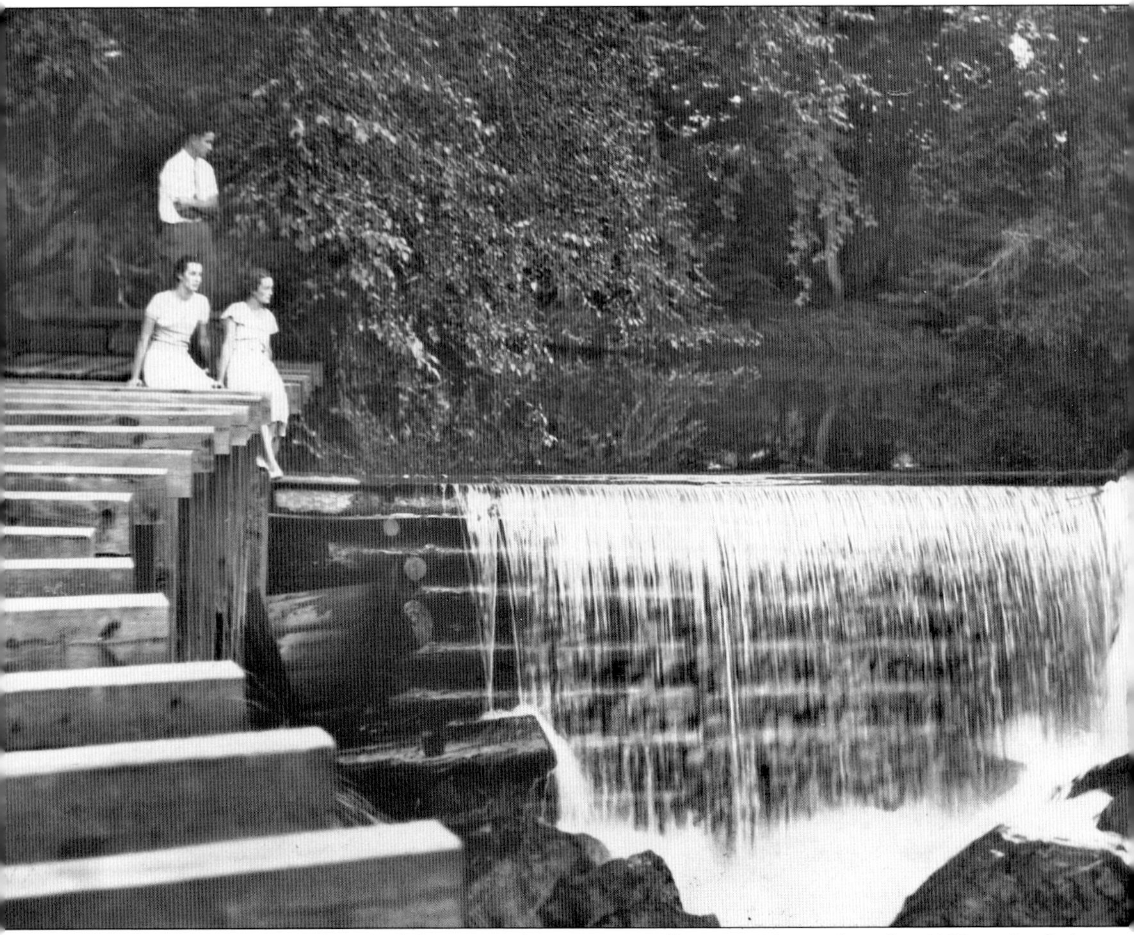

Nora Mill in Nacoochee had functioned as a grain mill since 1824, and in the 1930s, it had also become an attraction for travelers and visitors. With the Mountain Ranch Hotel still in business and smaller guesthouses available for those who could afford to come, the mill was a "must see" for guests. The mill is still in operation by the family of the late Ron Fain, who brought back traditional stone-ground corn and grain products with great success. Local residents, restaurants, and visitors enjoy the traditional taste and texture of products that include Dixie Ice Cream and Pioneer's Porridge.

This c. 1932 image, from a brochure for Greear's Lodge, faces west toward Hamby Mountain. The view shows the Gainesville & Northwestern Railroad tracks along the west side of the Chattahoochee River. Though seeing very little use by this time, the rails did service rail buses, handling whatever mail, express, and package-freight traffic that was needed. The rails were totally abandoned and removed by 1936.

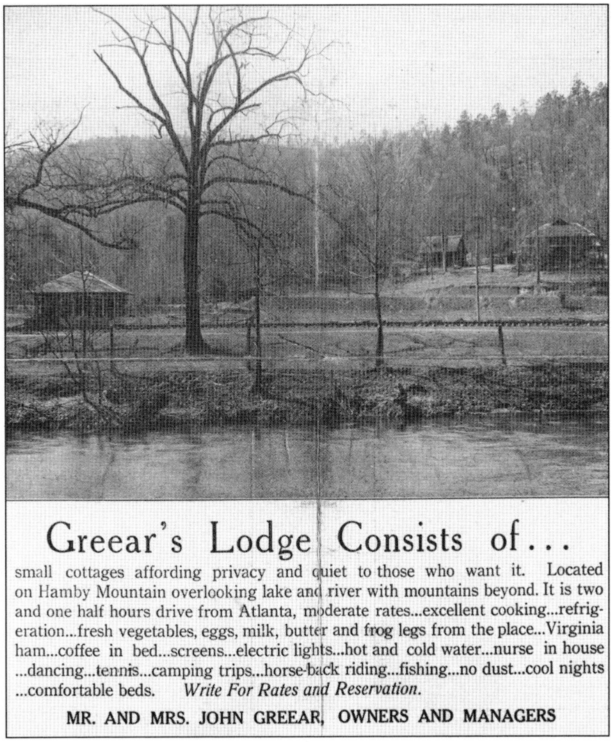

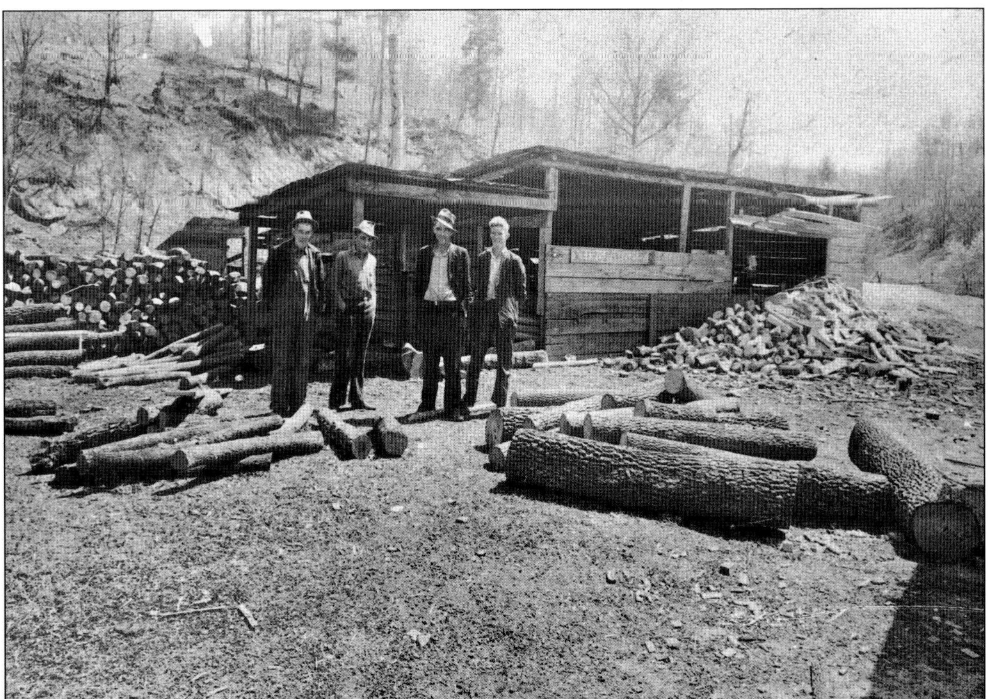

After the larger sawmills left the area, smaller mills appeared in and around the Helen area. This shuttlecock mill, operated by T.J. Tallent, made weaving-loom shuttles from the dense wood of native dogwood trees. The mill was in operation from 1936 until the early 1960s.

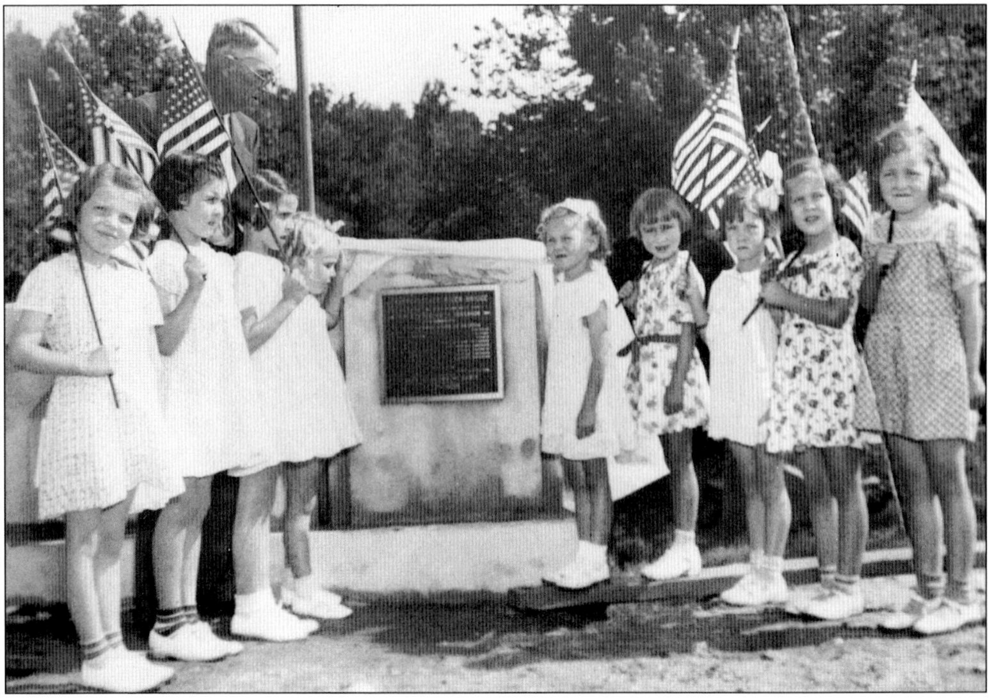

In 1938, the steel bridge that had served Helen since the early days of the Byrd-Matthews Lumber Company was replaced with a concrete bridge. The new bridge was located downstream from the original, and Main Street was rerouted over the new bridge. The triangle that formed between the new and old sections of Main Street is now the site of the Helen Marketplatz. Photographed at the bridge dedication are, from left to right, Evelyn Blackburn, Henrietta Howard, Jeannie Lusk, Gwendolyn Vandiver, Euzella Blackburn, Augustus Holmes, Maxine Lusk, Nell Holmes, and Thelma Sims. W.A. Allison stands behind the girls on the left.

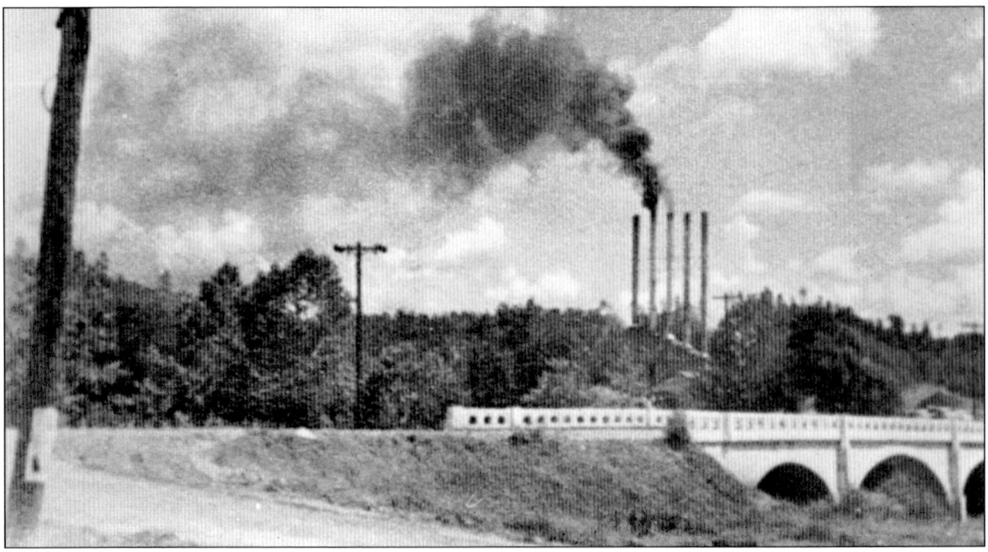

Charles Maloof, a Lebanese immigrant who had established other local retail businesses, purchased the mill site after the Morse Brothers Land and Lumber Company moved to Mexico. In 1938, he opened a smaller hardwood-flooring mill, providing needed jobs.

A Hotel Where Friendly Hospitality Will Please You

LACES
H SEEING
wee Falls
chee Valley
. Yonah
Creek Falls
t. Tray
Ruby Falls
'd Mines
'abin Falls

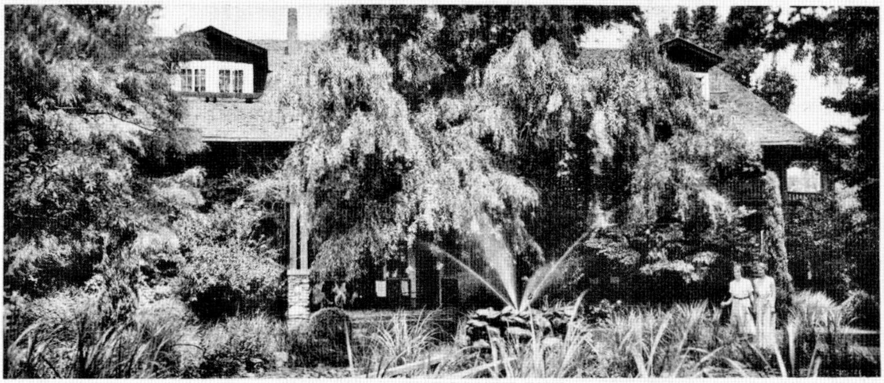

FRONT VIEW OF MOUNTAIN RANCH HOTEL

Riding
Swimming
Dancing
Tennis
Golf
Hiking
Fishing
Shuffle Board

an invitation to visit the MOUNTAIN H HOTEL in the beautiful mountains of H GEORGIA; where the climate, natural and bracing mountain air are unsurpassed.

tel contains fifty guest rooms, attractively ed—with or without bath—and is sur-d by beautiful shaded blue grass lawns. INING ROOM is one of the chief attrac-Specializing in fresh fruits and vegetables, pring chickens, and country cured hams. ndidly trained Chef is in charge of the chen—a master of Southern cooking.

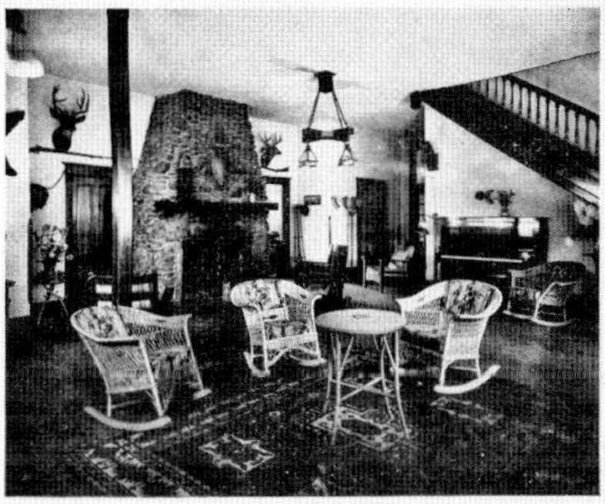

The main lounge with its large open fireplace . . . cheery and comfortable at all times.

The cheerful home-like lounge with its huge fire-place, the inviting verandas, attractive dining room, the cordial friendliness of guest and per-sonnel encourage contentment and complete ease.

THE MOUNTAIN RANCH is located at the head-waters of the Chattahoochee—so beautifully described by Sidney Lanier — 88 miles from Atlanta, over a perfectly paved highway — 33 miles north of Gainesville, Georgia. If arriving by rail notify the management and a car will meet you in Gainesville.

The Mountain Ranch Hotel continued to operate after the Morse Brothers Land and Lumber Company closed, and it remained successful through the 1930s. New Deal road-building projects improved the mobility of people who had automobiles, and travel and tourism to the mountains gradually increased.

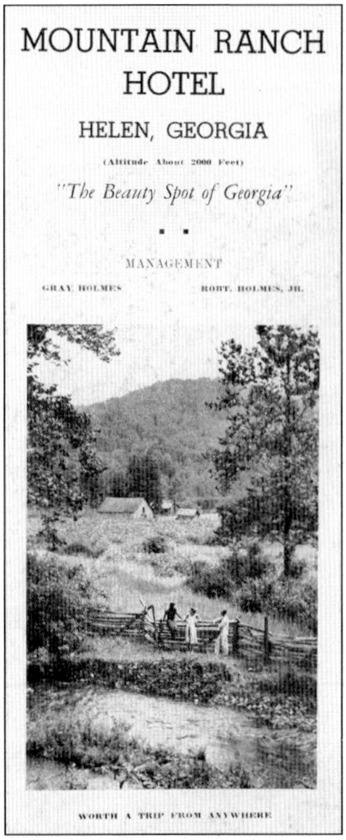

When W.A, and C.W. White purchased it, the name was shortened to the Mountain Ranch Hotel. The 1940 brochure declared it "Worth a Trip from Anywhere." The Mountain Ranch Hotel offered room and meals starting at $3 a day. Horseback riding, swimming, dancing, tennis, shuffleboard, golf, and hiking were featured activities.

Shown here from the 1940 brochure is the lobby of the Mountain Ranch Hotel. The stone fireplace is typical of many seen today in older homes in the region. Regrettably, the Mountain Ranch Hotel was lost to a fire in 1945, never to be rebuilt.

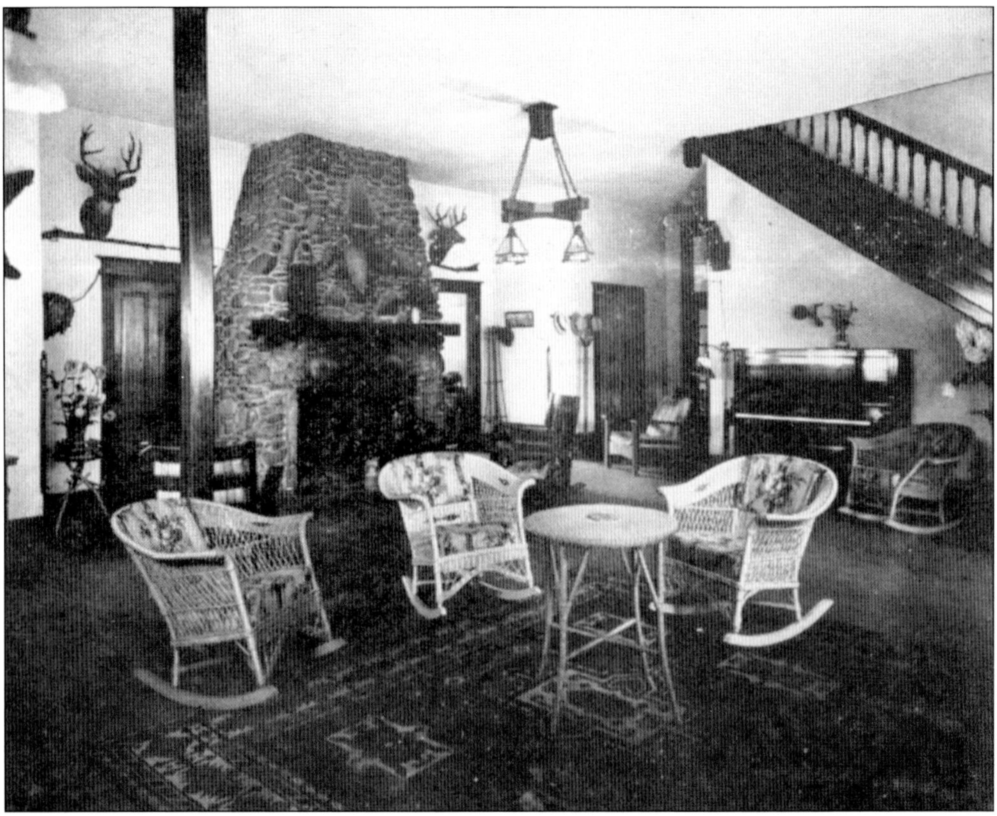

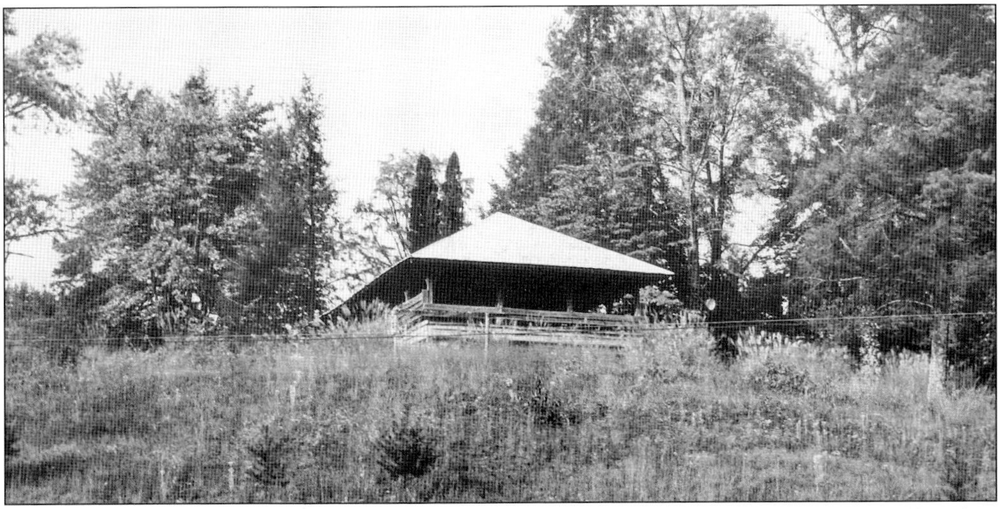

The covered pavilion of the Mountain Ranch Hotel escaped damage from the 1945 fire that destroyed the hotel. The structure became a meeting place for residents to gather and enjoy live music and dancing. Many residents today have fond memories of evenings spent at the 1950s venue, which overlooks the downtown area.

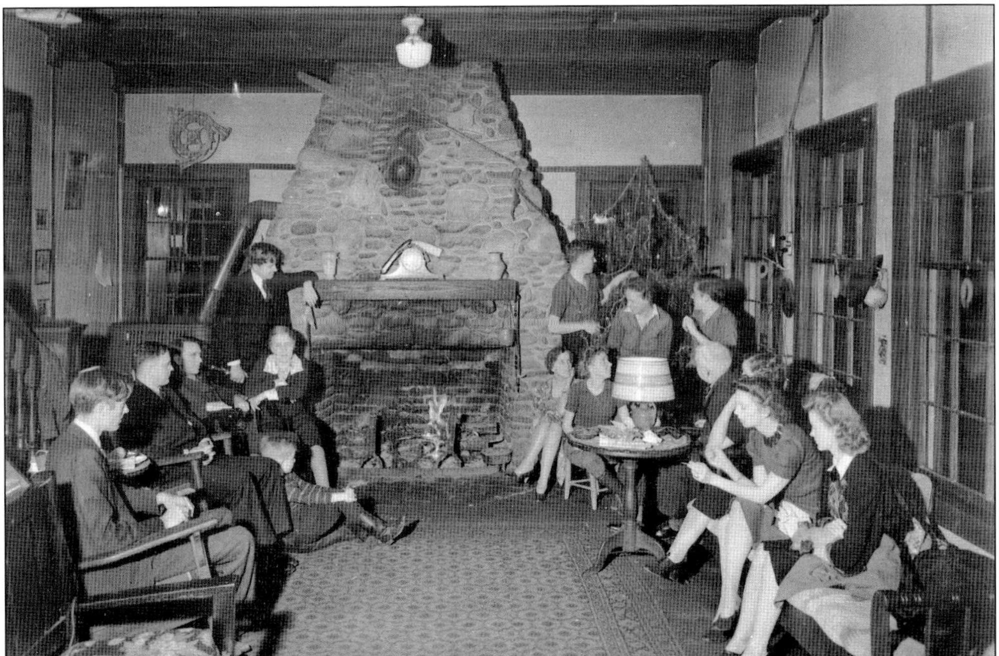

This 1940 Christmas gathering at the Helen home of John and Caroline Greear was attended by poet and author Byron Herbert Reece, seated at far left. Later nominated for the Pulitzer Prize and twice winning the Guggenheim Award, Reece became good friends with Philip and Mildred Greear. Mildred herself became an acclaimed poet. The Greears operated a guest lodge, offering activities similar to those available at the Mountain Ranch Hotel. From left to right are Byron Reece, Joe McGinty, John F. Greear, Joe McGinty Jr, Caroline Greear, David Greear, unidentified woman, Josh Greear, Jean McGinty, Anna Miller, Philip Greear, Charles Miller, Mary Miller, Mildred Greear, and Virginia Greear.

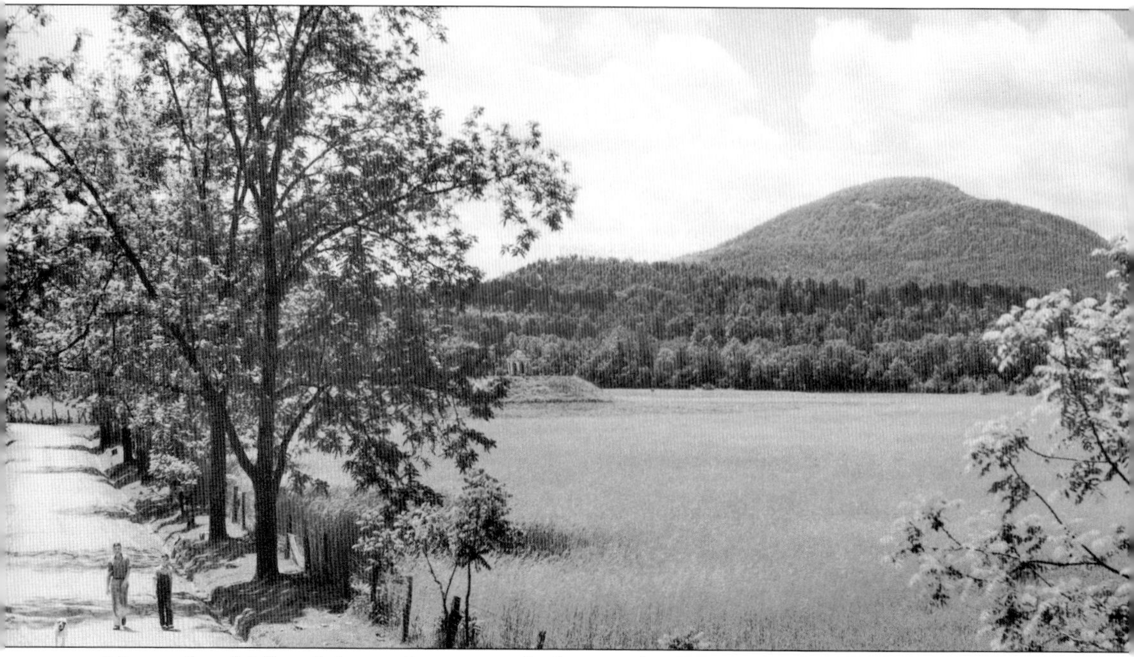

Nacoochee Valley did not change much during the Depression. Dominated by agricultural operations, there were a few guest boardinghouses and inns. This view shows the Unicoi Turnpike as it passed through the Nichols-Hardman property. In the near distance is the Nacoochee Indian Mound, and beyond is Mount Yonah.

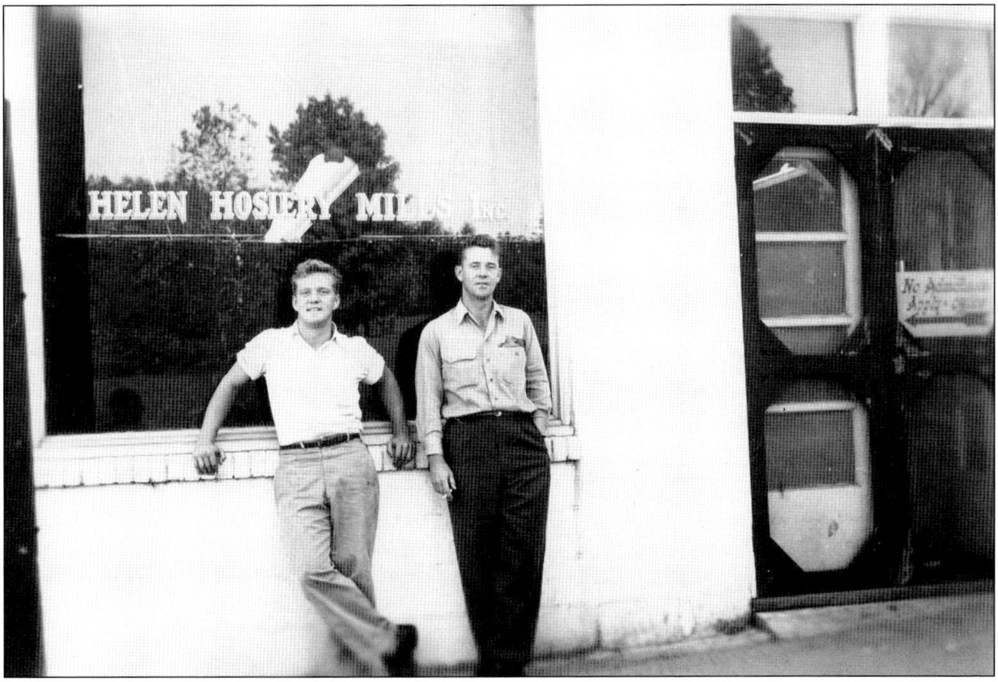

In an effort to boost the local economy in 1946, Charlie Maloof rallied the Helen community to build a facility to accommodate a hosiery mill. The community responded, and within three months, Helen Hosiery Mills began producing a wool and cashmere blend of argyle socks. Later becoming Wilco Hosiery Mills, the company was known as the world's largest manufacturer of hand-darned argyle socks. The mill was operated by Jimmy Wilkins. Here, Jim Wilkins (right) and brother Buddy (left) pose outside the Helen Hosiery Mills.

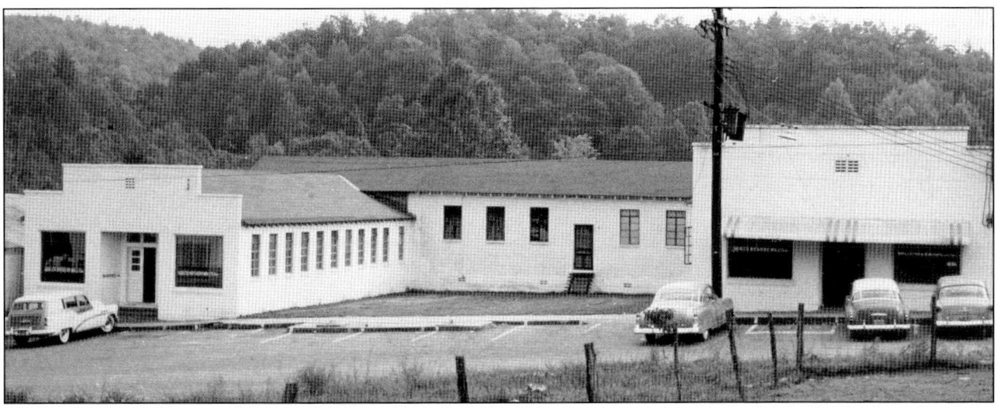

By the time the Helen Hosiery Mills came to town in 1946, there was very little to keep the local economy going. The timber industry was gone, and the Mountain Ranch Hotel had been destroyed in a fire. Charlie Maloof, determined not to let Helen fade away, worked to bring the hosiery mill to Helen, appealing, "We had to have an industry or die." The mill provided employment for almost 12 years.

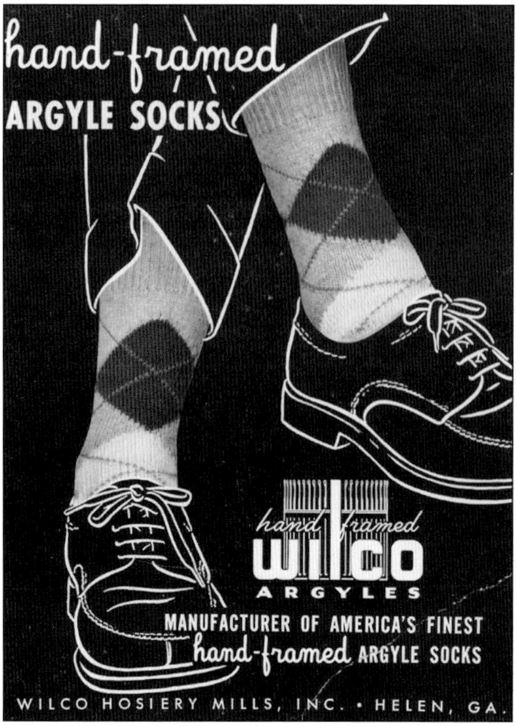

This full-page advertisement for Wilco Hosiery Mills appeared in *Esquire* magazine around 1950. The hosiery mill had an office and representatives in New York City. By the mid-1950s, Burlington and other textile manufacturers began making socks using automated methods, rendering hand-knit socks obsolete. In 1959, the Wilco Hosiery Mills closed, but in 1962, Jimmy Wilkins returned to Helen and opened Orbit Manufacturing, successfully producing ladies apparel until 1996, providing much-needed jobs.

Jim Wilkins (standing, center) oversees production at the Wilco Hosiery Mills around 1948. The women working in the mill were paid based on production. The company had an office in New York in the Empire State Building, and salesmen would make trips to call on buyers in the New York garment district. One of the major customers of the hosiery mill was Federated Department Stores, parent company of Macy's.

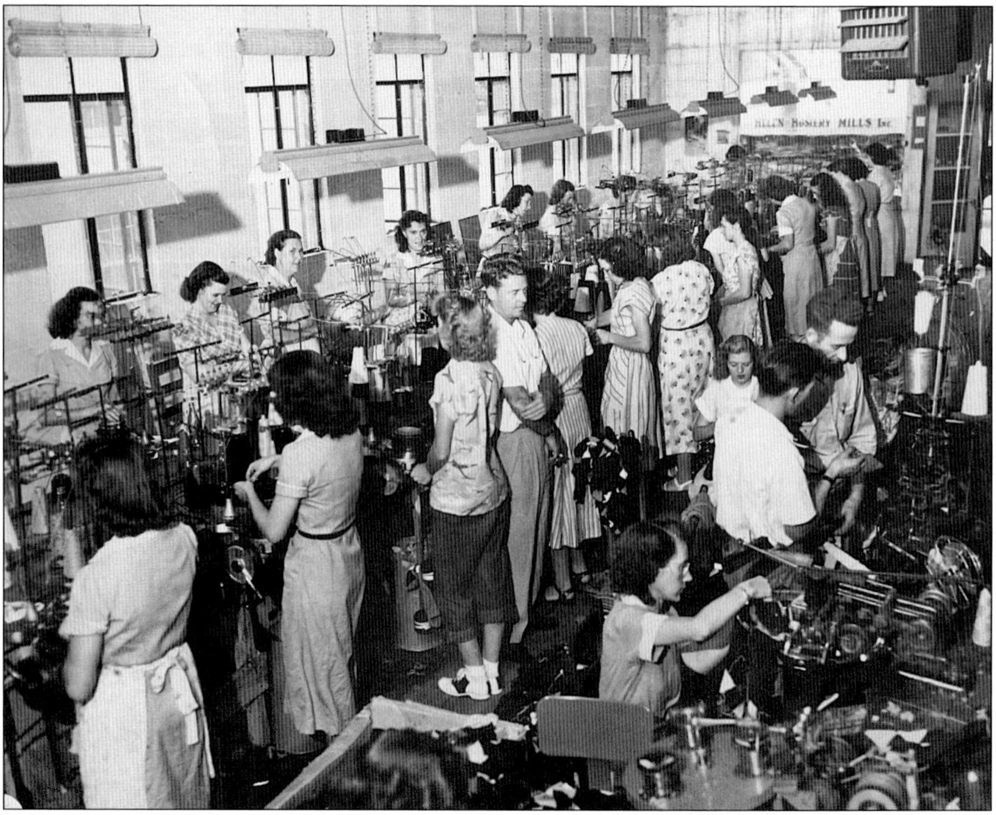

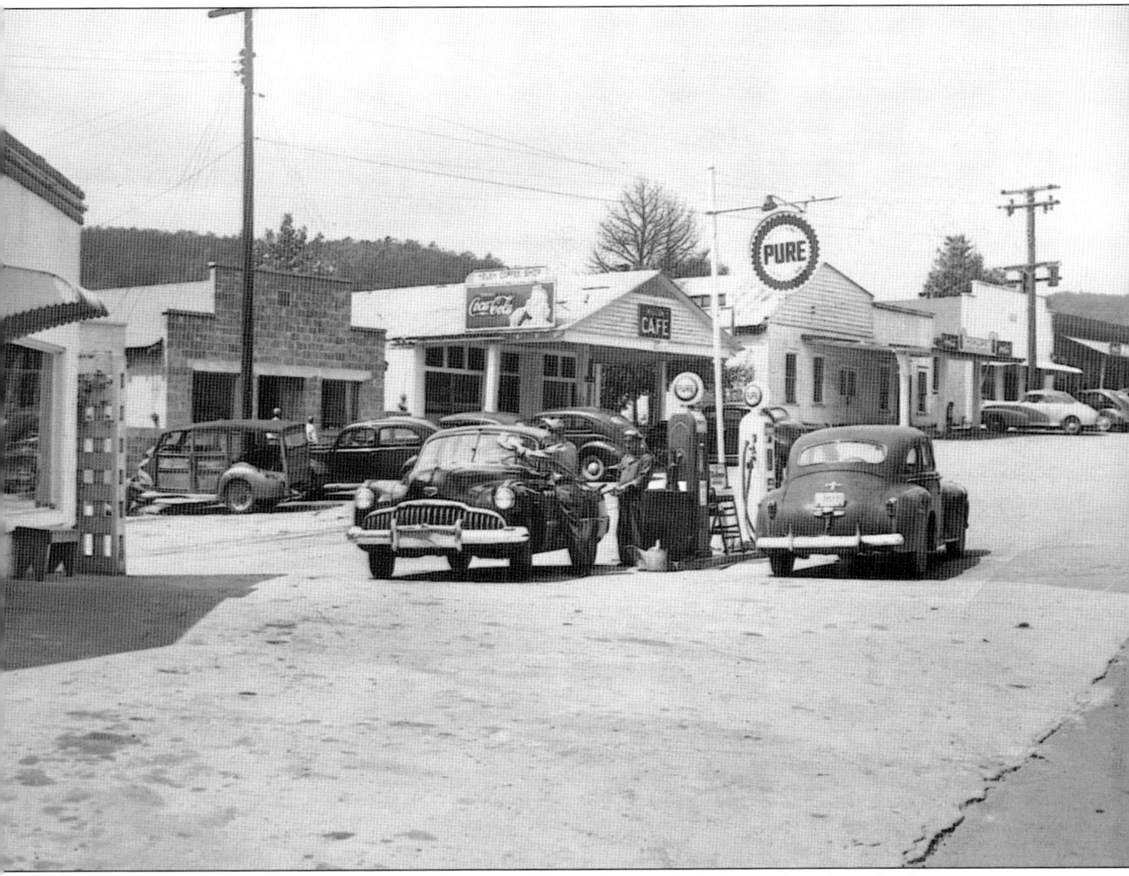

When the original steel bridge over the Chattahoochee River was replaced with the concrete bridge, Main Street was rerouted about 100 feet east and downstream, creating a triangular section of ground between the old and new streets. For more than three decades, the triangle existed. The Pure Oil service station, built by Bob Taylor in the triangle, featured uniformed attendants who would fill the tank, check the oil, and wash the windshield. In the background, the Helen Café advertises Coca-Cola. A 1939 Ford Woody Wagon in need of serious repair is visible in front of what would become Chief Westmoreland's Garage.

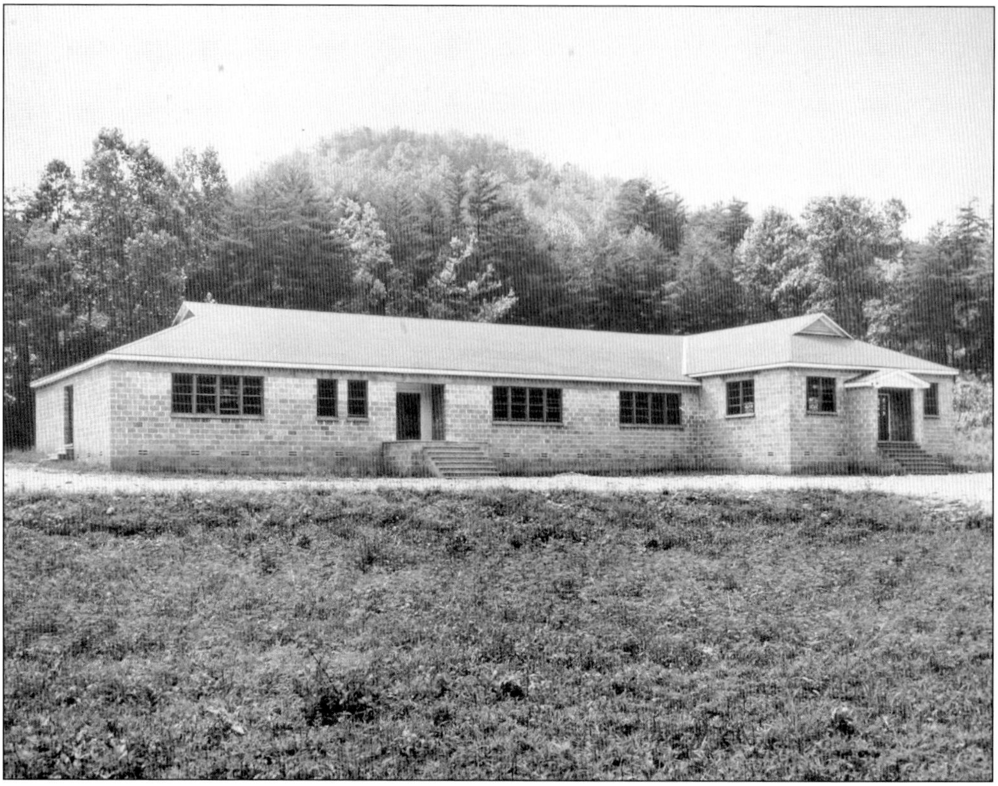

Around 1949, a second Helen school was constructed on Escowee Street, across the river from its original location. A nearly identical, cinder-block school was constructed in Robertstown about the same time. Both schools served their respective communities for over 15 years, but both closed and were consolidated at the Nacoochee School location. Kel New was the first principal at the school in Helen. The building would eventually become Orbit Manufacturing.

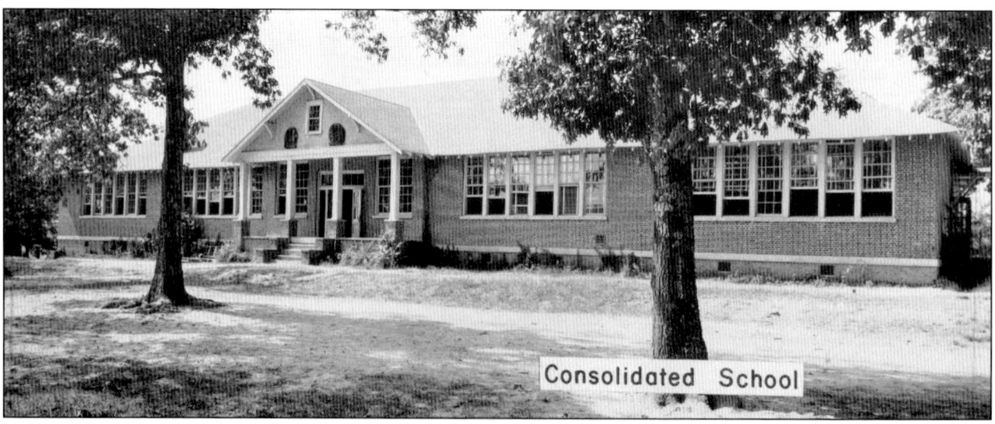

The Nacoochee Institute was destroyed by fire in 1926 and merged with the Rabun Gap Industrial School, forming the Rabun Gap-Nacoochee School at Rabun Gap. The Sautee-Nacoochee School was built in 1927 and operated until 1974. When the Helen School closed, children from Helen and Robertstown areas went to the school in Nacoochee. By the late 1970s, the building was occupied by the Sautee-Nacoochee Community Association.

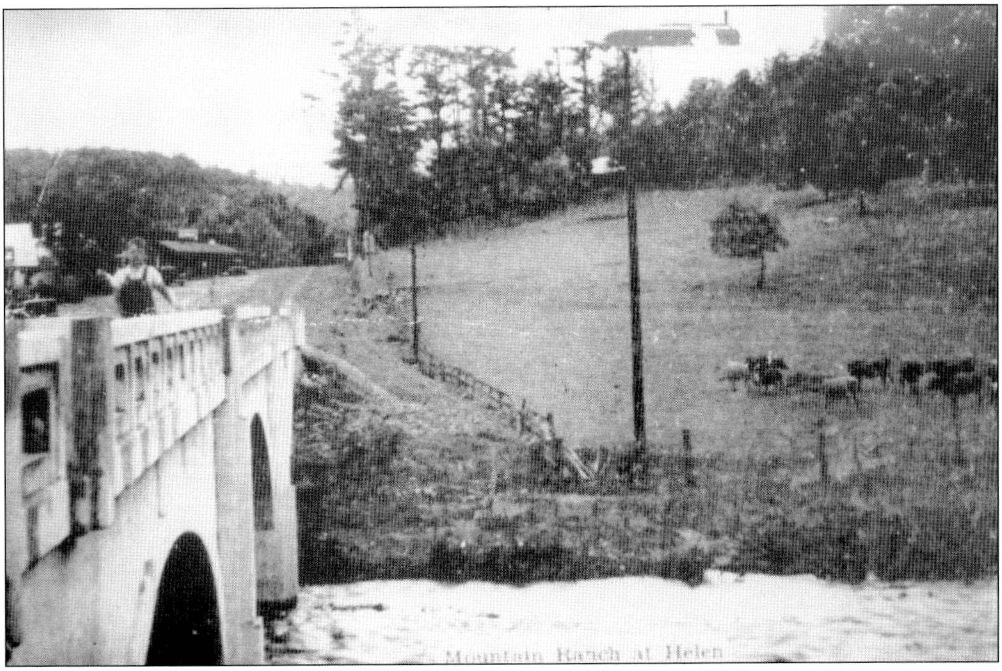

To the east of Main Street, cows briefly shared their field with the Helen baseball team, which revived for a short time in 1950. In this image, the Mountain Ranch Hotel is gone, but the pavilion where community dances were held is visible on the hill. This pasture area was also used in the church picnic scene in the 1951 film *I'd Climb the Highest Mountain*, starring Susan Hayward, William Lundigan, and Rory Calhoun.

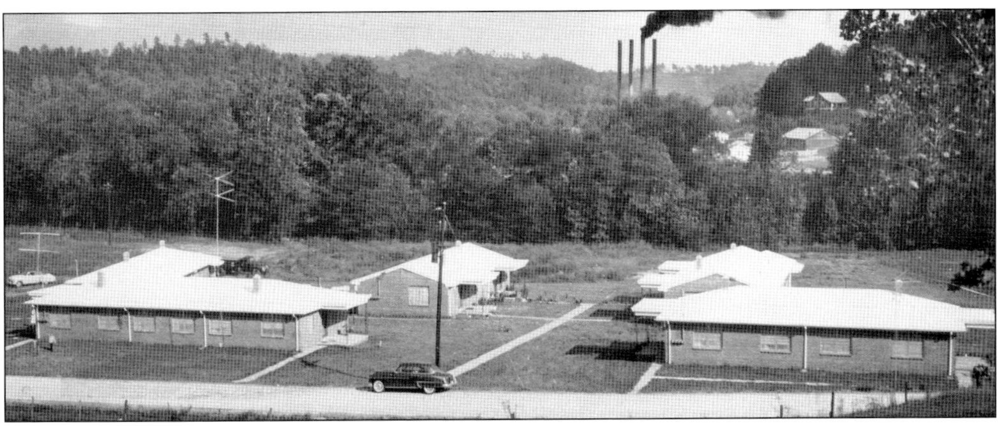

In the 1950s, the Toccoa Housing Authority constructed low-income housing units in Helen on Chattahoochee and Unicoi Streets. Charlie Maloof, while serving as mayor, once again was instrumental in bringing improvements to Helen by way of these affordable homes; his goal was to maintain the workforce in Helen for industries such as the Helen Hosiery Mills.

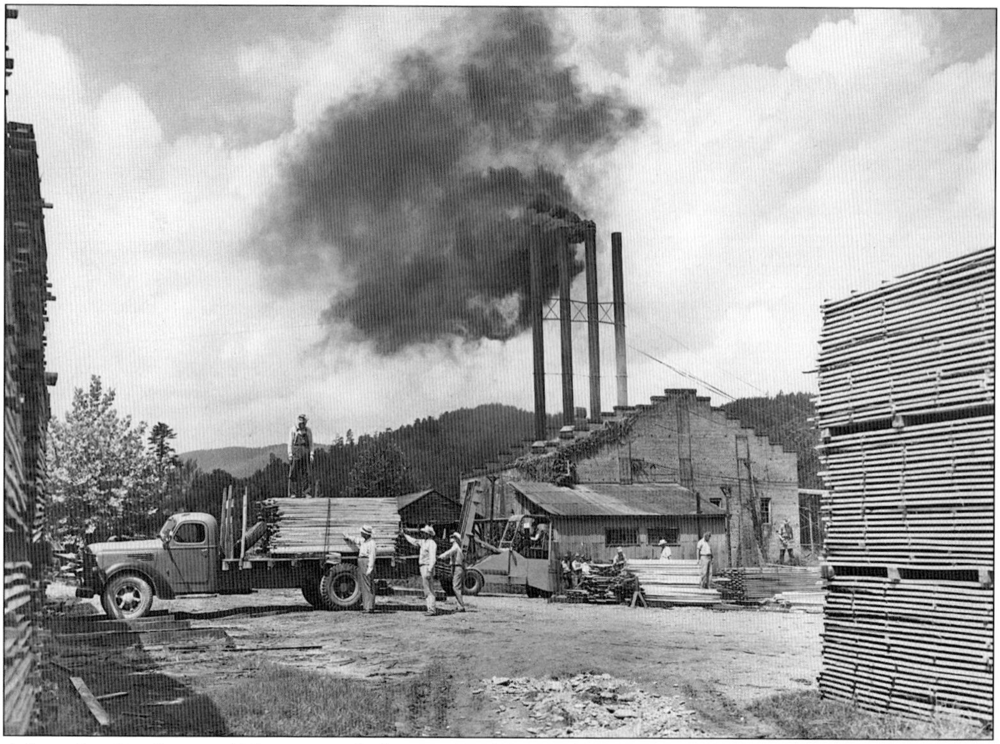

After the lumber mill harvested the profitable timber, it was dismantled and shipped to Mexico. The building that had housed the twin band saws was gone, but the brick powerhouse remained, and Charles Maloof converted it to a hardwood-flooring mill. Charles Miller managed the enterprise.

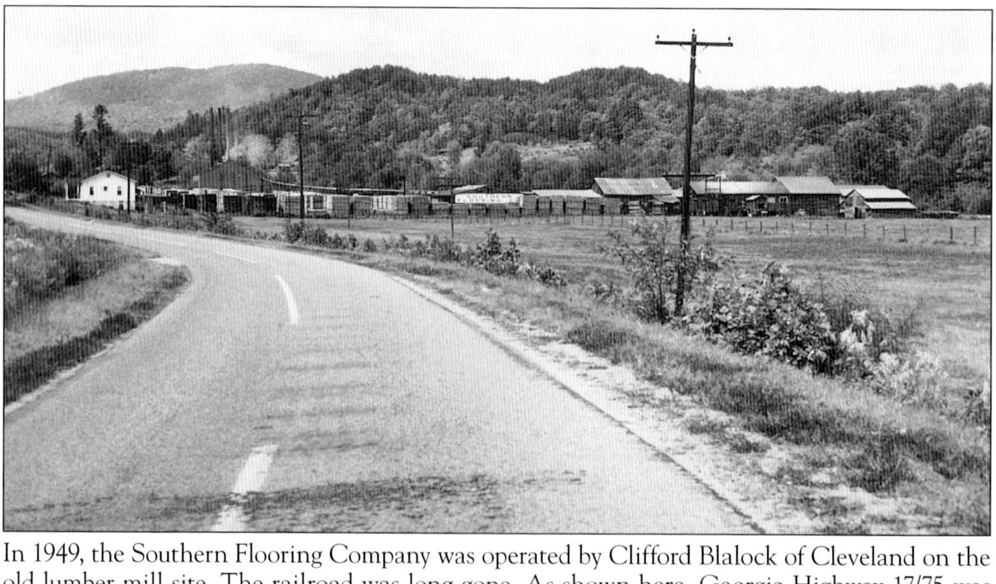

In 1949, the Southern Flooring Company was operated by Clifford Blalock of Cleveland on the old lumber mill site. The railroad was long gone. As shown here, Georgia Highway 17/75 was paved but was barely wide enough to accommodate two cars. The brick powerhouse at the mill had only four smoke stacks instead of the original five. In the early 1950s, the flooring mill caught fire and the business moved to nearby Cleveland, Georgia.

The Chattahoochee United Methodist Church was established in 1860 and was the focal point of Robertstown religious and social activities. The church was featured prominently in the film *I'd Climb the Highest Mountain*. The church is one of the oldest in the area.

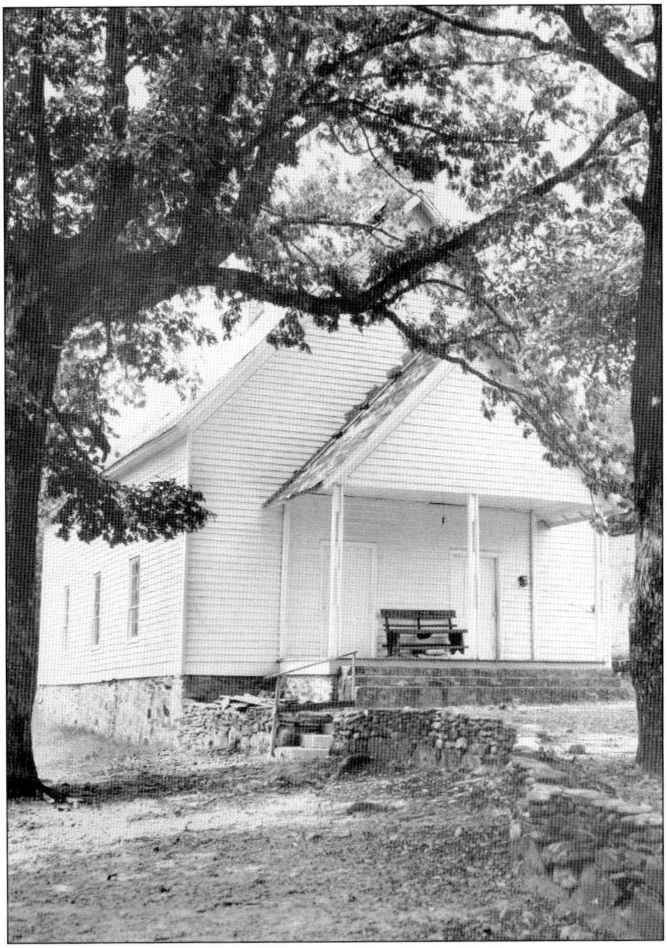

Outside Nora Mill, local boys wait to be called for their scene during the filming of *I'd Climb the Highest Mountain*. The film was directed by Henry King and cost $4 million to produce. Some Helen area residents had speaking roles, including Jerry Vandiver and Dottie Sims-Jackson. Shirley Black-McDonald was a stand-in for Susan Hayward. A number of local residents were employed as extras, including June Westmoreland-Parks, Lois Brown, Fred Stovall, Neal Sims, Skip Cathy, Winston Lusk, Joyce Allison, and James Rogers.

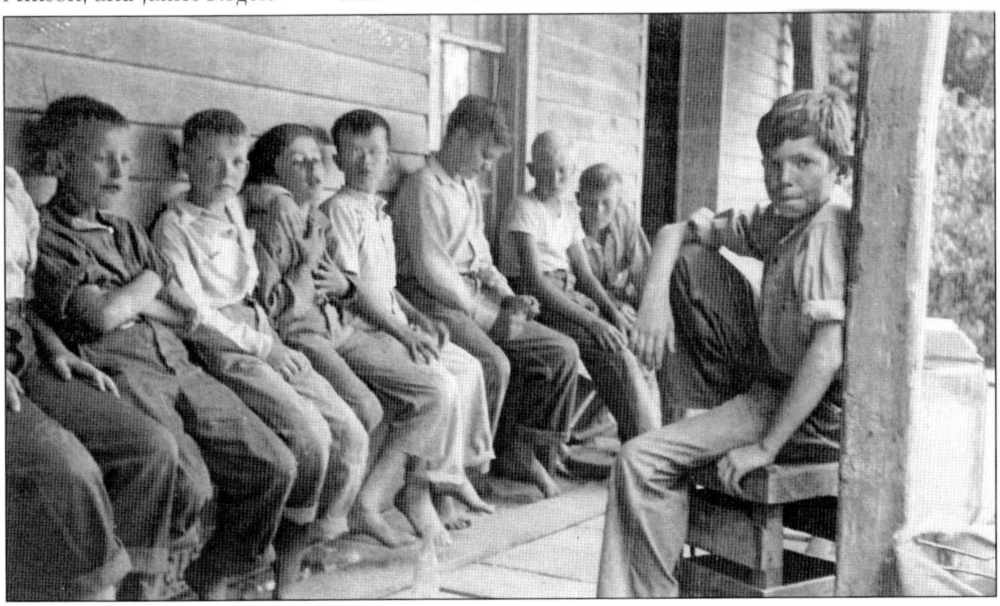

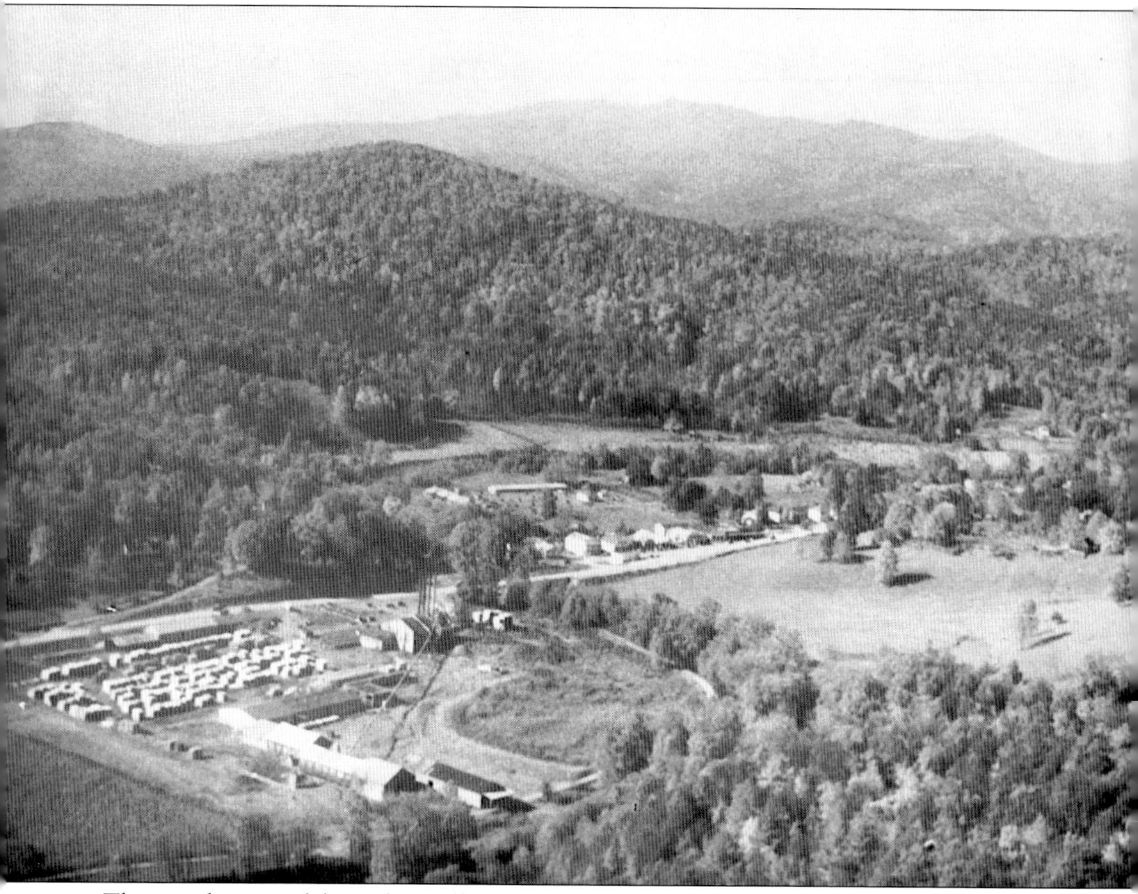

This aerial image of the Helen Valley from about 1949 shows the hardwood-flooring mill still in operation. Only four of the five tall smokestacks are standing. The millpond is gone, but there is a large inventory of finished flooring ready for delivery. There are no buildings on the east side of Main Street. Behind downtown, Hamby Mountain rises from the river bottom and Horse Range is on the horizon.

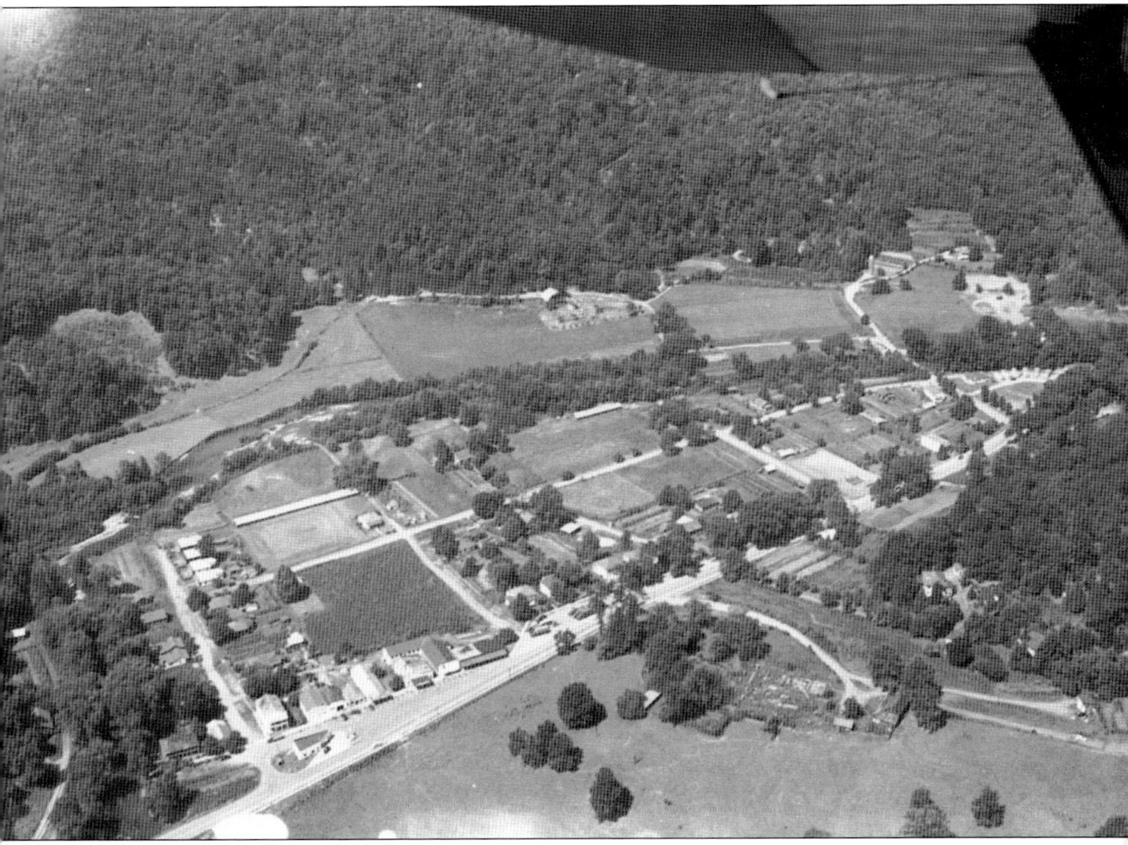

In this aerial view, looking west toward Hamby Mountain, the remnants of the Mountain Ranch Hotel can be seen in the foreground. From White Street south to the Chattahoochee Bridge, there are no structures on the east side of Main Street. Much of the land was used as small farm plots, planted with corn. Chicken houses are visible along the river, off Unicoi Street.

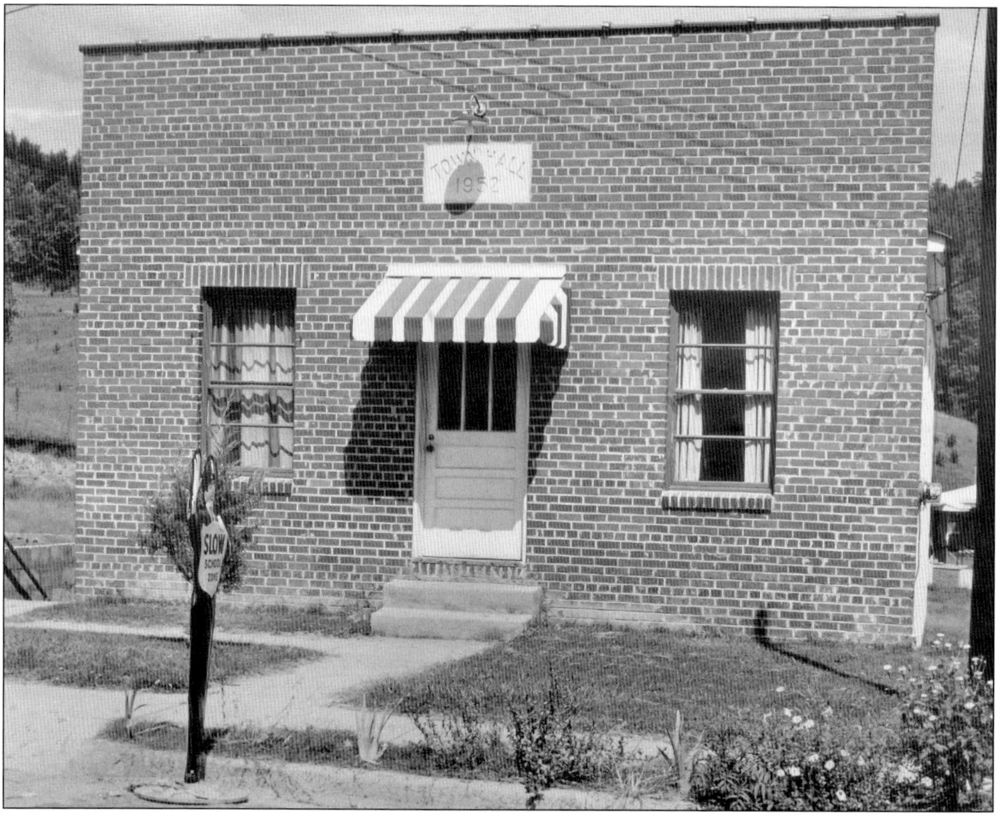

In 1952, city hall was located in this brick building on the east side of Main Street, next to Brown's Standard Oil service station. It later moved to the west side of Main Street next to the south wing of the hosiery mill, then to a new municipal building on Chattahoochee Street, and finally to the current location at 25 Alpenrosen Strasse.

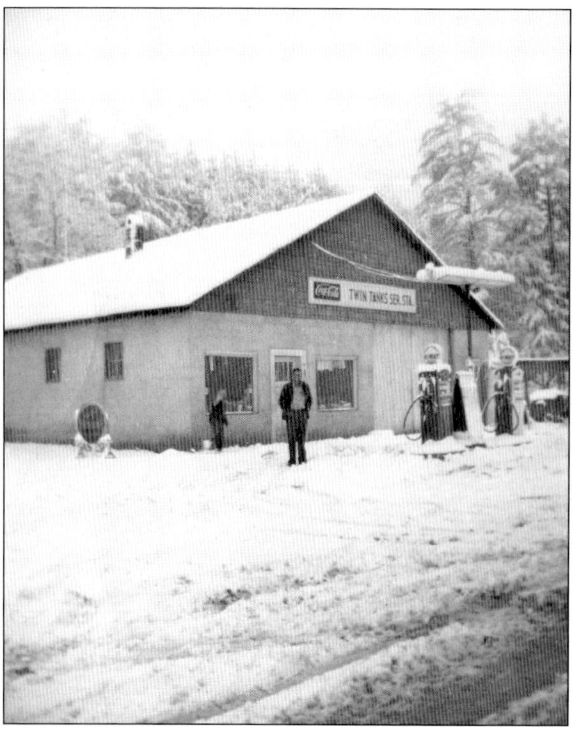

Garland Vandiver poses at the Twin Tanks Service Station in 1960 after a heavy snowfall. Vandiver operated the station from 1947 to about 1974. Later, Ron and Rita Fain operated Fain's Antiques from this location, before Ron took over milling operations at Nora Mill.

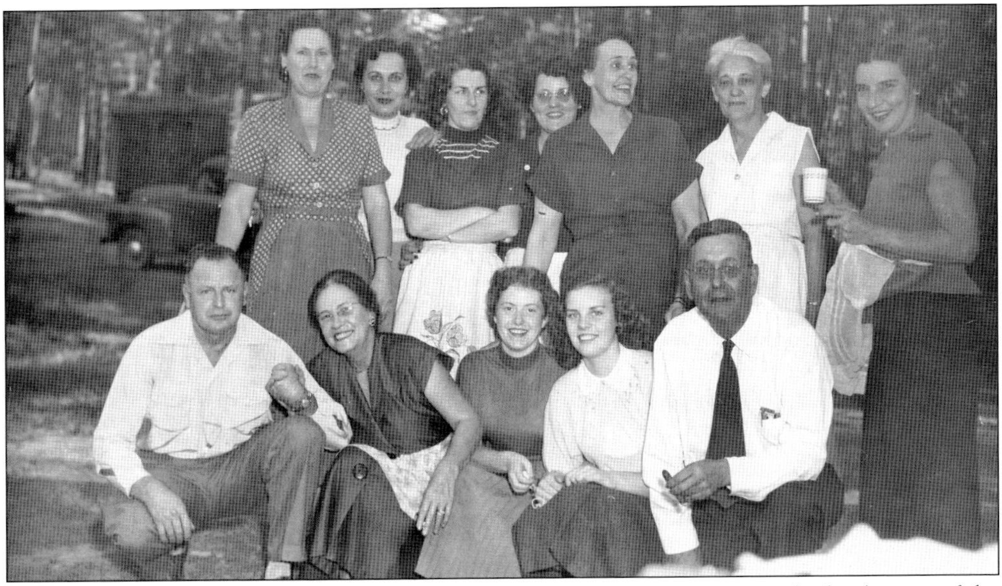

Late in the 1940s, Charlie Maloof realized that for Helen to survive, tourism had to be part of the solution. Automobile travel to North Georgia was increasing. Maloof had political connections in Atlanta, including Gov. Herman Talmage, and he proposed a new park and lodge just north of Helen. Unicoi State Park was opened in June 1954, and the lodge was built by 1969. This image was taken at the groundbreaking ceremony. From left to right are (first row) Roy Robinson, Blanch Maloof, Barbara Ann Allison, June Westmoreland, and Charlie Maloof; (second row) Martha Allison, Della Westmoreland, Doris Ruth Cathy, Billy Adams, Beatrice Westmoreland, Arispa Palmer, and Sue Vandiver.

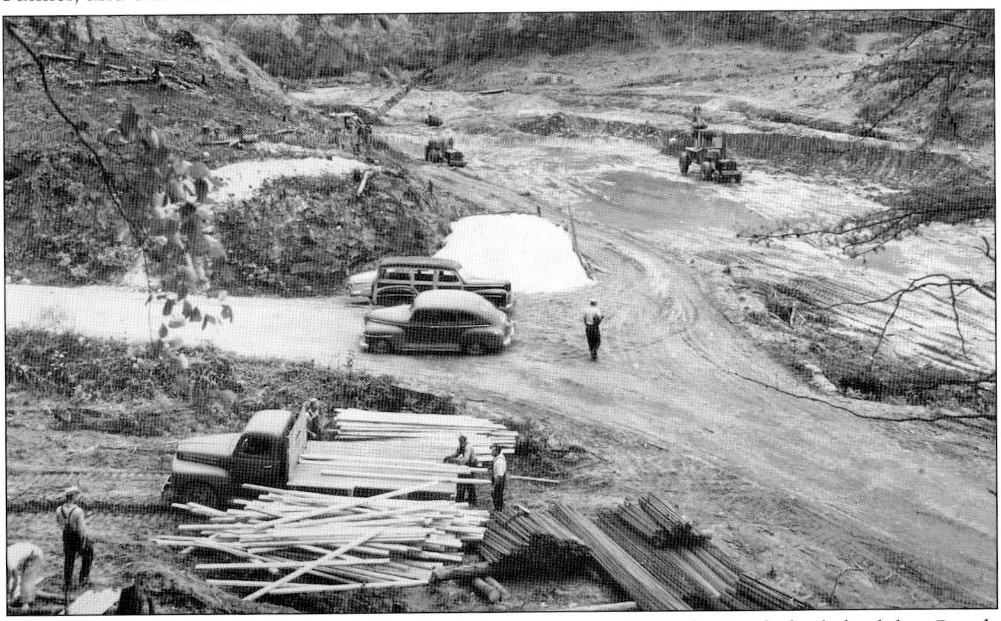

Construction of Unicoi Lake began in 1951. The waters of Smith Creek feed the lake. Smith Creek is formed at the confluence of York and Curtis Creeks at the base of Anna Ruby Falls. Smith Creek flows from Unicoi Lake and joins the Chattahoochee River in Robertstown, at the intersection of Georgia Highway 17/75 and State Route 356.

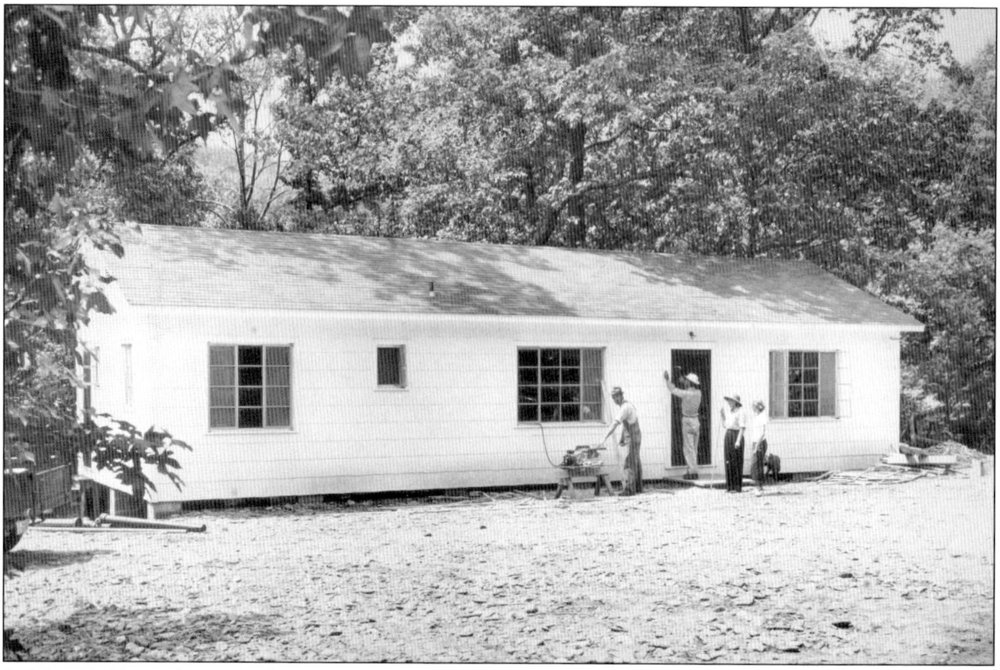

Zebbie Phillips, photographed here wearing dark slacks and a hat, supervises work on the building that would become the Chattahoochee Grill. Both the Chattahoochee Motel and Grill were built in anticipation of tourists visiting Unicoi State Park, north of Helen.

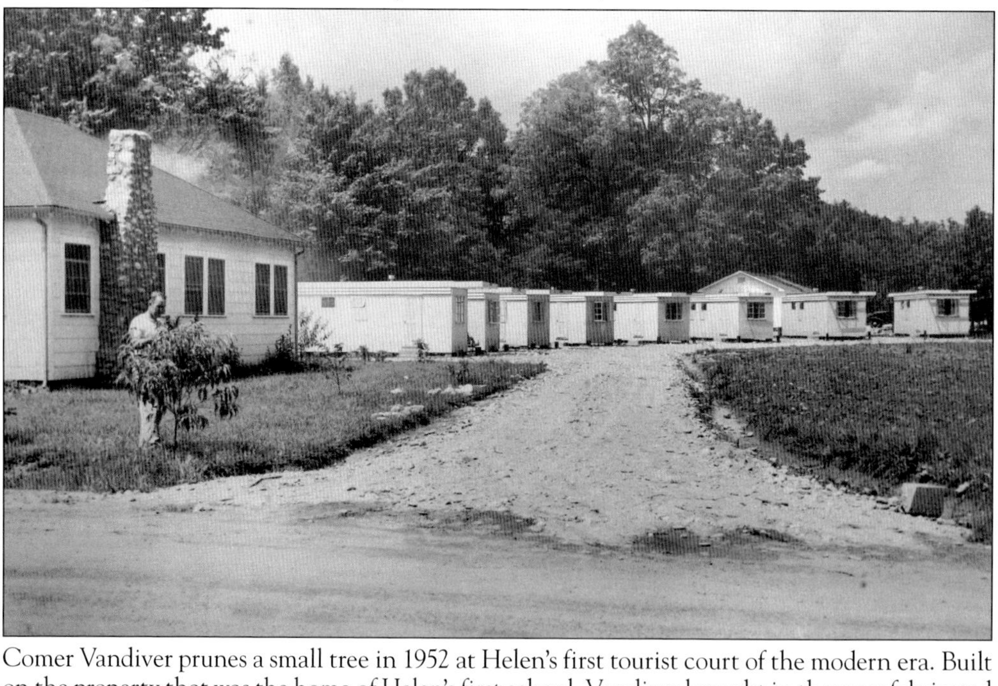

Comer Vandiver prunes a small tree in 1952 at Helen's first tourist court of the modern era. Built on the property that was the home of Helen's first school, Vandiver brought in these prefabricated cabins and furnished them to accommodate overnight guests. Zebbie Phillips's Chattahoochee Grill is visible in the background. Currently, the Hofbrauhaus River Front Hotel and Restaurant occupy the site.

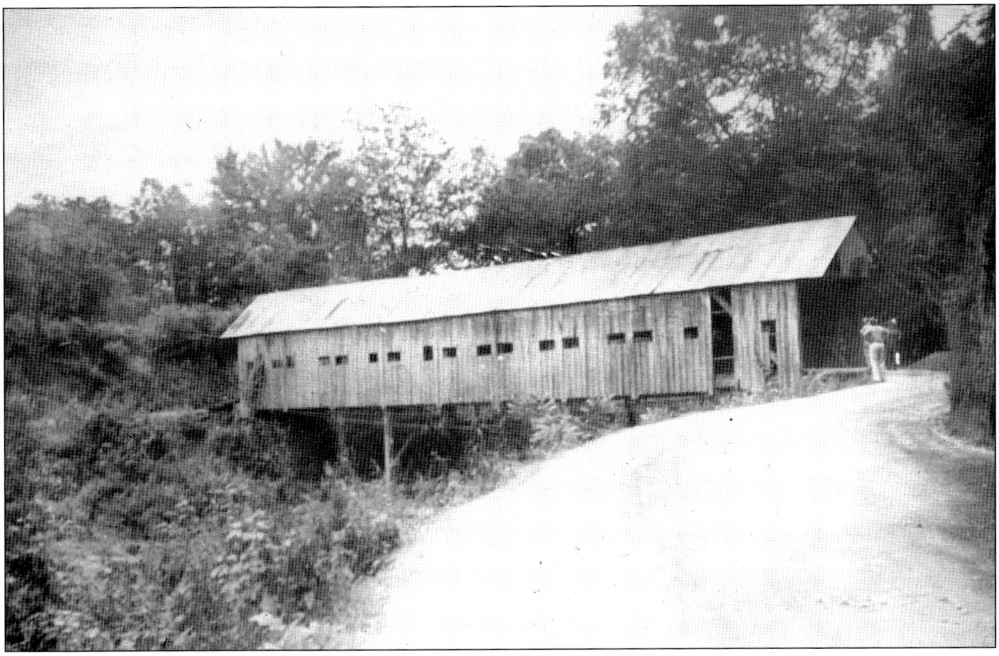

At one time, this covered bridge crossed the Chattahoochee River in Nacoochee Valley. Originally constructed to accommodate buggies, wagons, and riders on horseback, the bridge fell into disrepair and was torn down by the early 1950s.

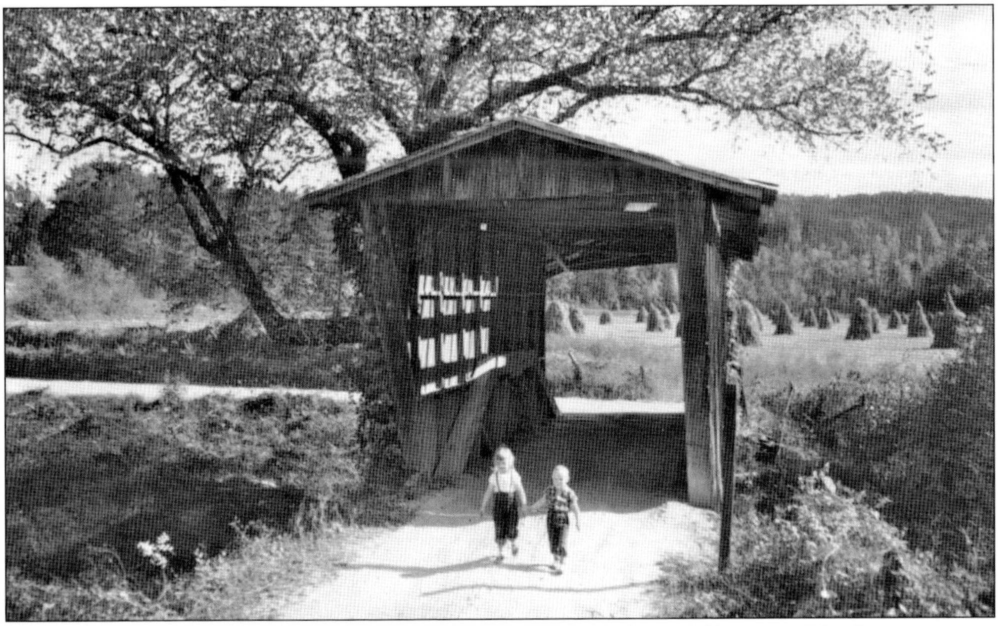

The covered bridge over Chickamauga Creek on Georgia Highway 255 is one of the few remaining original covered bridges in northeast Georgia. Currently maintained as a roadside park by the Georgia Department of Transportation and the White County Historical Society, the bridge harkens back to a time when life moved at a slower pace. In this mid-1950s image, barefooted Joyce and Tommy Tallent stroll down the dirt road hand-in-hand, as hay bundles dry in the pasture beyond.

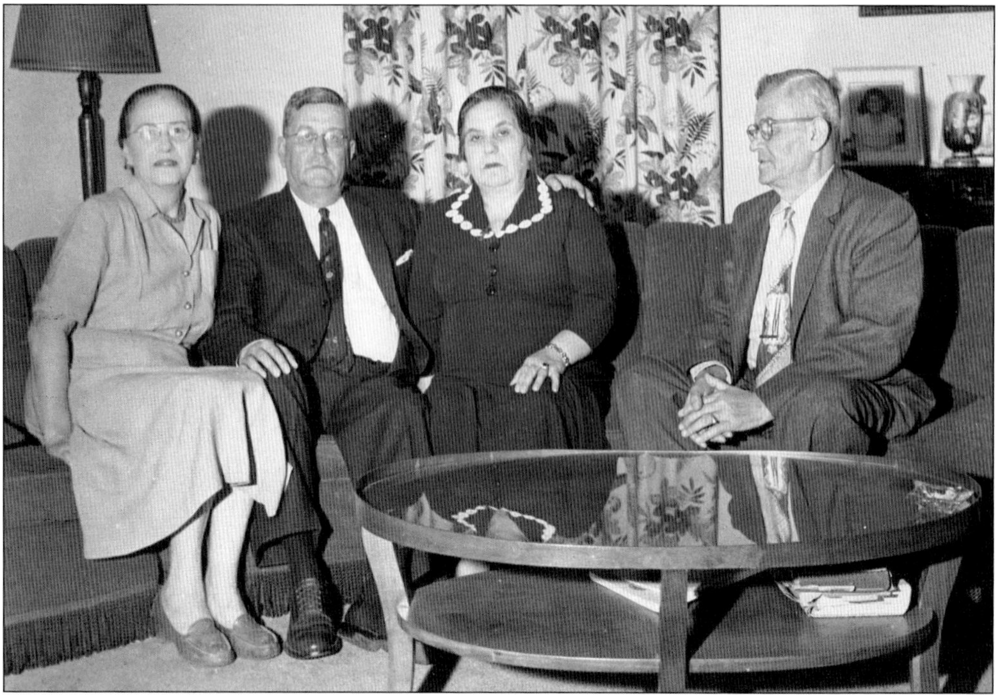

Charlie Maloof is credited with helping Helen residents survive the tough Depression years. His dedication to the town continued over the following decades. In 1956, Charlie's sister Sadie Ferhart made a rare journey to Helen from the family homeland in Lebanon. Charlie's brother Sol, who lived in Bryson City, North Carolina, joined the reunion. Shown from left to right are Blanch Westmoreland-Maloof, Charlie Maloof, Sadie Maloof-Ferhart, and Sol Maloof.

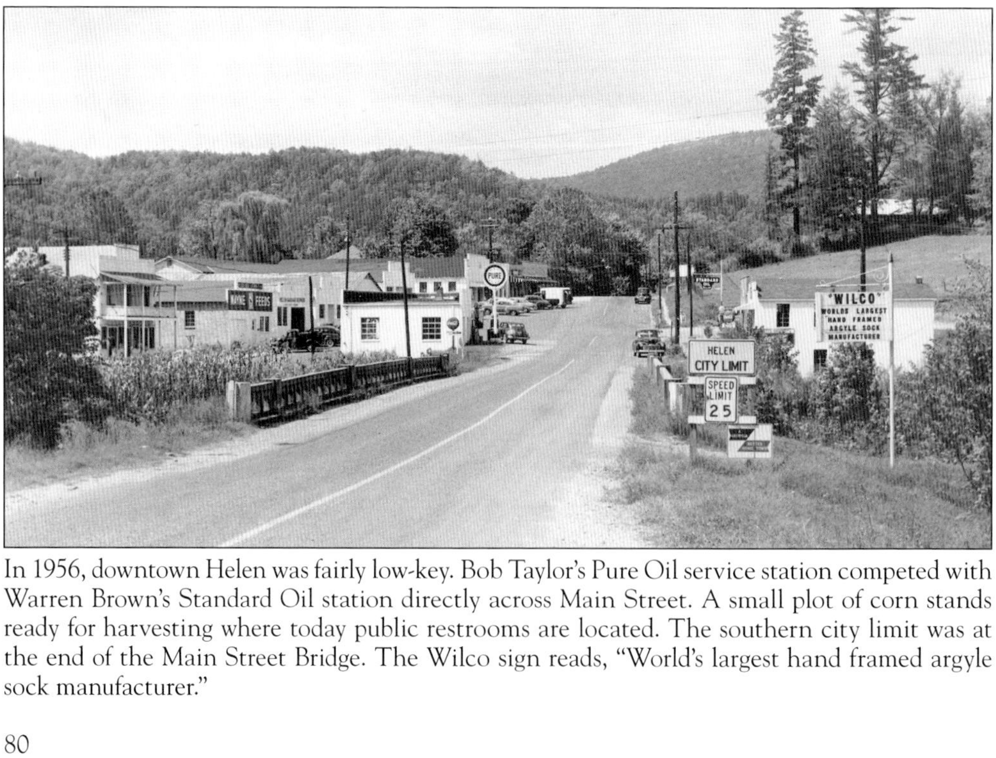

In 1956, downtown Helen was fairly low-key. Bob Taylor's Pure Oil service station competed with Warren Brown's Standard Oil station directly across Main Street. A small plot of corn stands ready for harvesting where today public restrooms are located. The southern city limit was at the end of the Main Street Bridge. The Wilco sign reads, "World's largest hand framed argyle sock manufacturer."

Four

Images of Tourism in Northeast Georgia 1860–1969

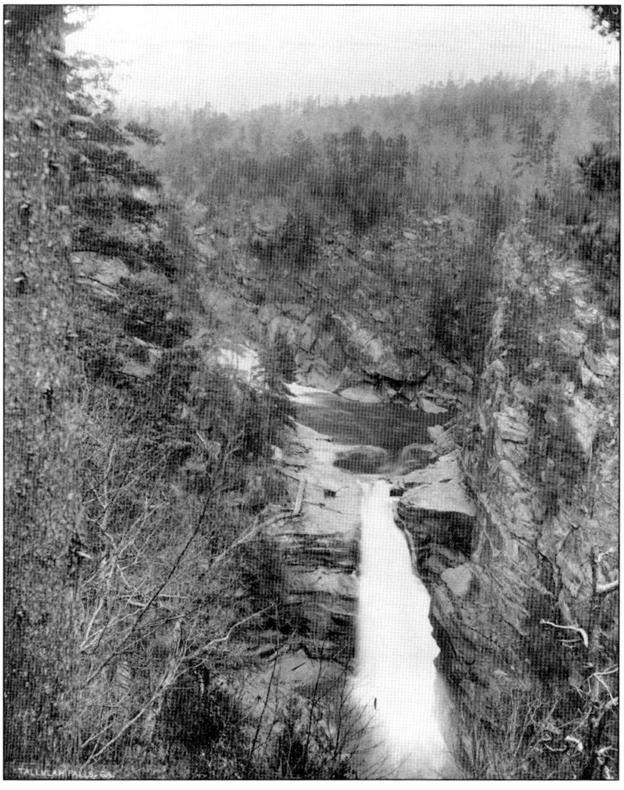

Having been a point of interest in northeast Georgia since the early 1800s, Tallulah Falls and Tallulah Gorge were among the first tourist destinations in the region. Accessible by train in the late 1800s and then by automobiles in the early 20th century, the area became extremely popular. Nearly 20 hotels and resorts, along with restaurants, churches, and a railroad depot, were built to serve visitors. Wealthy individuals from the lower part of the state, escaping the heat and yellow fever outbreaks, would arrive via the Tallulah Falls Railroad and spend their summers in the cool mountain air.

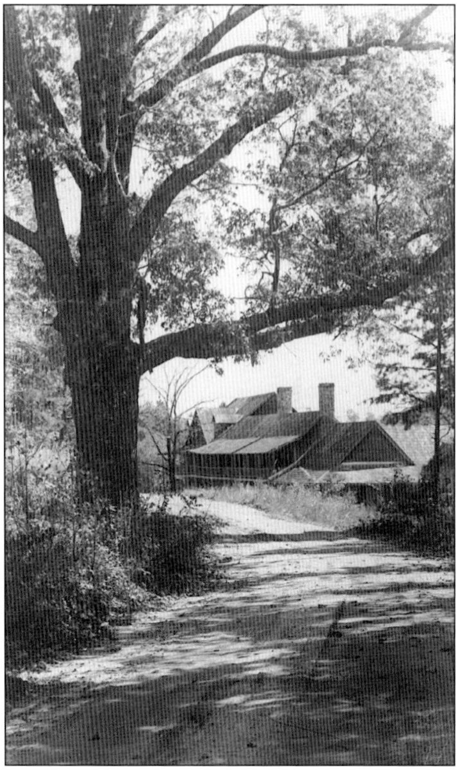

Beginning in 1890, Glen-Ella Springs, north of Clarkesville, became a popular lodging establishment for visitors to the falls and gorge. The popularity of Glen-Ella and Tallulah Falls as tourist destinations convinced developer John Mitchell to build his hotel in Helen.

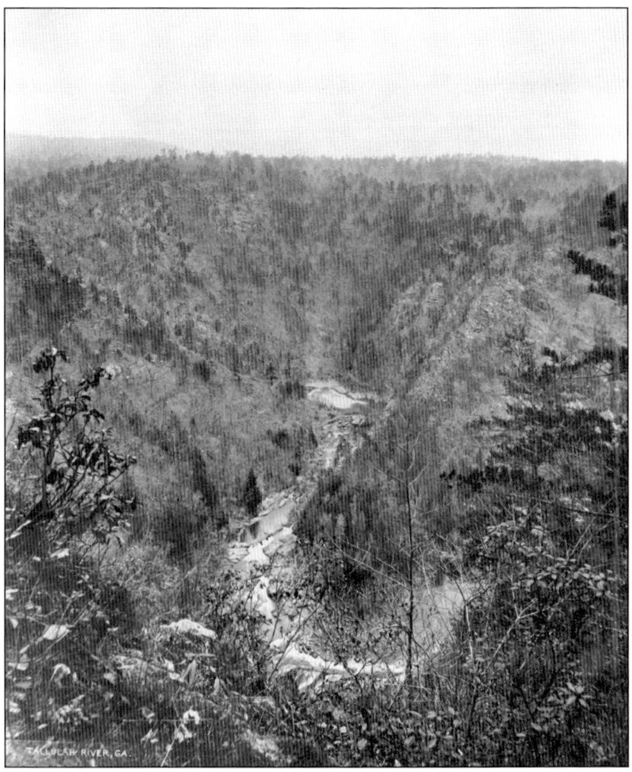

Known as the "Grand Canyon of the South," Tallulah Gorge remained an attraction into the 20th century. Then, despite vehement objection of notable citizens like Helen Dortch Longstreet, the Tallulah River was dammed in 1919, silencing the roar of the majestic falls and marking the onset of tourism's decline. The railroad discontinued passenger service, and most of the hotels and resorts closed by the mid-1930s.

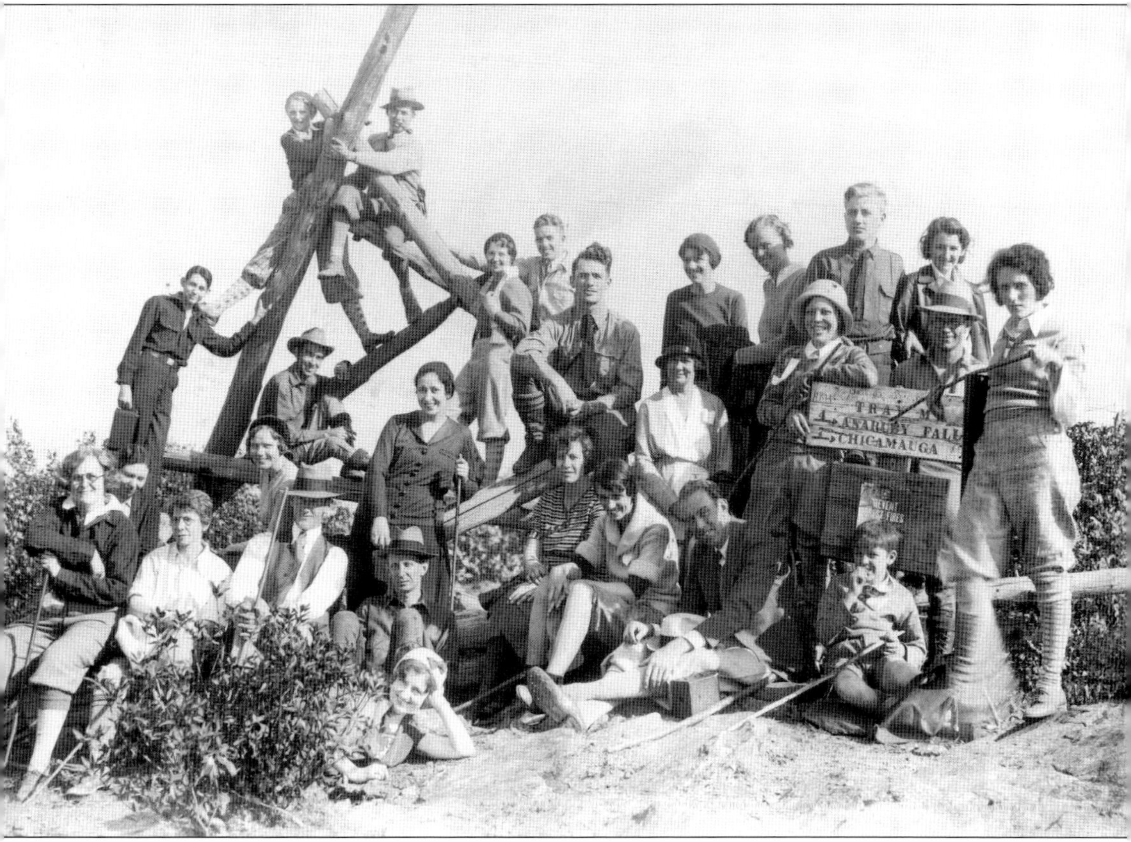

The Appalachian Trail was completed in 1937, but Georgia sections of the trail were established as early as the late 1920s. The Georgia Appalachian Trail Club started in 1930. This c. 1932 photograph shows club members on top of Tray Mountain, north of Helen. Club members held meetings in homes or inns, such as Greear's Lodge in Helen, then spent the day hiking and maintaining the trail. Today, the trail attracts thousands of visitors each year, both day-hikers and the more ambitious thru-hikers.

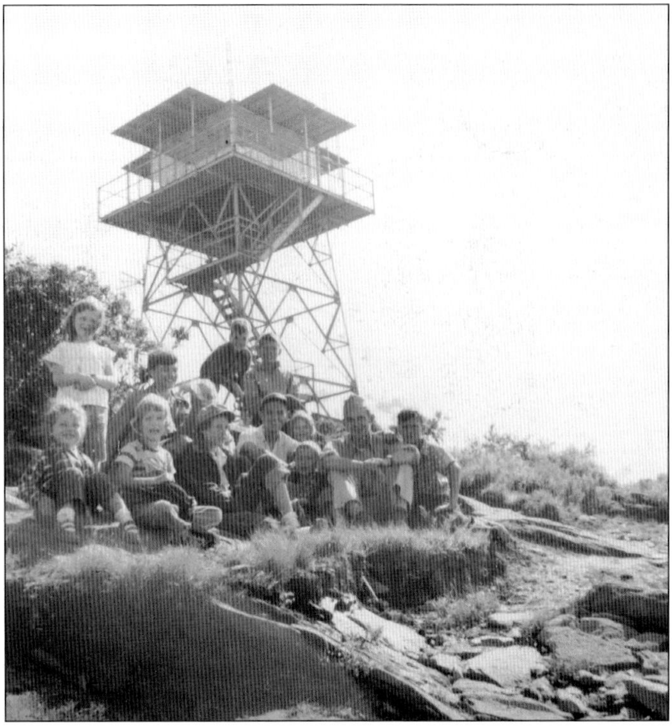

Known as Enota by Cherokee natives, Brasstown Bald is Georgia's highest peak and is only 20 miles from Helen. Arthur Woody, who was instrumental in establishing the Chattahoochee National Forest, oversaw construction of a rock observation platform for visitors. The original rock platform was later replaced with the metal structure shown here from the 1940s. The current rock building was constructed in 1965.

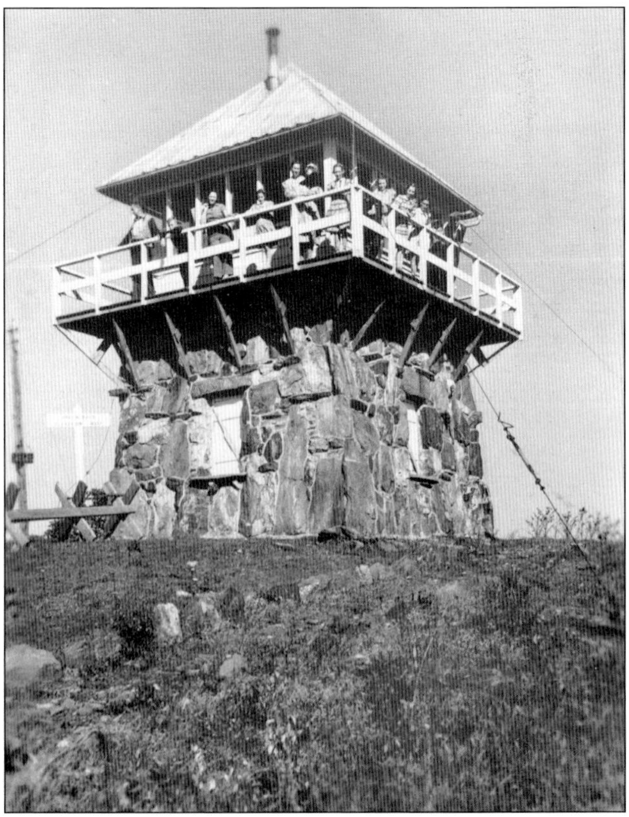

The rock structure at Rabun Bald, Georgia's second-highest peak, was built in the same style as that of the Brasstown rock tower, but unlike Brasstown, the Rabun Bald rock foundation is still in use.

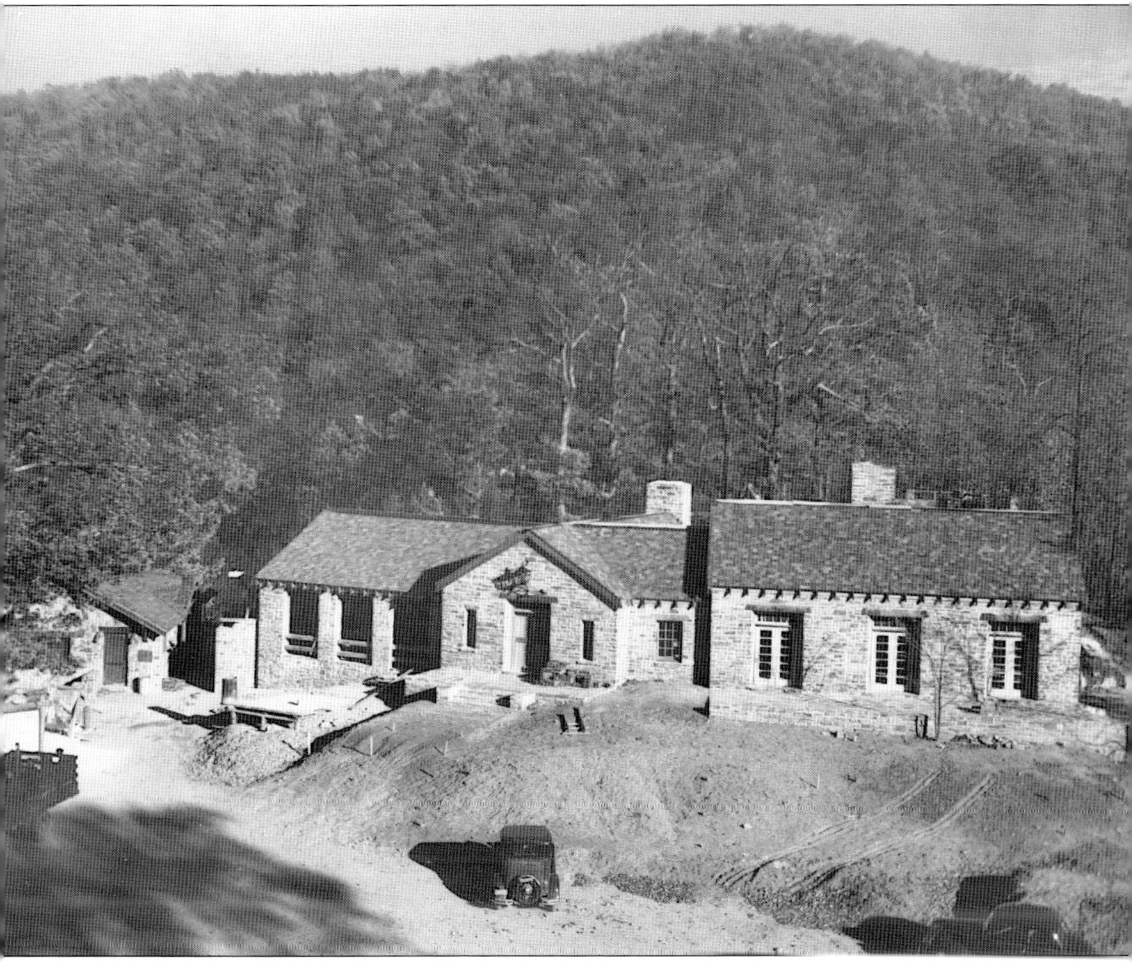

Originally a log structure built by the Morse Brothers Land and Lumber Company, Walasi-Yi Inn at Neel's Gap was rebuilt in 1939 by the Civilian Conservation Corps. It was a restaurant and inn until 1965 and then abandoned. By the mid-1970s, the building was slated for demolition, but a group of conservation-minded residents intervened in 1977, and the structure was entered in the National Register of Historic Places. It is a popular stop-off for Appalachian Trial hikers and day-trippers driving one of the routes from Helen to Blairsville.

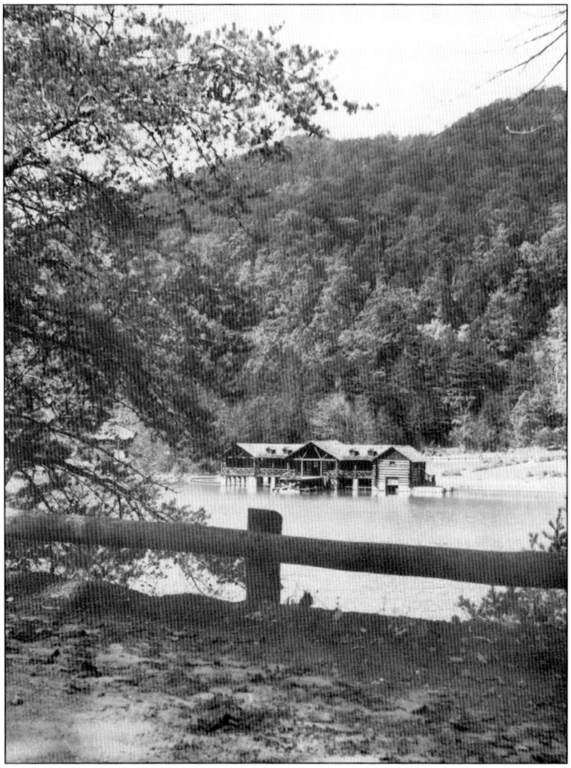

Only 20 miles from Helen, Vogel State Park was founded in 1931 and is the second oldest state park in Georgia. Augustus Vogel and Fred Vogel Jr. of Milwaukee, Wisconsin, were heirs to the Phister Vogel Leather Company, a Wisconsin tannery founded by Frederick Vogel. The Vogel family harvested bark from oak and hemlock trees located on thousands of acres they owned in North Georgia. Lake Trahiyta, located in Vogel State Park, was named for a legendary Cherokee maiden. The rugged buildings at Vogel State Park, constructed by the Civilian Conservation Corps, remain today.

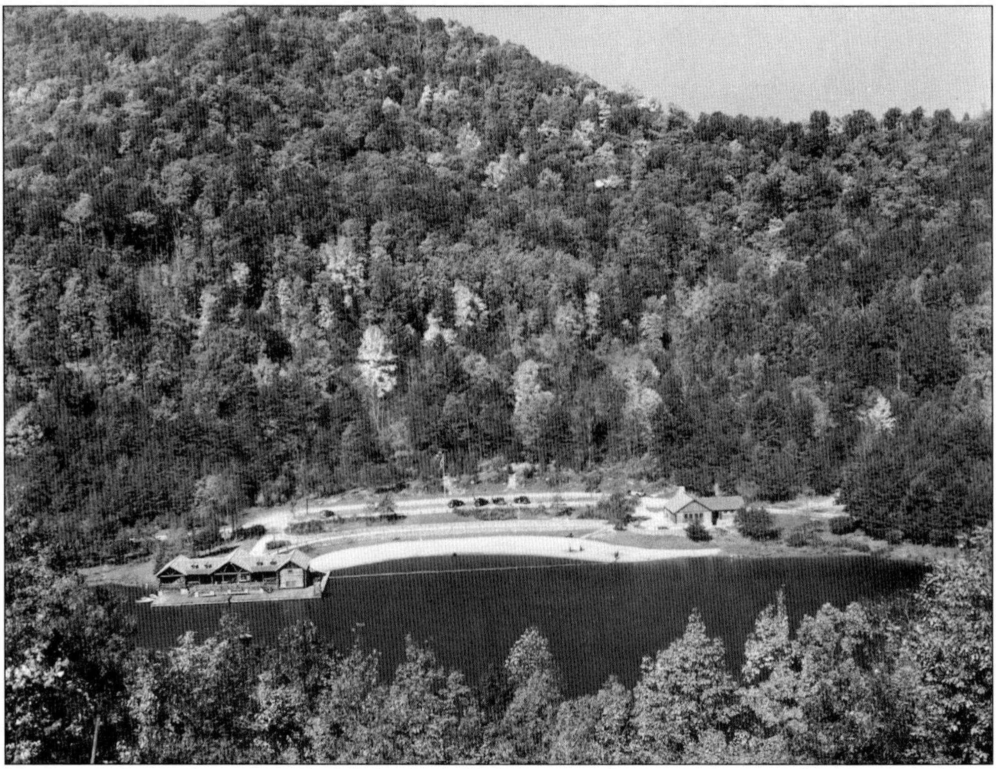

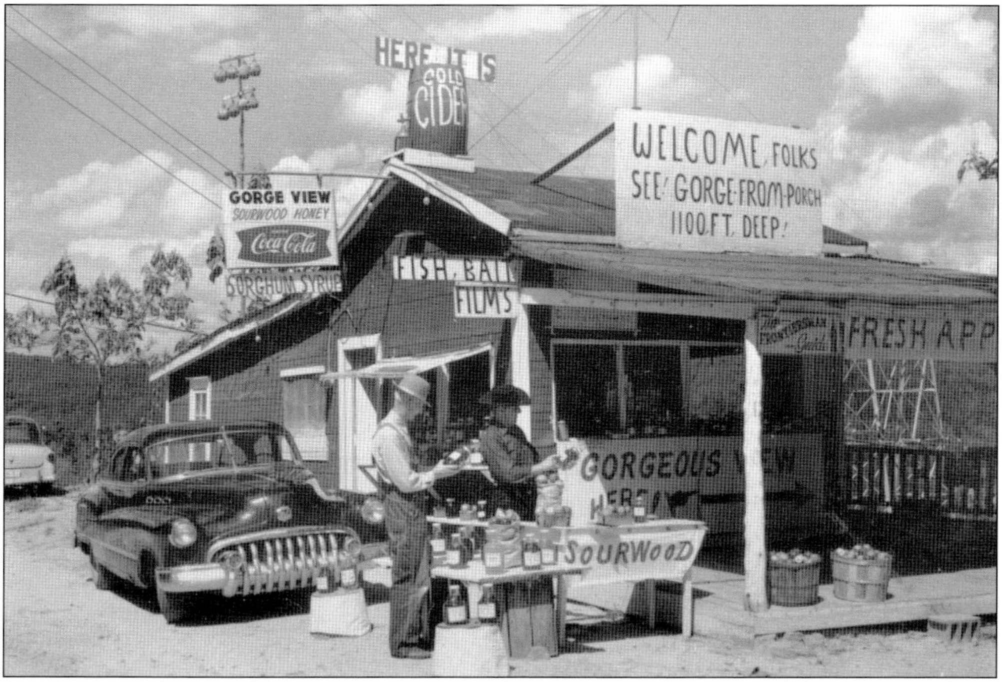

Because of improved highways and automobiles, Tallulah Gorge had a resurgence of popularity in the early 1950s. Roadside attractions offered fresh produce and mountain crafts not available in metropolitan areas. But increasing completion from nearby towns like Dahlonega and eventually Helen made tourism a tough market for businesses at the gorge.

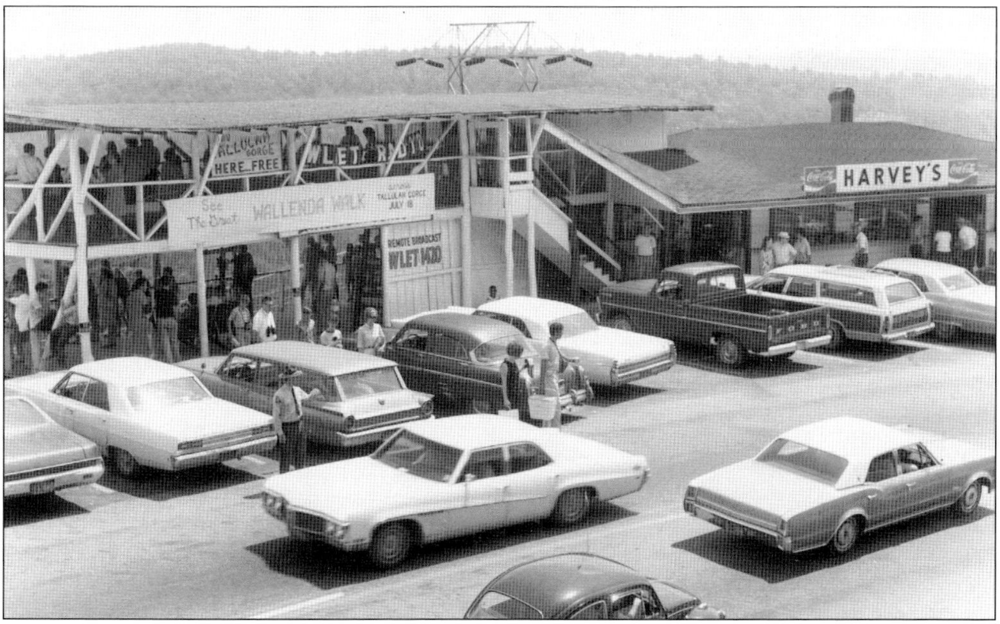

On July 18, 1970, a 65-year-old Karl Wallenda performed a high-wire walk across Tallulah Gorge. An estimated 30,000 people came to Northeast Georgia and watched Wallenda perform two headstands as he crossed the quarter-mile-wide gap. Many of those who came to watch Wallenda also made their first visit to Georgia's Alpine Village, only 30 miles from the gorge.

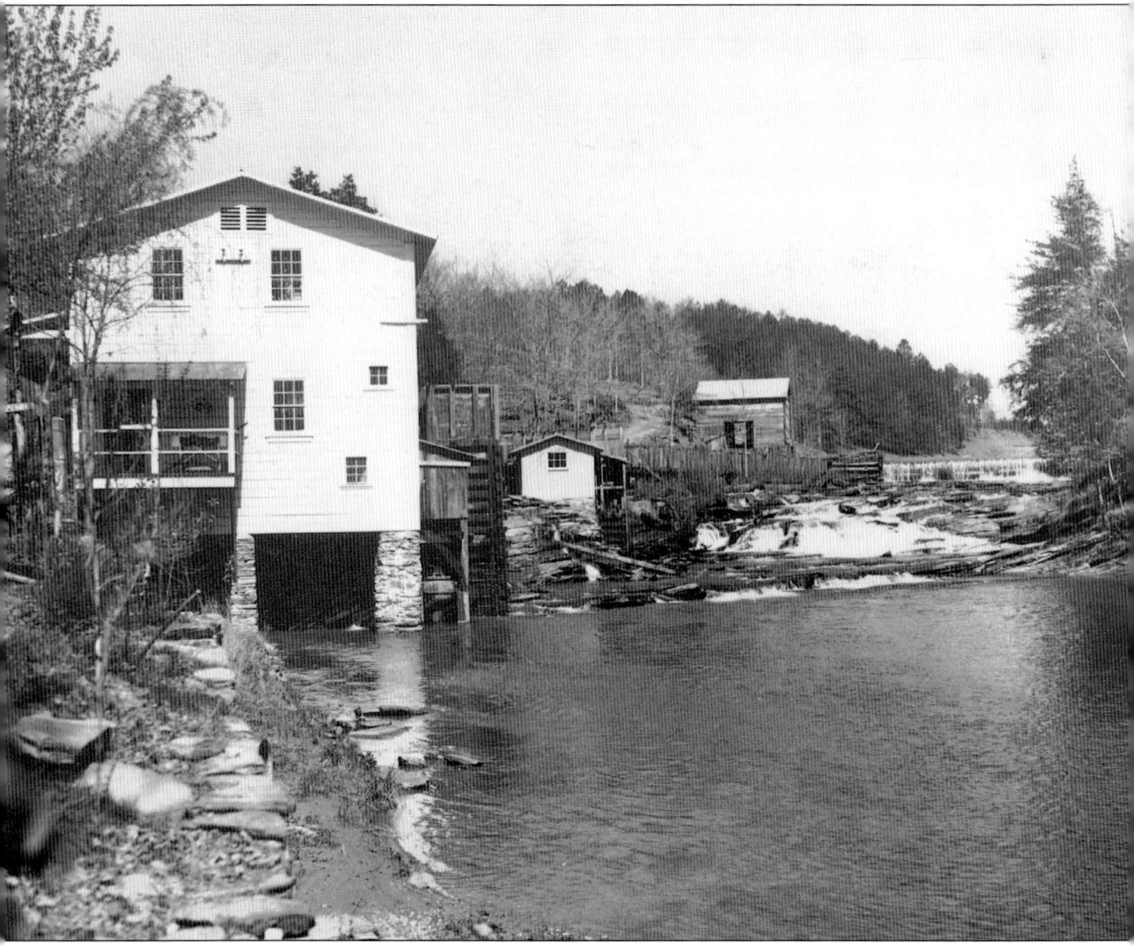

Watts' Mill on Georgia Highway 197, like Nora Mill outside Helen, had been an operating gristmill since before the beginning of the 20th century. Rebuilt once in 1930, then again in the mid-1960s, the mill has been a favorite stop for folks going to lakes Burton, Rabun, and Seed for decades. John and Glen LaRowe had the vision to turn the mill into a tourism destination and had great success offering handcrafted pottery at the rustic mill site. Family members over several generations have the fond memory of feeding the trout from the porch of the mill.

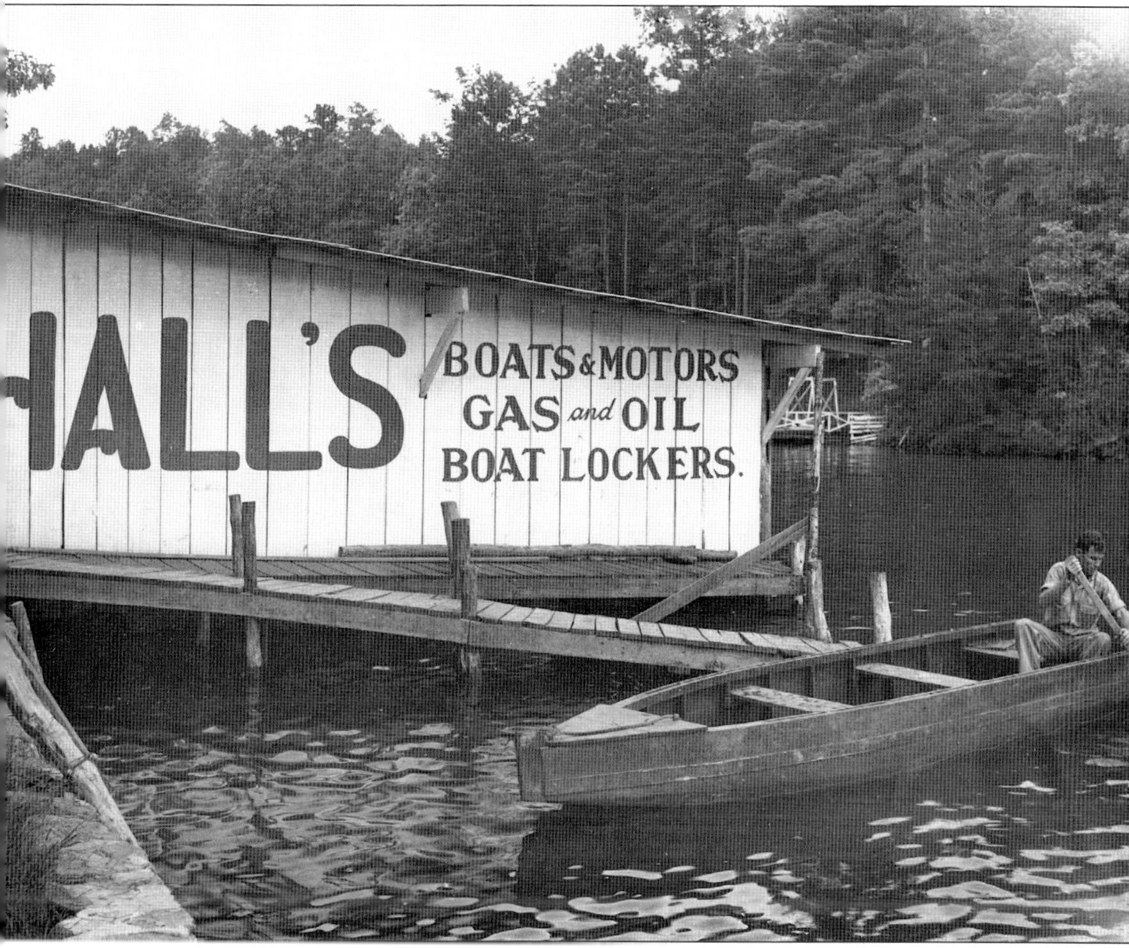

Built in 1919, Lake Burton is the first of six lakes in the Tallulah River watershed. Lake Seed, Lake Rabun, Lake Tallulah Falls, Lake Tugalo, and Lake Yonah make up the remainder. Owned and operated by the Georgia Power Company, at one time the lakes were the largest producers of electricity in the state. The lake area also quickly became a popular recreational destination. Before Helen was rejuvenated in the early 1970s, visitors on their way to the lakes would pass through town without even slowing down. This late-1930s image shows Hall's Marina on Lake Rabun.

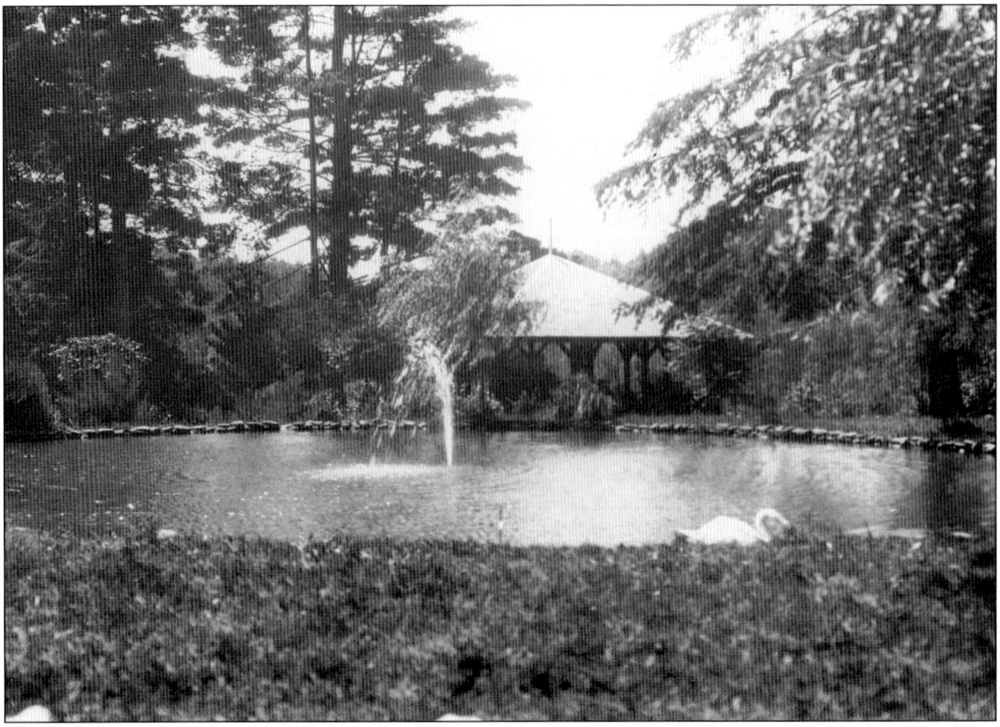

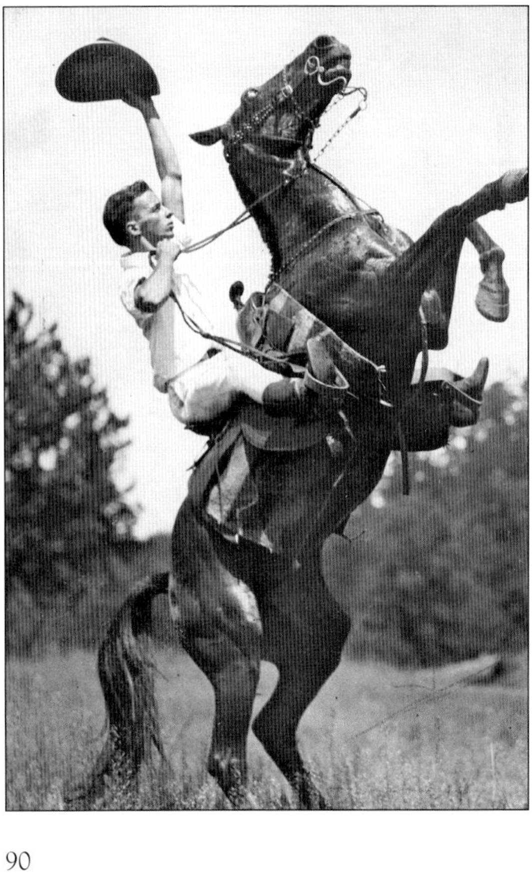

Originally built to accommodate the needs of the Byrd-Matthews Lumber Company in Helen, the Mountain Ranch Hotel became a major attraction of its own. Outlasting the lumber mills, the hotel eventually offered 50 lodging rooms, golfing, horseback riding, and swimming.

In 1942, the Beau Gay Dude Ranch in Helen was another pre-alpine tourism-oriented enterprise. Trails through the mountains, valleys, and down to the river gave riders an opportunity to enjoy the natural beauty of the Helen area. The more intrepid riders had a chance to be a real cowboy for a day. In this image, Kip Mayrick demonstrates his riding skills.

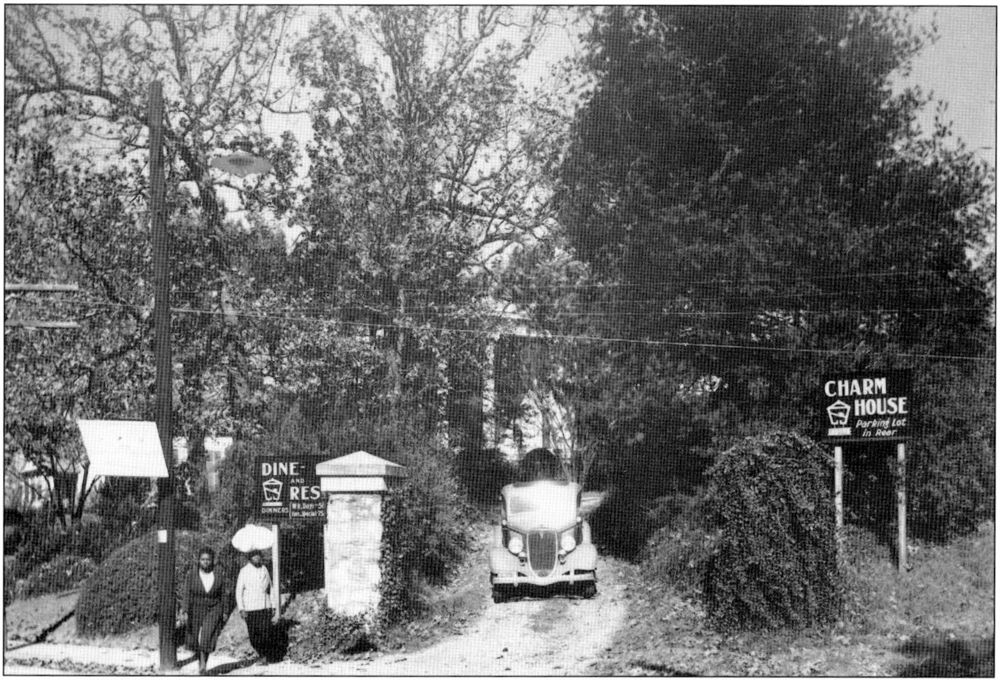

Clarkesville, Mount Airy, Demorest, and Clayton also catered to tourists of the 20th century. Early residences, including the Charm House in Clarkesville, were converted to restaurants, inns, or guesthouses.

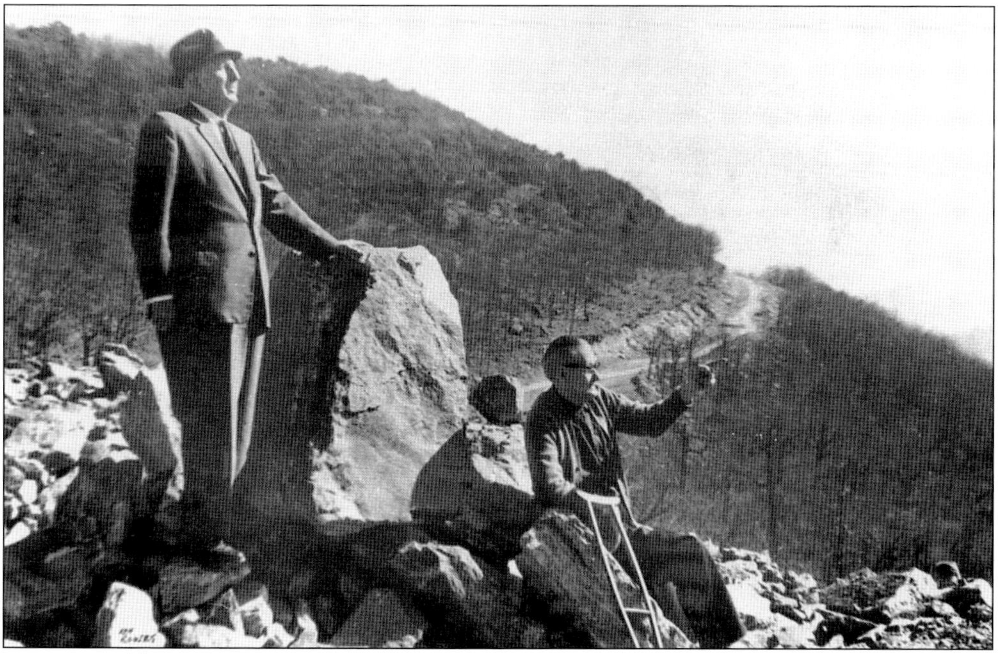

Visionaries like Arthur Woody realized northeast Georgia's future depended on preserving the natural beauty of the mountains. Through his efforts, the Chattahoochee National Forest was created and wildlife populations were restored. James Davidson (seated), posing here with Sen. Richard Russell, proposed scenic byways so more people could enjoy the beauty of the mountains.

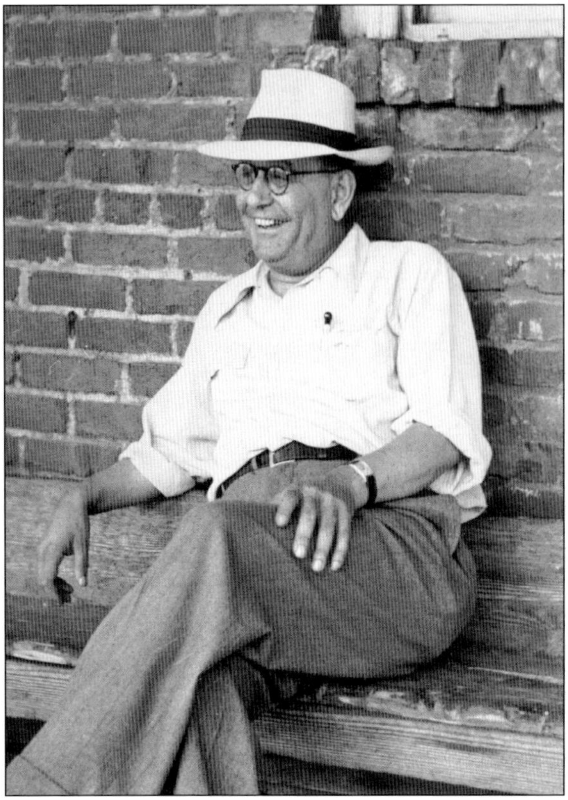

Charles Maloof understood the value of the natural surroundings and what it meant to nearby communities. Primarily a merchant and businessman, he envisioned what became Unicoi State Park, and he understood the direction Helen needed to go to thrive. With the help of Georgia's county unit system, Maloof was able to leverage his political influence by promising White County reelection votes to Gov. Herman Talmadge, if he would build a state park near Helen.

The beach house and swimming area at Unicoi Lake became a popular spot for both visitors and residents. Local young adults worked in the summer as lifeguards at the beach house. There was a swimming dock, diving boards, and a waterslide. Other jobs became available as the Unicoi area expanded. A number of residents spent their entire life working at the park.

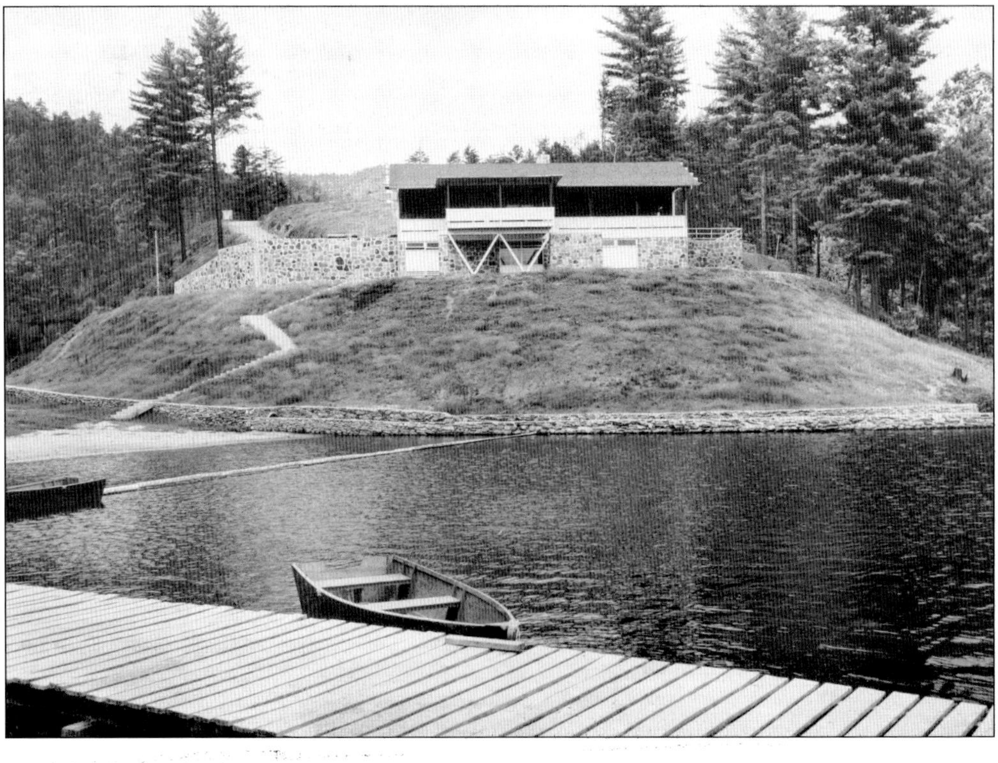

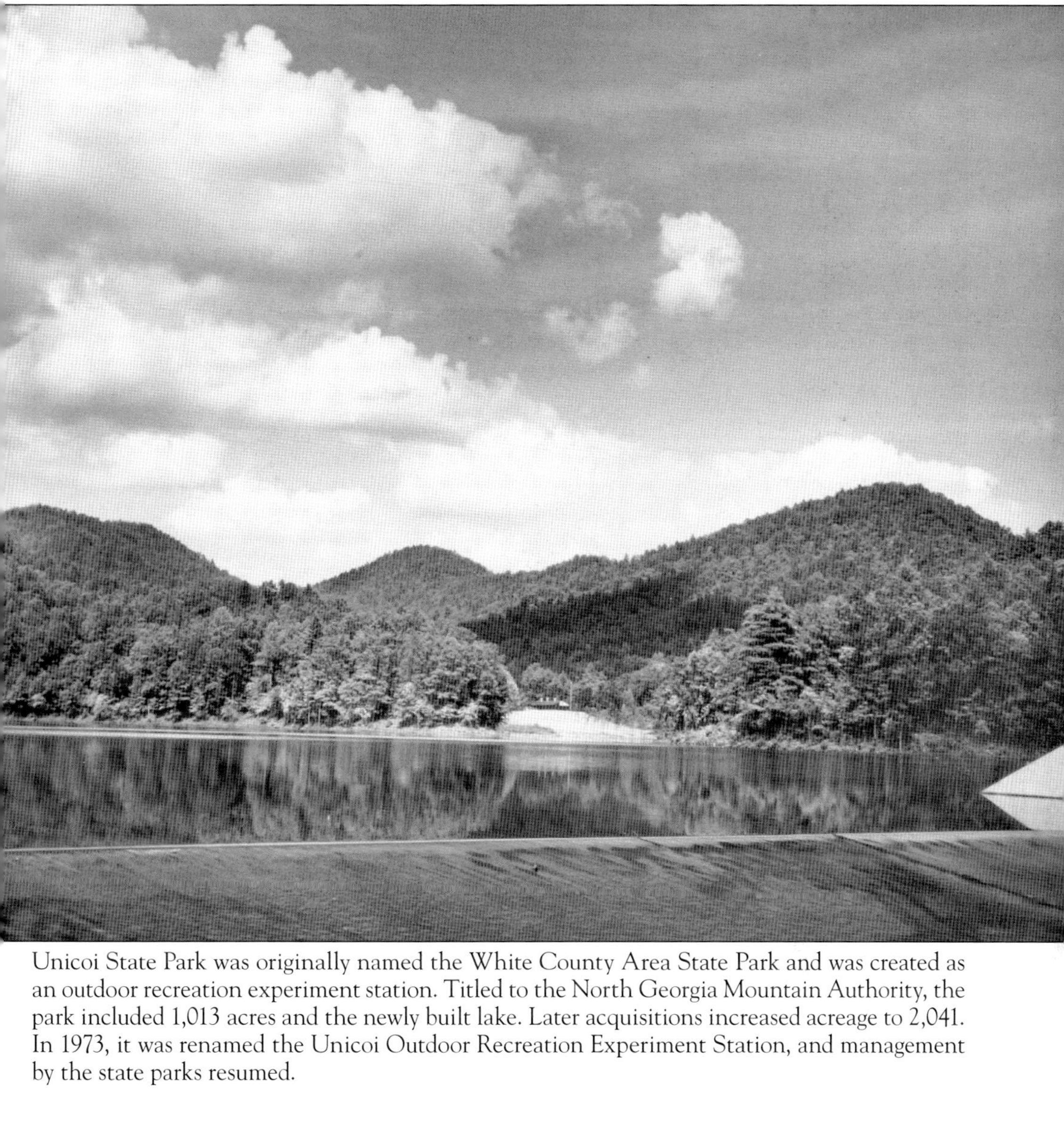

Unicoi State Park was originally named the White County Area State Park and was created as an outdoor recreation experiment station. Titled to the North Georgia Mountain Authority, the park included 1,013 acres and the newly built lake. Later acquisitions increased acreage to 2,041. In 1973, it was renamed the Unicoi Outdoor Recreation Experiment Station, and management by the state parks resumed.

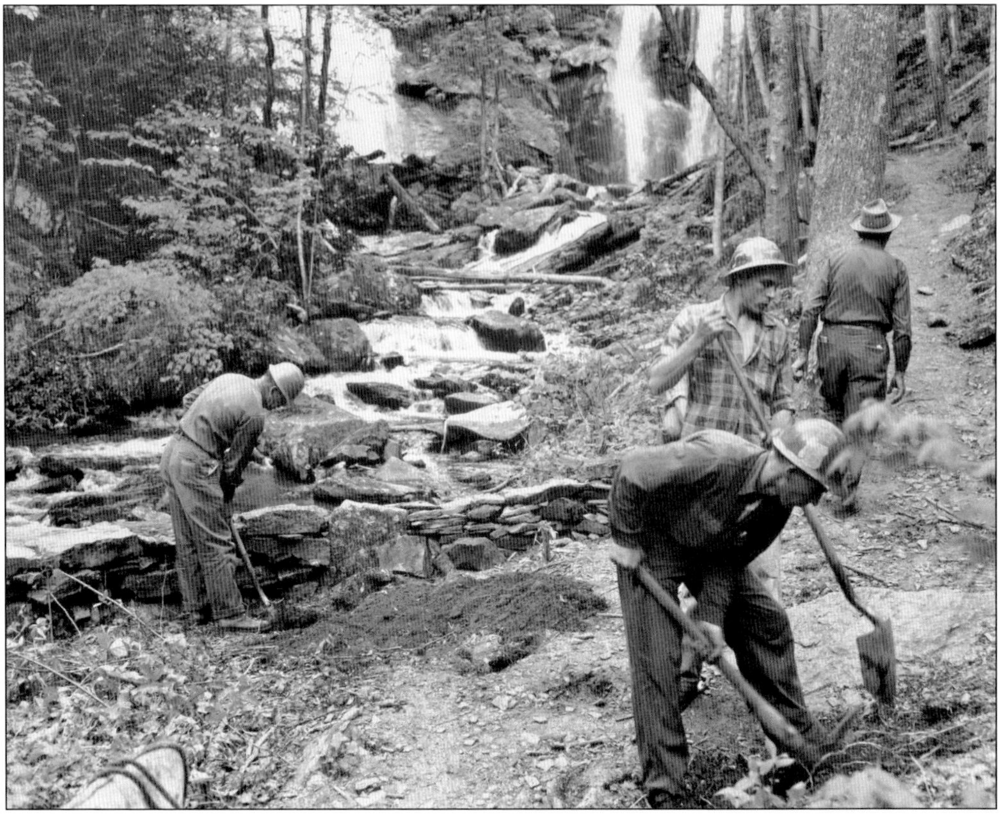

Anna Ruby Falls became a part of the Chattahoochee National Forest in 1925. Previous years of logging had left the area in distress, but by the 1950s, with the help of the Civilian Conservation Corps and US Forest Service, the area was gradually restored to its natural state. At the falls, Curtis and York Creeks meet to form Smith Creek, which supplies water to the lake at Unicoi State Park.

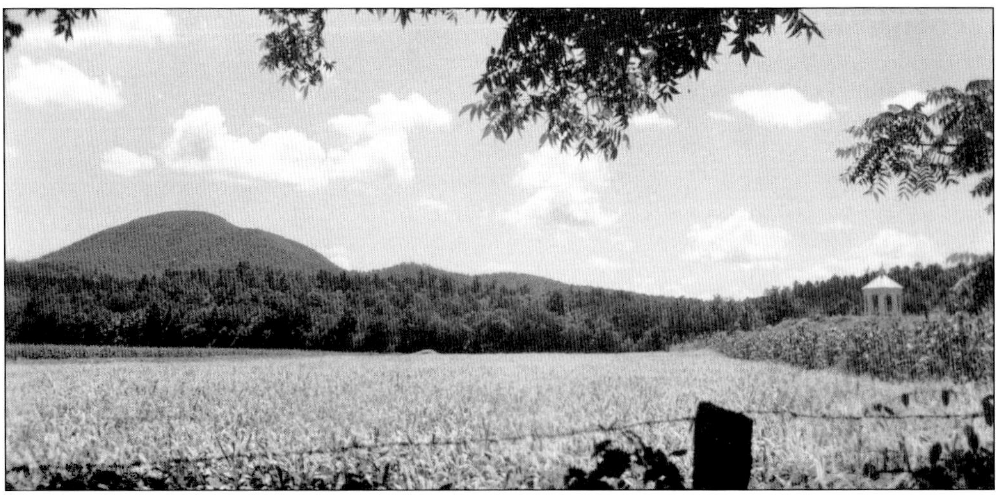

Nacoochee Valley's beauty and intrigue are obvious, but vision and foresight are needed to preserve that splendor and majesty. Special community groups, like the Sautee Nacoochee Community Association, formed to protect the area from overexposure and excessive development.

Five

Helen's Alpine Conversion 1969–Present

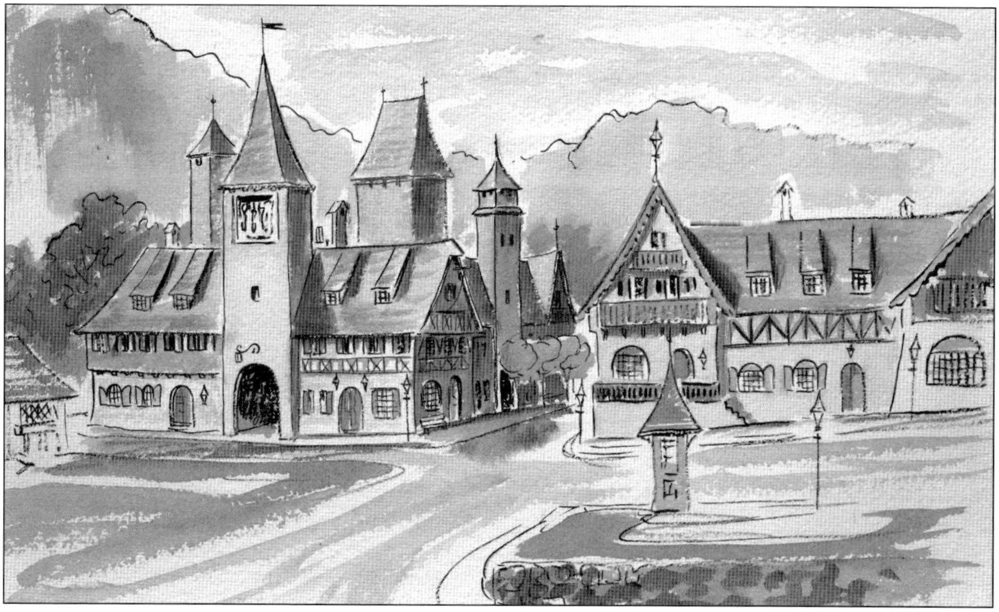

Helen's alpine conversion began as a pipe dream, but unlike many such dreams, it came true. John Kollock's visualization of River Street was quite a departure from the shacks and hastily built structures that lined the street during Helen's lumbering years. Original homes and hotels had no running water or bathrooms. Waste facilities consisted of shallow holes in the ground; more often than not, waste flowed into the river. Kollock envisioned a town where craftspeople, artists, and shopkeepers would live above their stores, much like the Bavarian villages he admired while serving in the military.

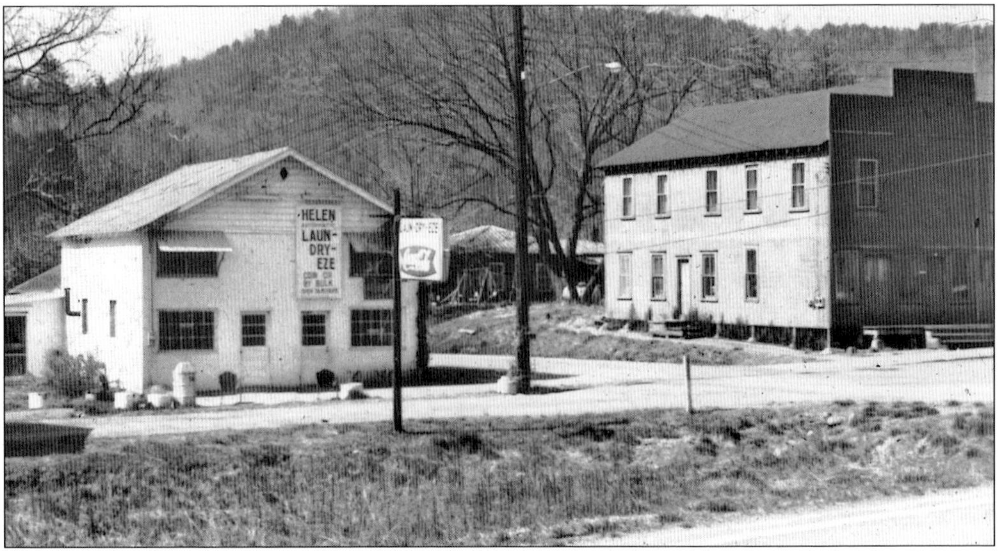

In 1967, most buildings in downtown Helen had not changed for three decades. Shown here are the Laun-Dry-Eze coin-operated laundry and the old Commercial Hotel. The laundry was owned and operated by Ed and Dot Gedney and was a welcome convenience for many families still using old-fashioned wringer washers. The hotel building was also occupied by the Helen telephone switching office. Later, it became a facility offering hot showers. It fell into disrepair in the 1960s and was torn down by 1970.

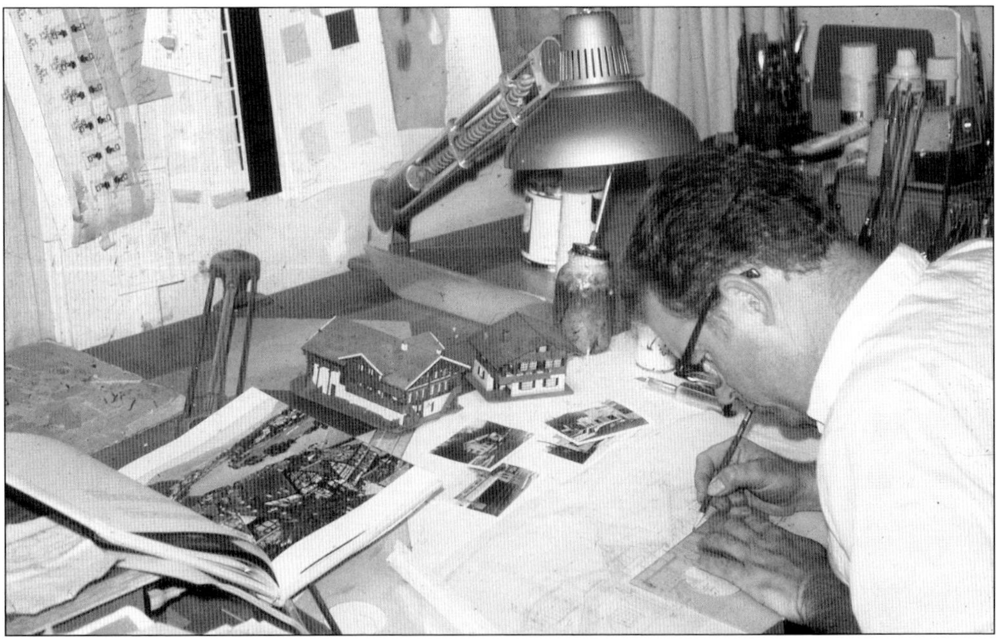

Artist John Kollock is photographed preparing a detailed elevation of a section of downtown Helen. The plans were based on images he had sketched in Bavaria years earlier. His artful eye, attention to detail, and enthusiasm for the project revitalized both the town of Helen and the citizens. Kollock, among others, had an "early-Disneyesque" vision for Helen, with cobblestone walkways, fountains, hand-painted murals on exterior walls, and shopkeeper residences above their stores.

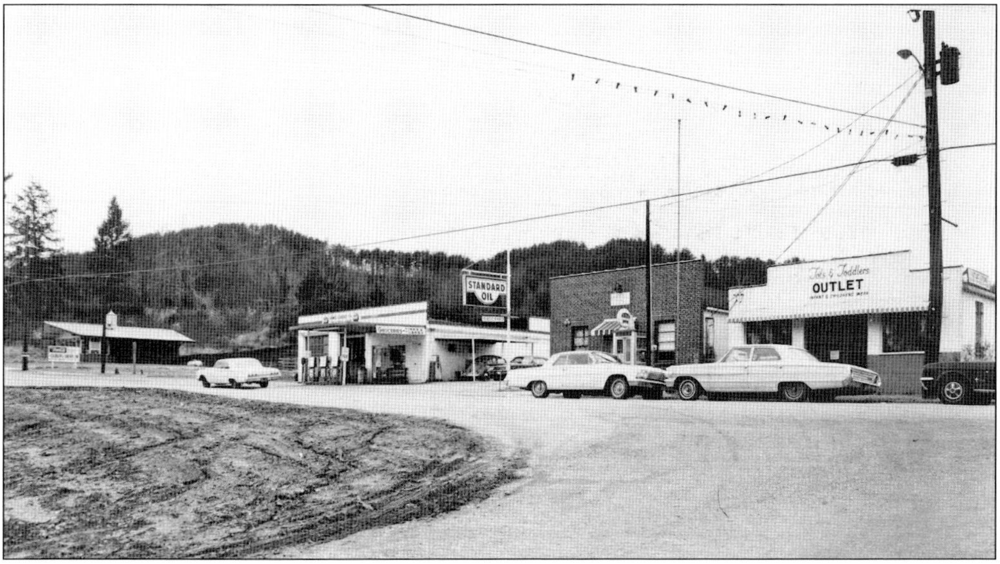

This Main Street image was taken about 1968, before Helen's alpine rejuvenation. Shown from left to right are the Ice-Burg Drive-In, Warren Brown's Standard Oil station, the Helen Town Hall, and Tots and Toddlers Outlet. The drive-in later became the Wurst Haus and Brown's station eventually became Granny's Funnel Cakes. The hill just above the drive-in is where the Mountain Ranch Hotel stood.

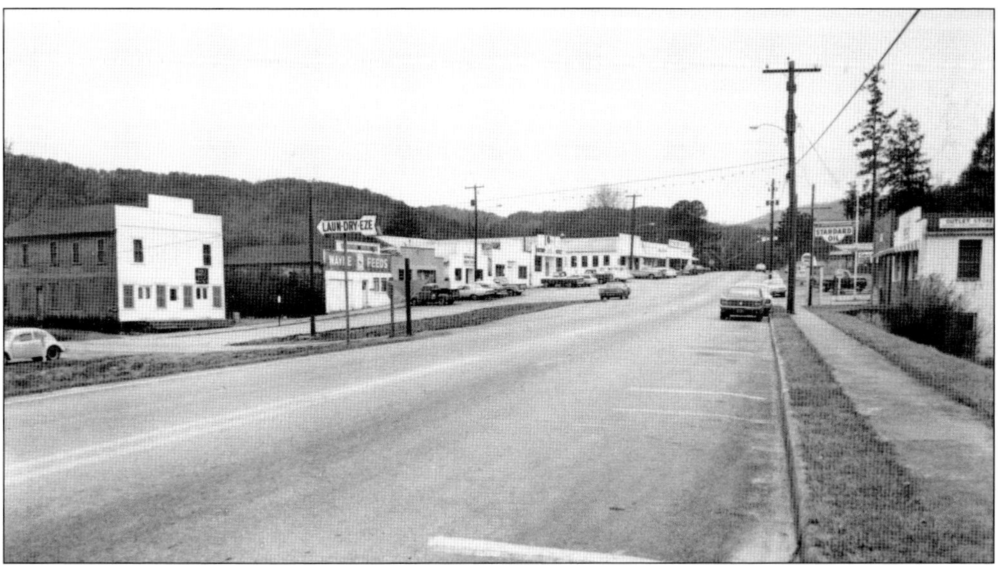

This 1968 image facing north on Main Street shows, from left to right, the Commercial Hotel building, Wayne's Feed Store, Chief's Garage, the Mountaineer Dress Shop, the Orbit Factory Outlet, and Pittman's Pharmacy. Charlie Maloof's office was at the corner of Main and Dye Streets.

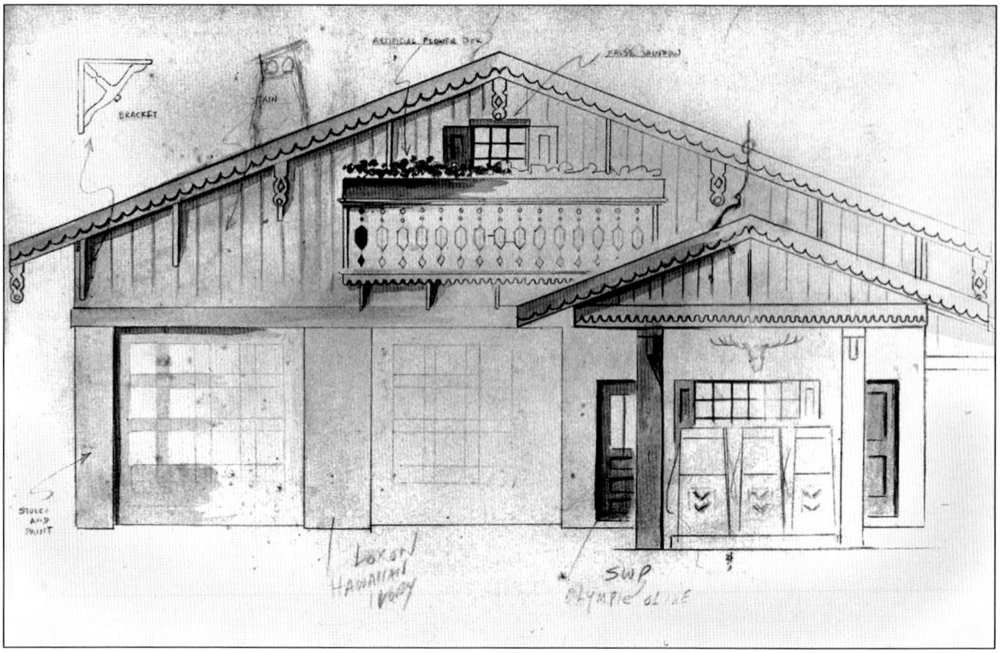

This was John Kollock's 1969 concept for the alpine motif to be applied to Warren Brown's Chevron service station on Main Street. Kollock was selected by Pete Hodkinson, Bob Fowler, and Jim Wilkins to conceptualize a new image for Helen in an effort to attract tourists. While Wilkins owned several buildings downtown and was fully on board with the project, both he and Hodkinson knew that everyone needed to agree on the plan for it to work.

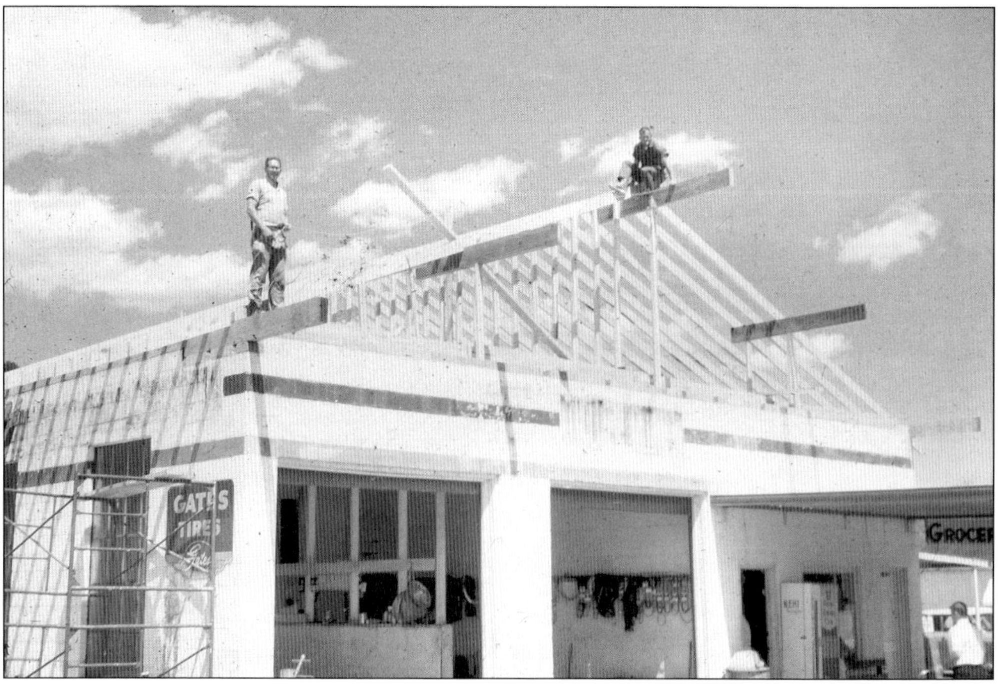

Work began on Brown's Chevron station in 1969. Work had also started on Jim Wilkins's buildings on the other side of Main Street.

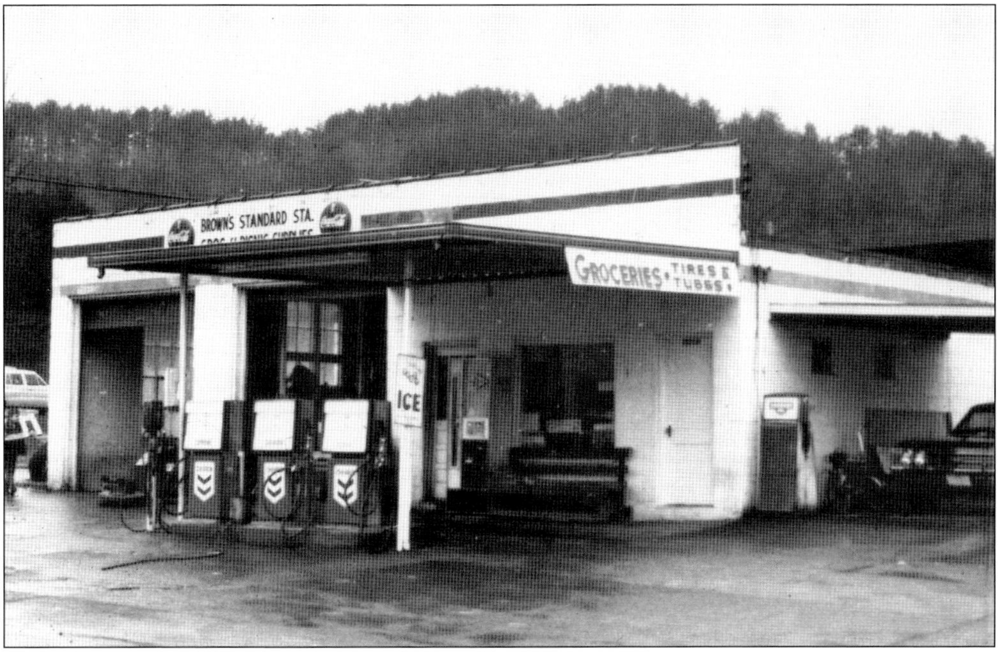

Shown here is Warren Brown's Chevron station in 1968, just before the alpine conversion commenced. The station had two service bays, three gas pumps, and a bench to sit and watch traffic go by. Brown also sold canned goods, dry goods, and some groceries. In the summer, Brown sometimes allowed residents to sell produce from their gardens in the parking lot next to the station.

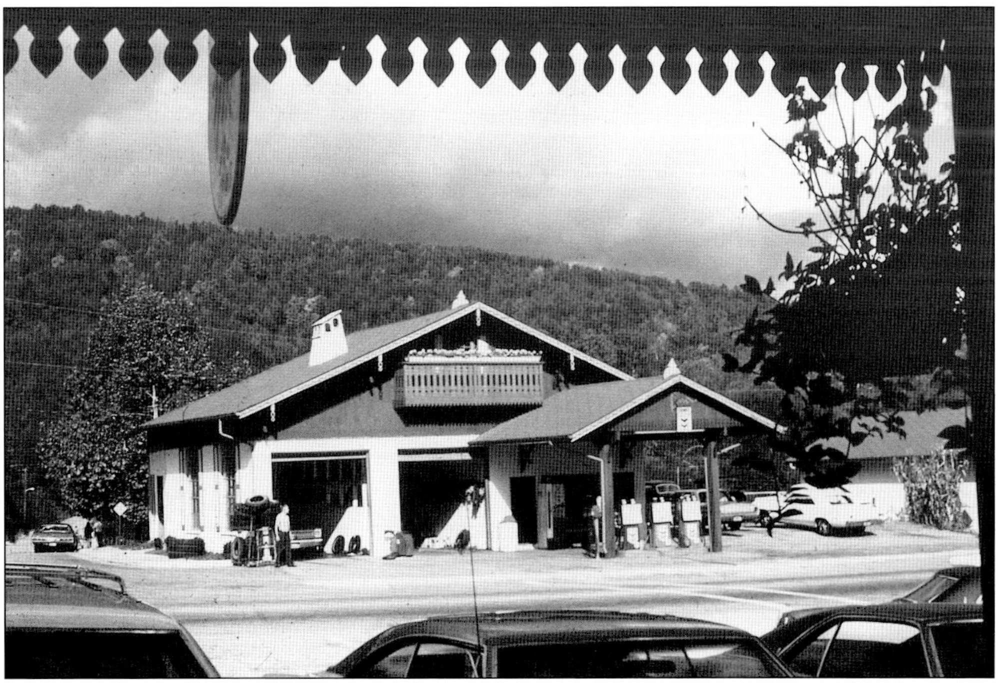

This image shows Warren Brown's Chevron Station in 1970, just after its alpine conversion. Brown, wife Lois, and family continued to operate the service station until the mid-1980s, eventually converting all of the property into retail shops geared toward the tourism trade.

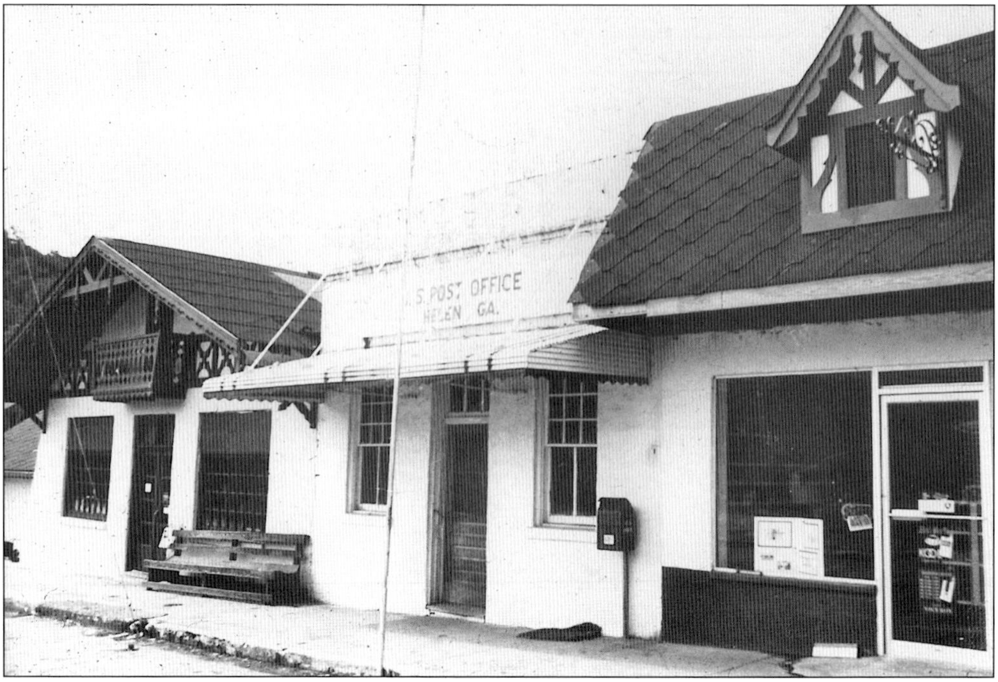

In 1969, the old Helen Post Office was sandwiched between the remodeled Pittman Pharmacy and what was to become the Helen Music Hall, formerly the north end of the hosiery mill. By 1970, the post office moved to the new municipal building on Chattahoochee Street.

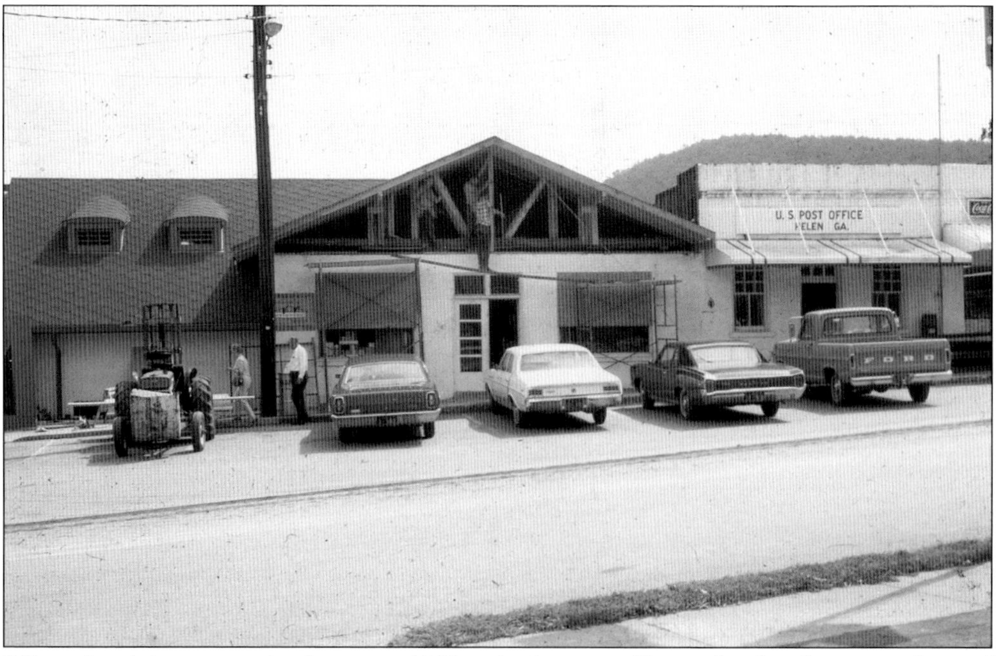

When the alpine conversion began in 1969, only the post office and a few shops were located downtown. There was a dress store, feed store, pharmacy, and menswear outlet. The former hosiery mill was one of the first buildings to be converted, becoming the Theatre Helen, where *The Sound of Music* was staged for several years.

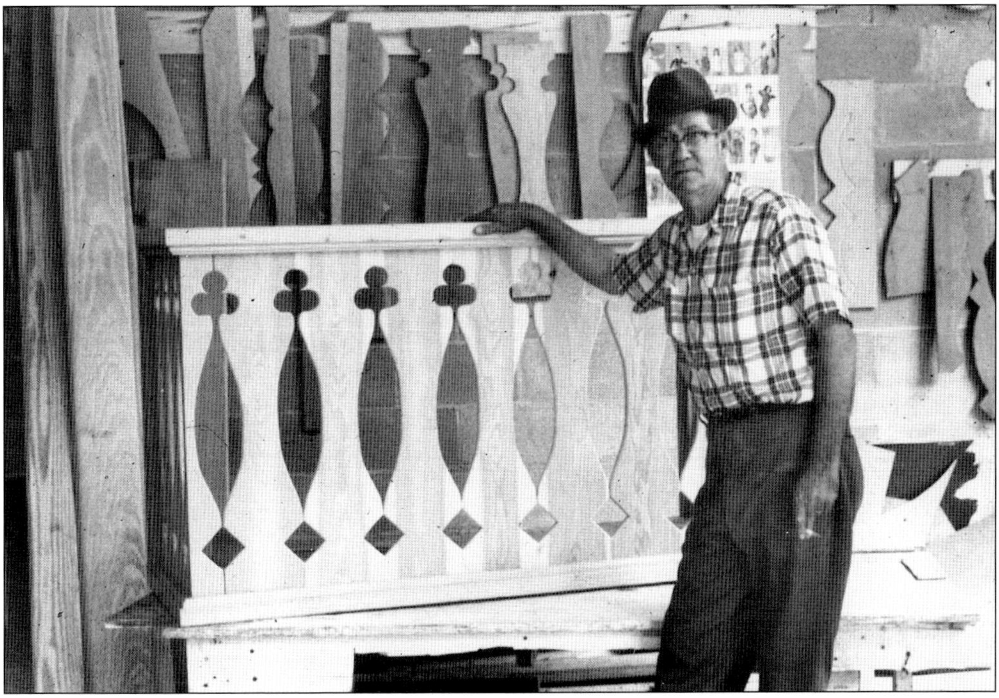

Hayne Sims, local business owner and contractor, immediately adopted the new style. His sons Roy and Neal went on to build many of the new commercial and residential structures in the Helen area. The willingness of local builders to embrace and apply the new architectural imperative demonstrates their ingenuity and community spirit.

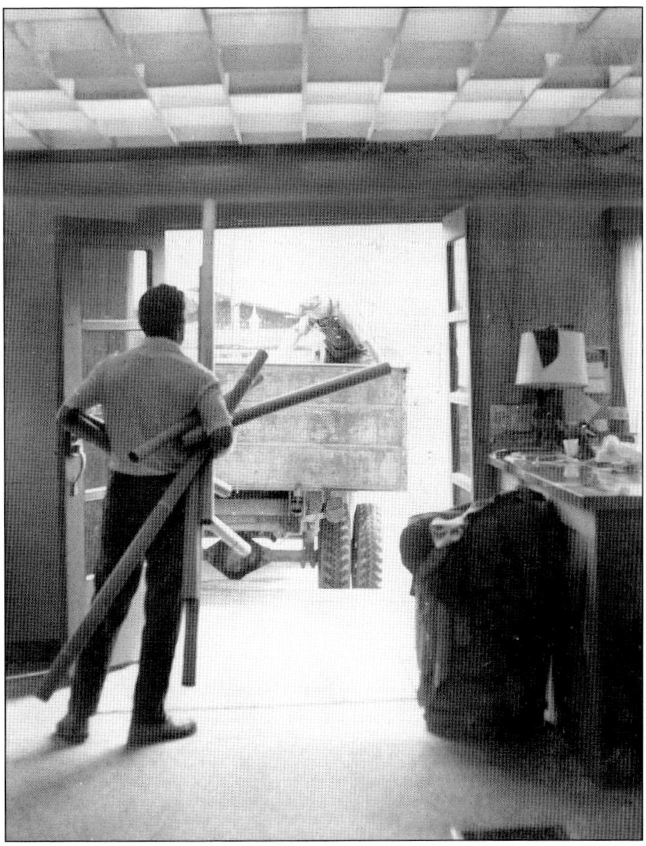

Out with the old and in with the new became the town theme, once the alpine motif was adopted. The building formerly occupied by the Wilco Hosiery Mill was remodeled and converted into a theater. In the late 1970s, this building became Hansel and Gretel's Candy Kitchen.

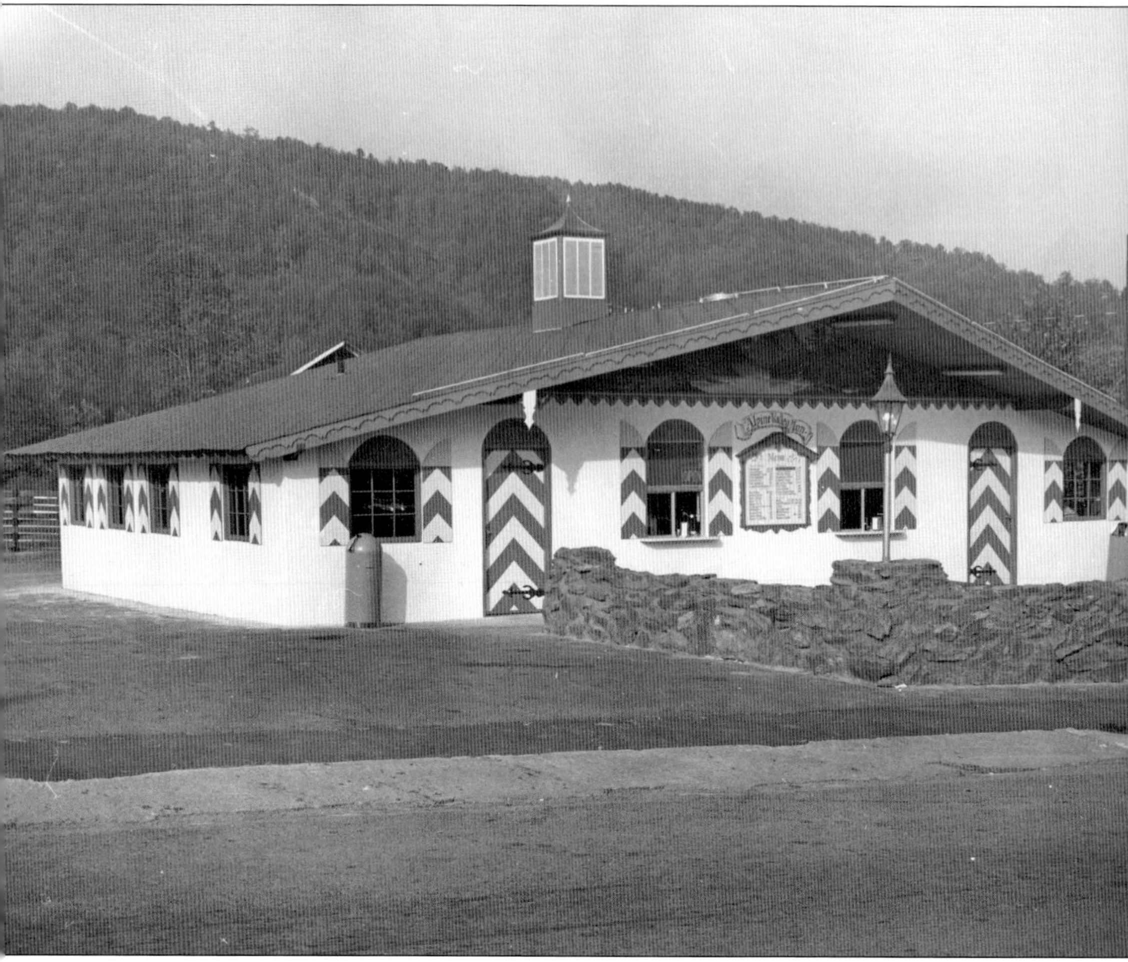

Briefly known as the Alpine Valley Inn, the former Ice-Burg Drive-In shines in alpine glory in 1969. Built in 1962 by Robertstown resident Ross Cathy, Athens restaurateur Sid Short purchased the structure in 1974, known by then as the Wurst Haus. The restaurant featured an outdoor beer garden and was a popular gathering spot for over 30 years.

Chief Westmoreland operated an automobile repair shop in Helen for over 30 years. Well established before Helen's alpine transformation began, some thought Westmoreland might be reluctant to decorate his garage with gingerbread trim, wall murals, and hanging baskets. When he enthusiastically agreed, everyone knew that it would be just a matter of time before all property owners would join in.

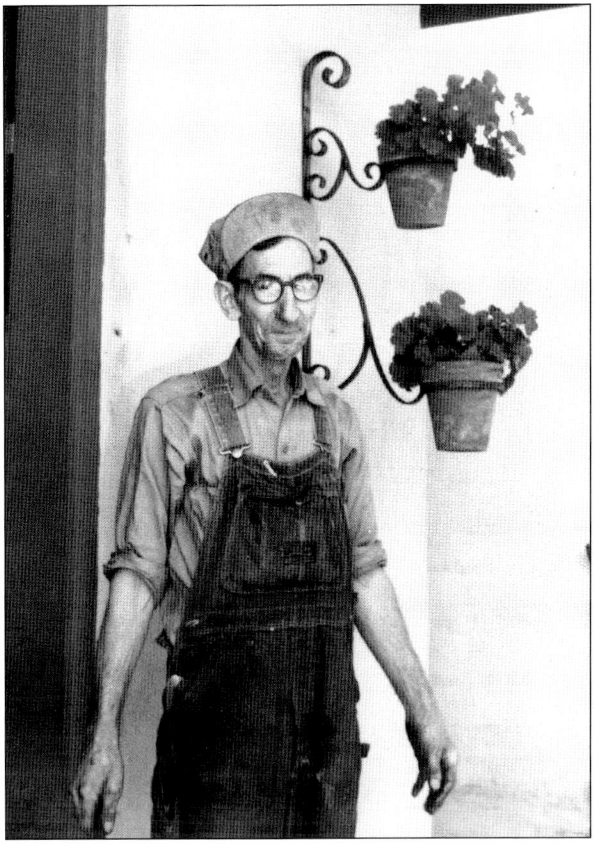

Jokingly referred to as "Georgia's first alpine phone booth," even the smallest structures took on the alpine theme. The phone booth and landscaped green space were installed on the site of the former Pure Oil service station.

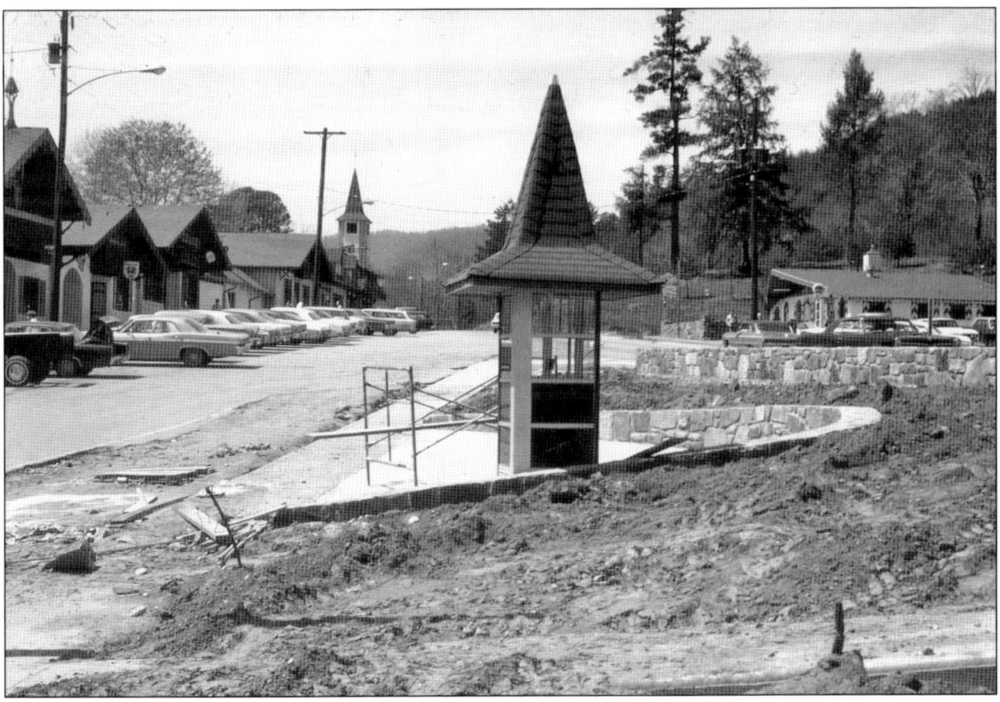

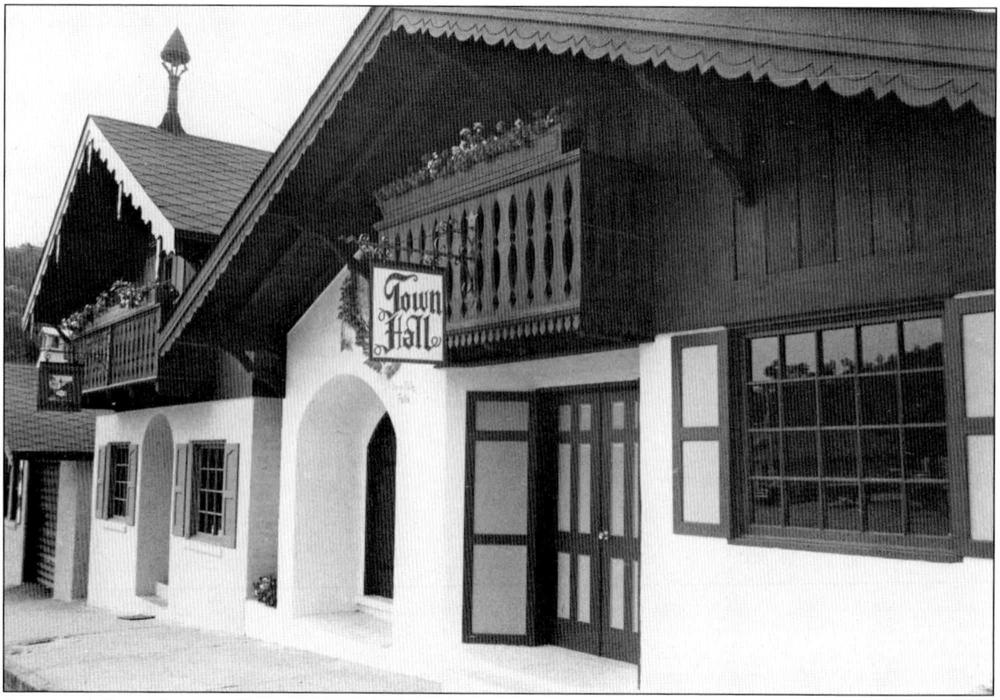

South of the old post office on Main Street was the former town hall. After both facilities moved into the new municipal building on Chattahoochee Street in 1970, the vacated spaces on Main Street became a bakery and the House of Tyrol. Currently, the Classics Gift Shop occupies the Tyrol building, and Lindenhaus Imports occupies the former post office site.

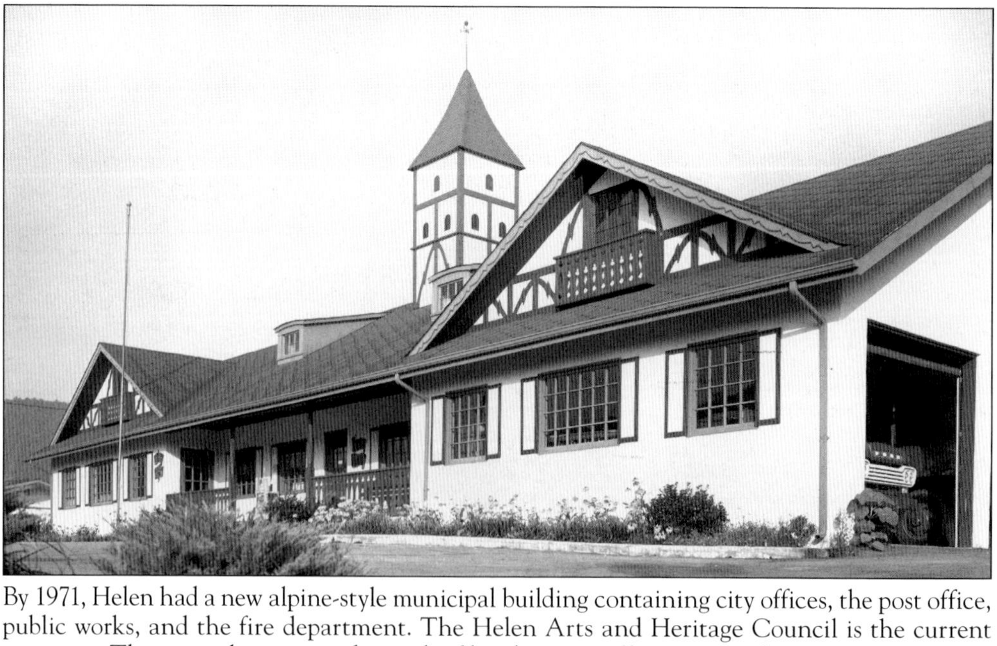

By 1971, Helen had a new alpine-style municipal building containing city offices, the post office, public works, and the fire department. The Helen Arts and Heritage Council is the current occupant. The council promotes the work of local artists, offers a curriculum of art instruction, hosts oral history presentations, and maintains a history and heritage room featuring images from Helen's past.

Not only did John Kollock design the alpine village, he worked on much of the decorative finishing. Shown here painting the entrance of the Alpine Music Hall, Kollock also painted additional murals depicting area attractions and historic events.

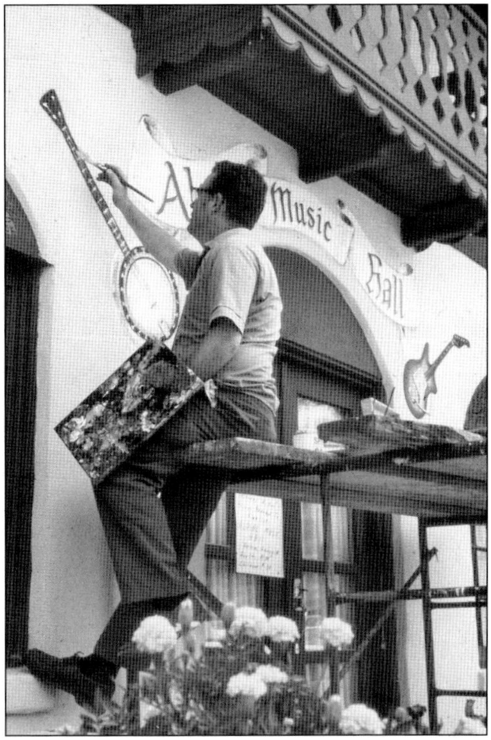

In this 1972 image, Bernd and Linda Nagy pose before the House of Tyrol. One of Helen's original shops after the alpine conversion, the House of Tyrol sold merchandise imported from Austria and Germany. A wall mural of nearby Anna Ruby Falls painted by John Kollock adorns the exterior wall.

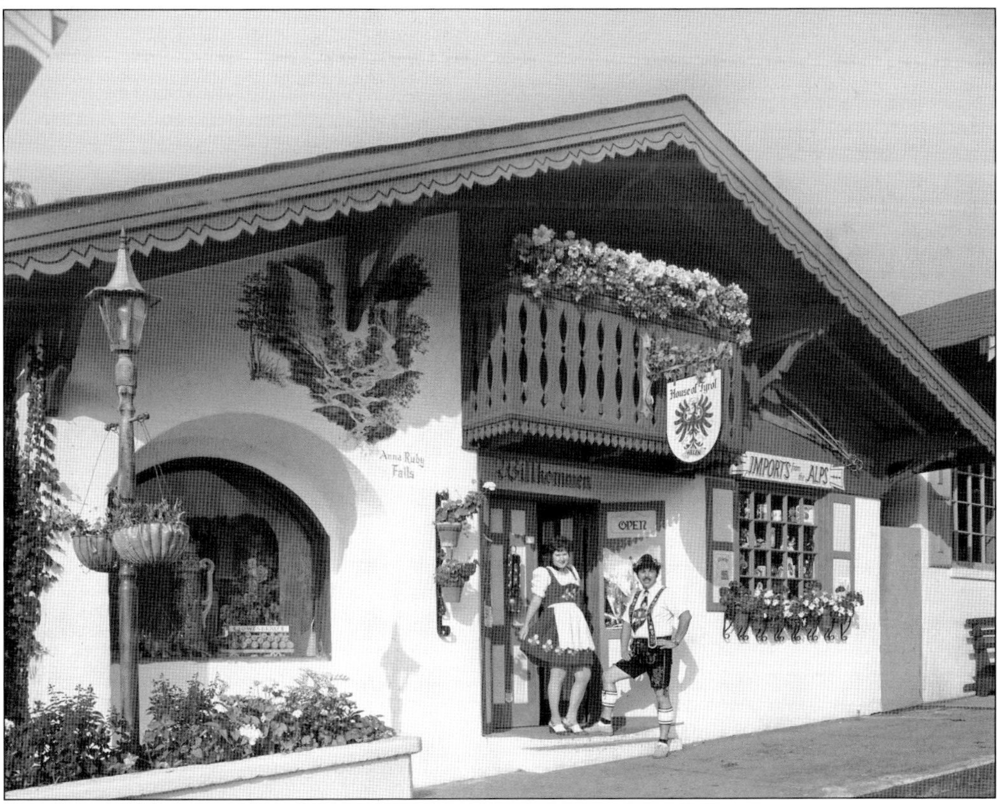

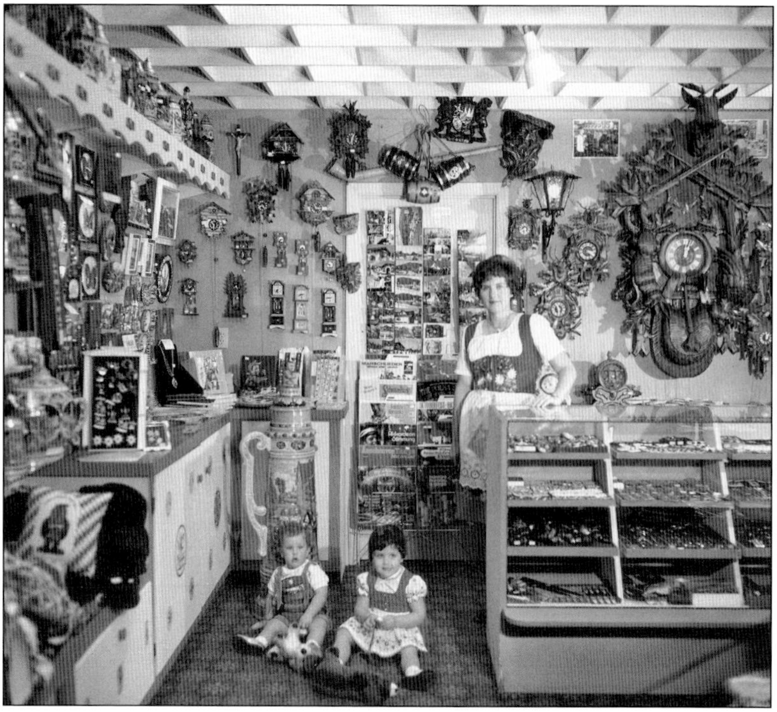

Inside the House of Tyrol in 1976, Linda Nagy stands behind her children, Markus and Christina, among Black Forest cuckoo clocks, giant beer steins, and Bavarian music records.

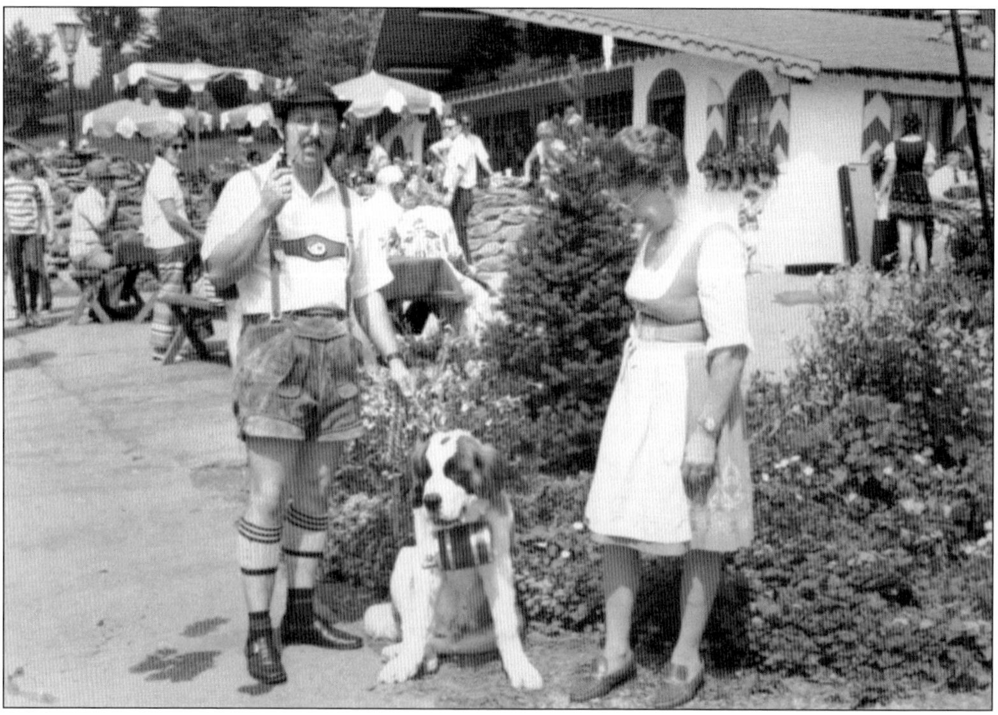

Bernd Nagy, an Austrian immigrant who made Helen his new home and established the first import gift store, the House of Tyrol, is shown in 1970 in front of the Wurst Haus. With him is St. Bernard puppy Barry and Bernd's mother, Irma. The House of Tyrol featured quality merchandise made in Bavaria and was one of Helen's most popular shops for over 30 years.

Pictured here driving to the green about 1984 is Jim Wilkins, who owned the successful apparel facility Orbit Manufacturing. But he wanted more for Helen. It was his determination, combined with the efforts of other businessmen like Bob Fowler and Pete Hodkinson, that converted Helen into a major tourist destination. Wilkins maintained this small private course at his home, and eventually he developed an 18-hole course, Innsbruck.

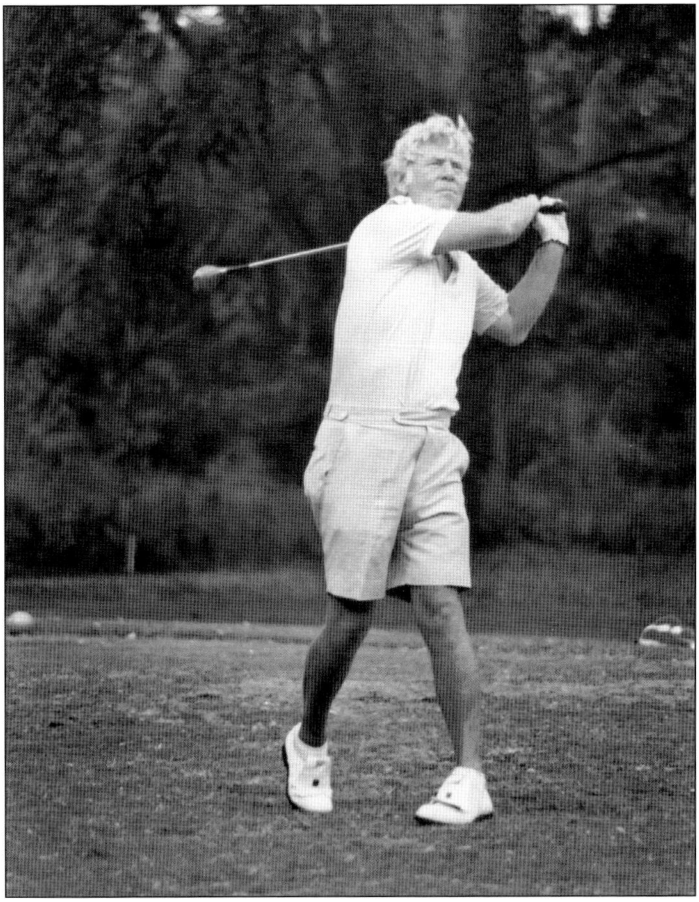

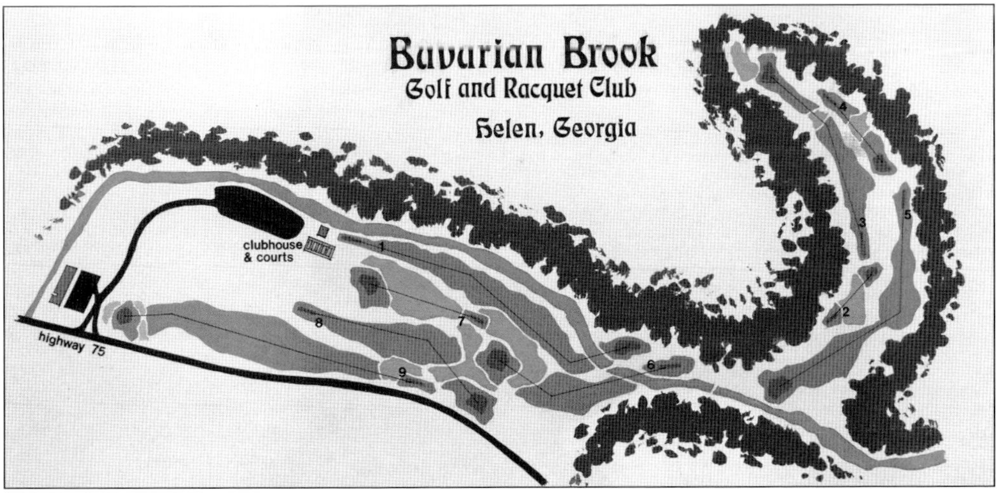

In 1973, under the direction of Helen entrepreneur Pete Hodkinson, a nine-hole golf course on the site of the old Helen sawmill was built. The course started where the Oktoberfest Festhalle is today, crossed the Chattahoochee River, bordered the home of Jim Wilkins, crossed back over the river, and ended at the Helendorf Motel. The course eventually gave way to the Island-area project, where Hugh Rainey constructed a townhouse complex named Bavarian Brook.

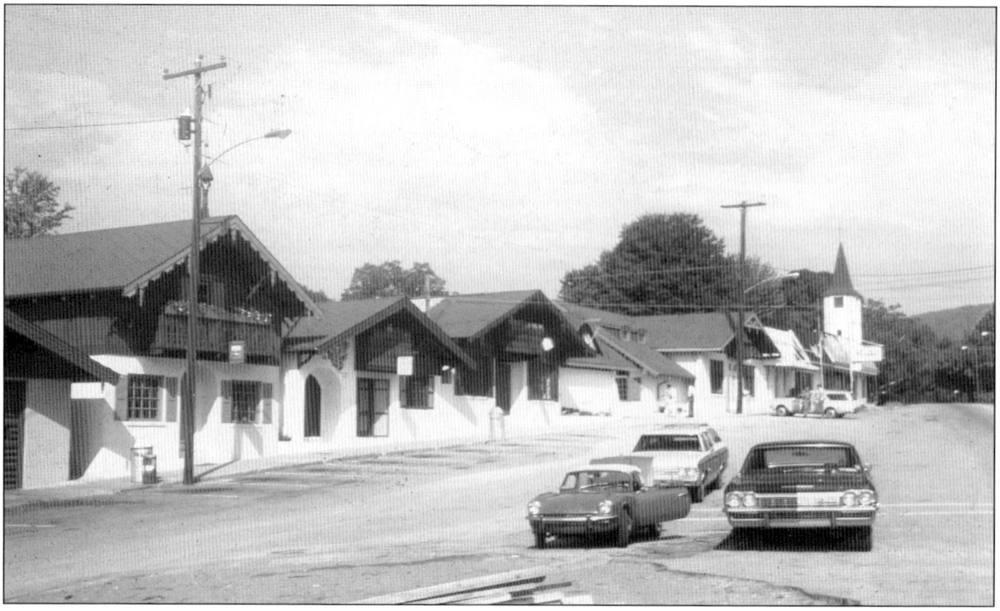

By the summer of 1970, most of the downtown buildings had been converted to the alpine theme. Town hall and the post office were still on Main Street, but construction of the new municipal building on Chattahoochee Street was under way. Utilities had not yet been buried. Newspapers were notified and invited to the area to report on the story of a town in the mountains that reinvented itself.

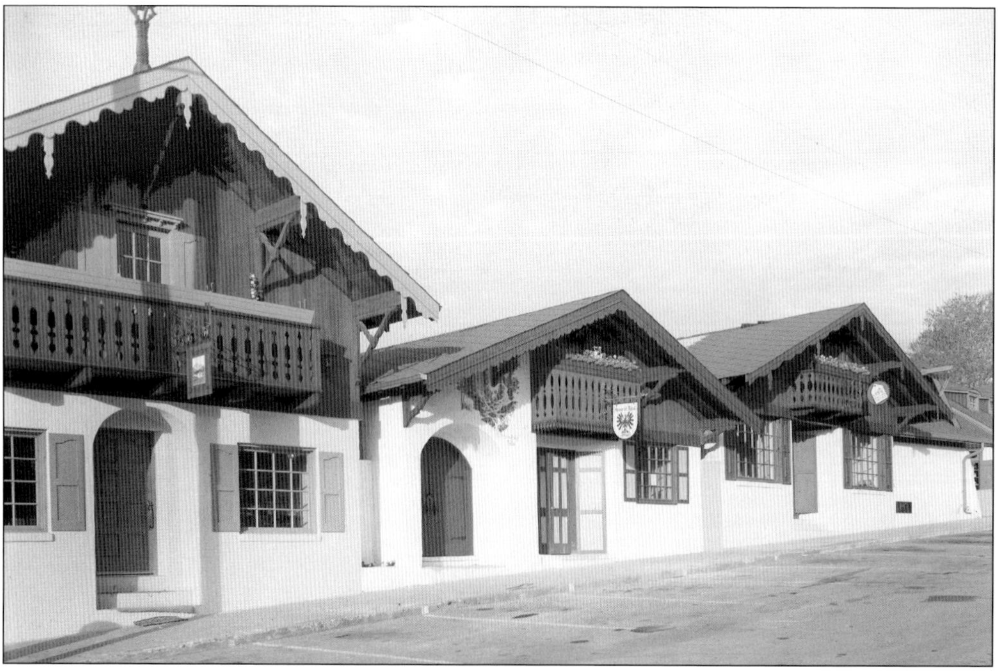

When the alpine conversion was complete, a request was submitted to the Georgia Power Company to bury and reroute utility lines running down Main Street. By 1971, all power lines had been removed from the downtown landscape, which greatly improved the aesthetics of the main walking district.

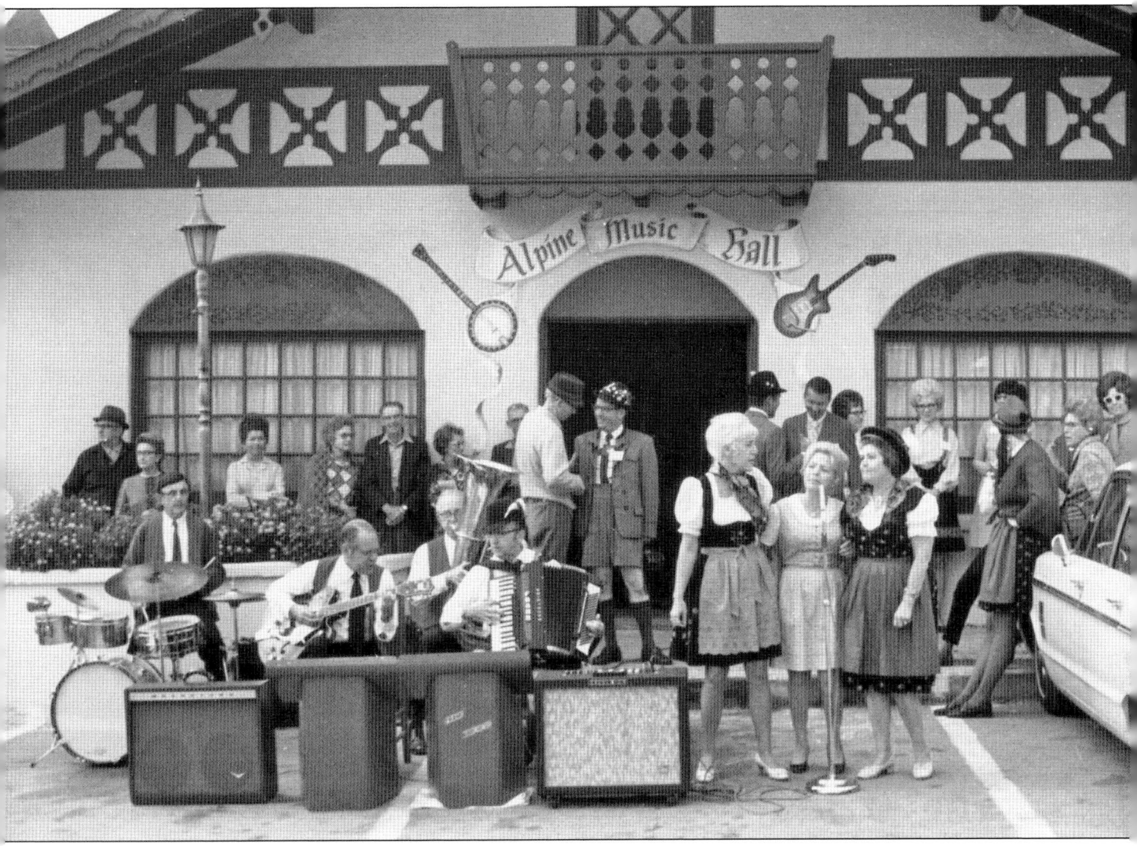

Helen's first Oktoberfest was held in front of the Alpine Music Hall, also known as Theatre Helen, on Main Street in 1970. Musicians and performers from Bavaria were recruited to perform. A small affair in its beginnings, Oktoberfest grew yearly to become Helen's biggest event. Helen's celebration is now the country's longest running Oktoberfest—spanning nearly seven weeks—from mid-September until the end of October.

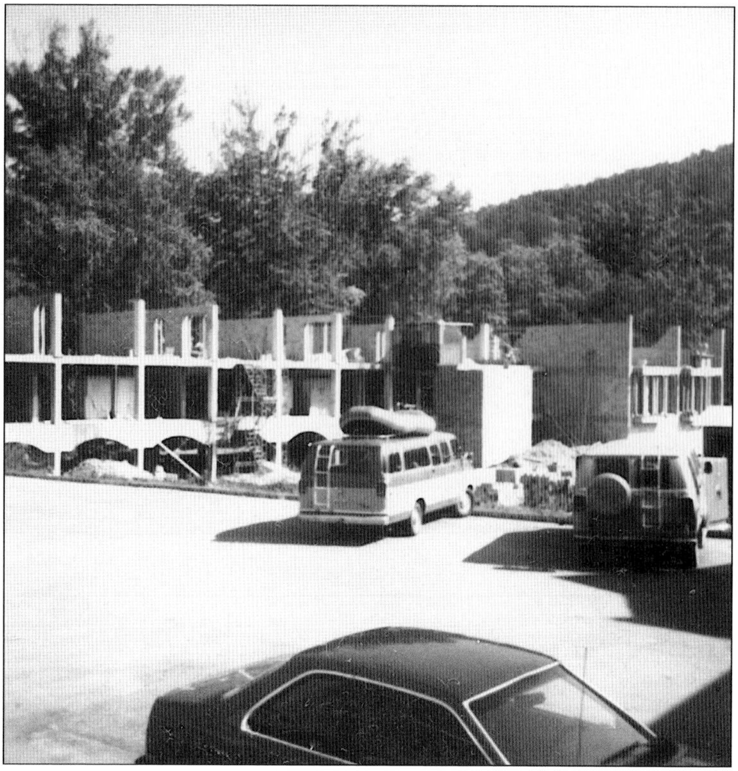

In 1973, the Helendorf was originally conceived and built by Pete Hodkinson as 30 individual condominium rentals to provide lodging for Helen's growing population of tourists visiting from throughout the Southeast. In 1974, Barbara and Dick Gay took over management of the facility.

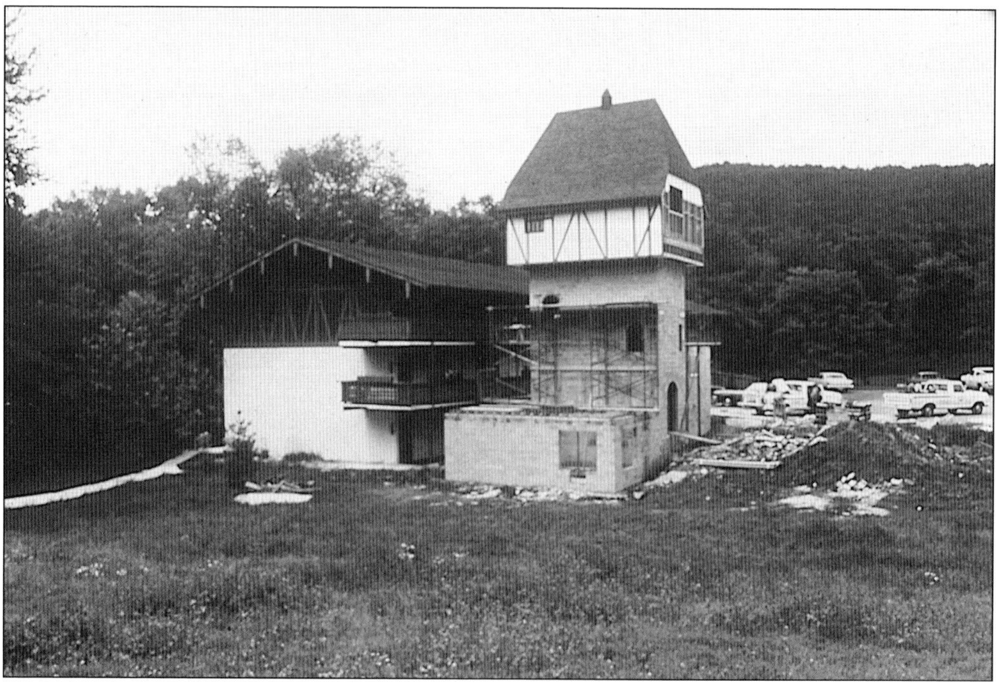

Here, Rapunzel's tower at the Helendorf nears completion in 1975. The Helendorf was one of the first buildings in Helen to be constructed after the alpine conversion took place. Gradually, it expanded to 100 guestrooms.

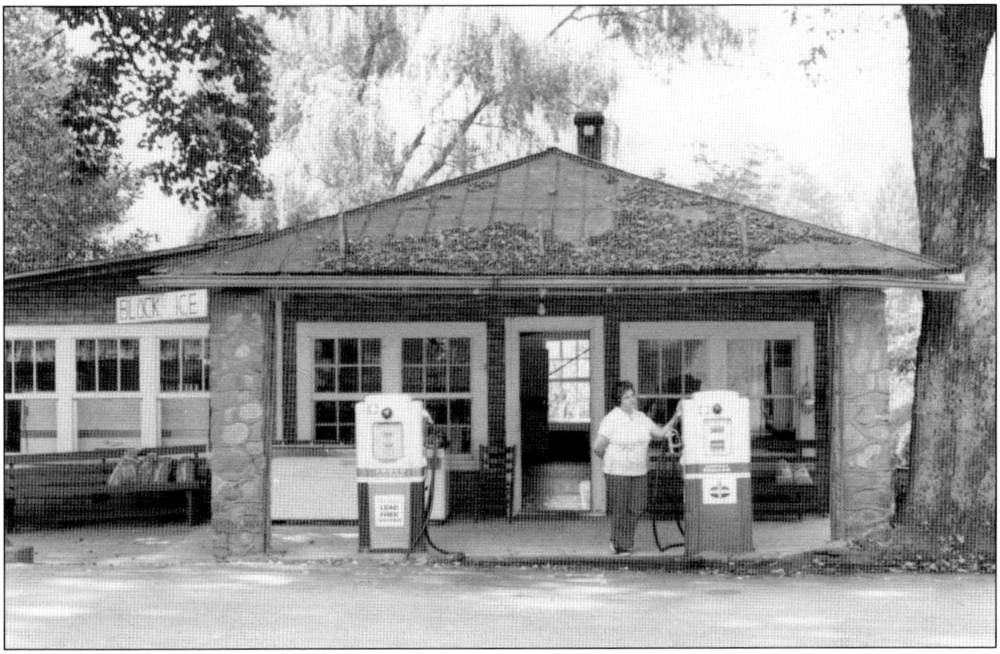

In 1972, Betty Fain poses outside the empty building formerly occupied by Bennett's Grocery. Betty, her husband, George, and the rest of her family operated Betty's Country Store at this location for 20 years before they moved to a new, larger location in 1992. The store is still owned and operated by members of the Fain family.

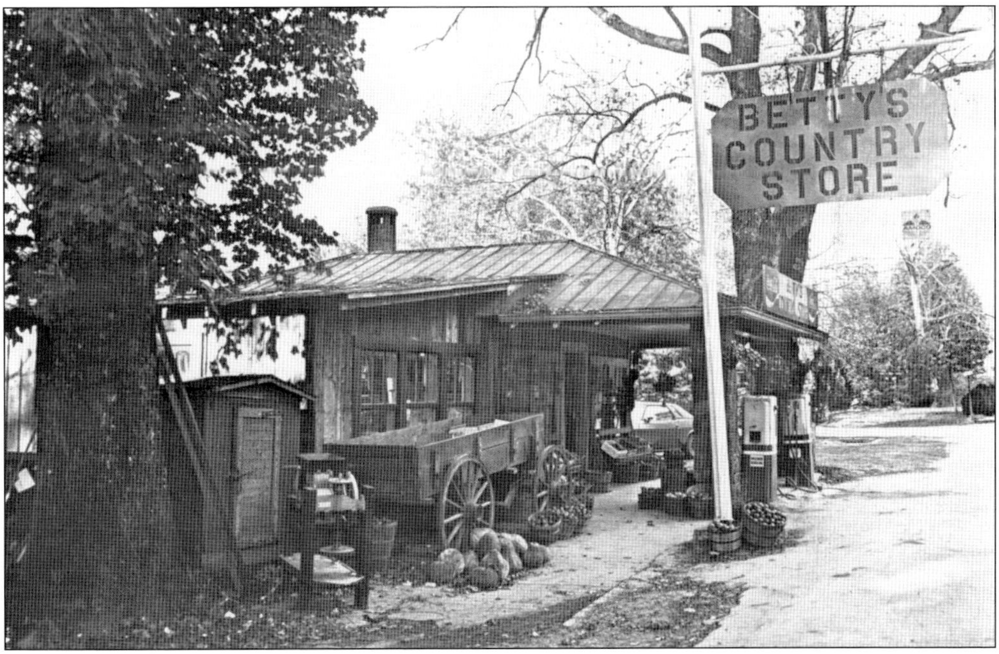

Betty's Country Store was among a handful of the old homes built during the sawmill days that retained their original appearance and did not adopt the alpine theme. While the town strongly encouraged businesses to adopt the motif, it was optional for existing buildings. New commercial buildings were required to adopt the motif.

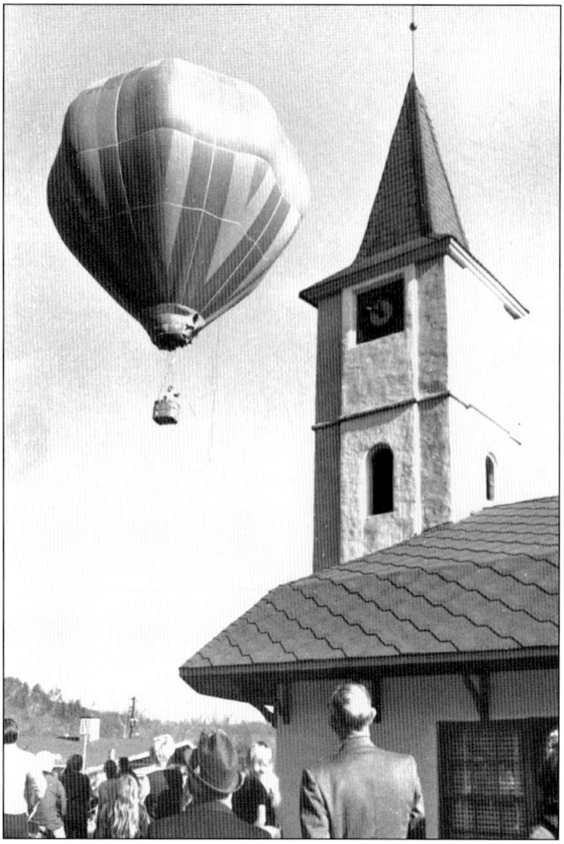

The first hot air balloon rises over Helen. Recruited by Pete Hodkinson and piloted by Ron Livley, the 1973 ascension marked the beginning of what was to become a fun, colorful activity associated with Helen to this day. The visual image of hot air balloons drifting over the village has become almost as iconic as Helen's alpine motif. The Helen to the Atlantic Balloon Race began in 1974 and is one of Helen's major events each year.

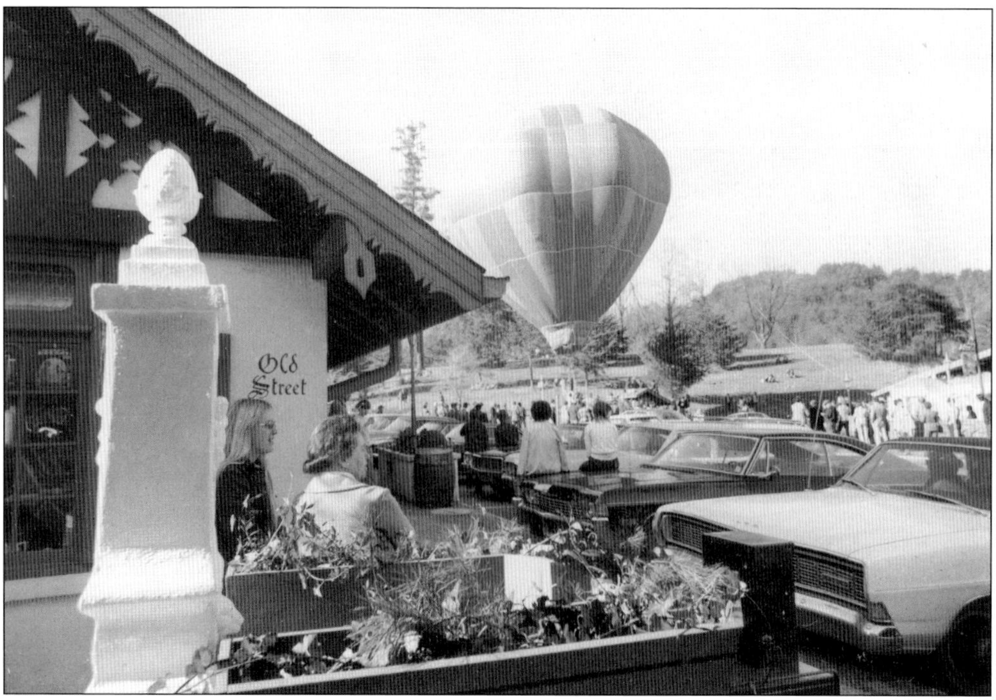

Ron Livley's balloon rises near the Wurst Haus. A popular spot for locals and visitors, the Wurst Haus hosted local musicians for over 30 years and served brats and beer. It was damaged by fire in October 2006 but reopened as King Ludwig's Beer Garden in 2010.

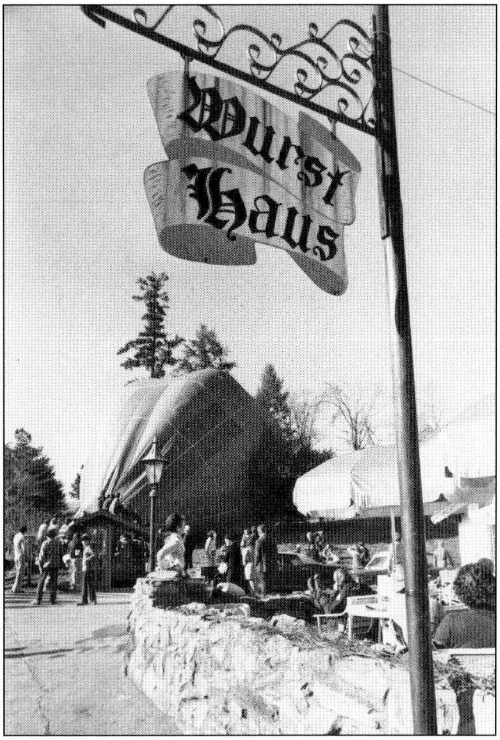

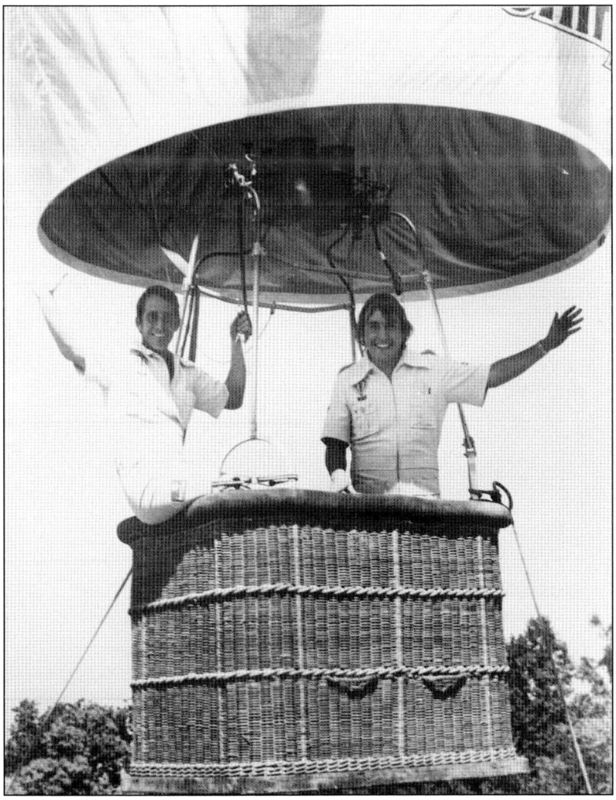

Balloonists Sid Cutter (left) and Tom Rutherford (right) won the first Helen to the Atlantic Balloon Race in 1974. Piloting the balloon sponsored by Budweiser, Cutter is considered the founder of the famous Albuquerque International Balloon Fiesta, which started in 1972. Rutherford, a state senator from New Mexico, also cofounded the famous Albuquerque event.

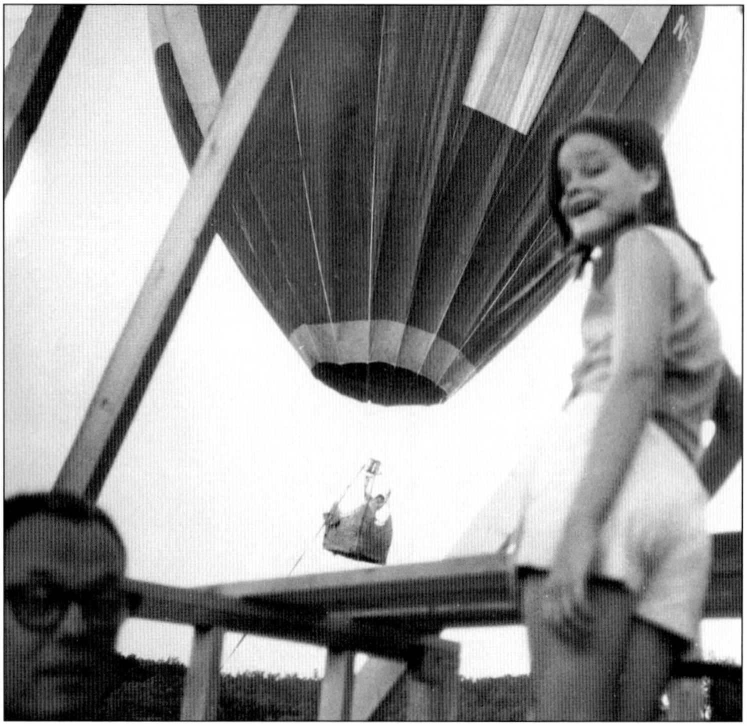

Richard Gay and his daughter Catherine pose as Pete Hodkinson lifts off in his Swiss Cross balloon. Hodkinson, dubbed the consummate promoter, coined a catchy tag for Helen's hot air balloon race: "From the center of the earth, to the edge of the world."

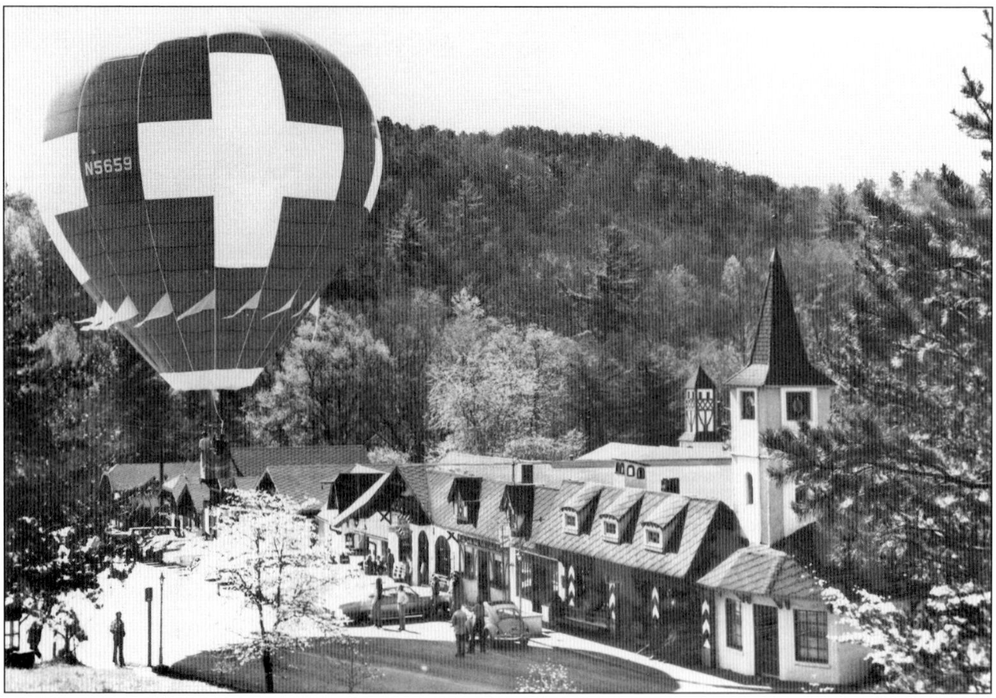

Pete Hodkinson's original Swiss cross balloon ascends from downtown Helen in 1974. The consummate promoter, Pete believed any publicity was good publicity. At the same time, his self-professed vision for Helen was to foil Gatlinburg village by offering quality merchandise while retaining a traditional alpine theme.

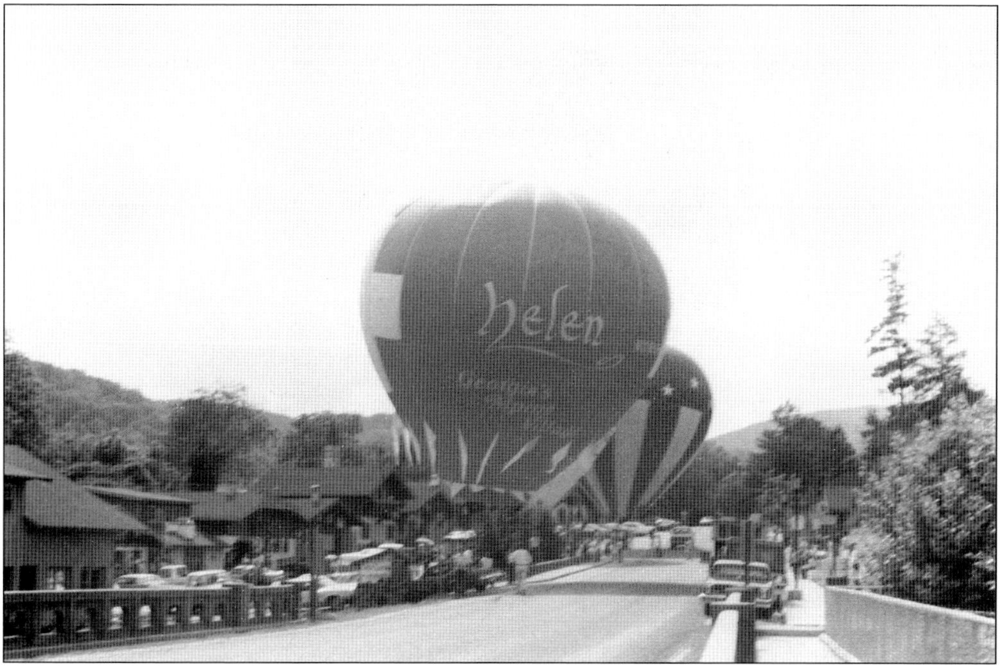

By the late 1970s, Helen had its own balloon. Early ballooning enthusiast and Hodkinson friend Tarp Head began manufacturing rugged, high-quality, handcrafted balloons in 1975. The Helen balloon, crafted by Head Balloons, featured Hodkinson's original Swiss cross emblem on two sides and the words "Helen, Georgia's Alpine Village" on the other two sides.

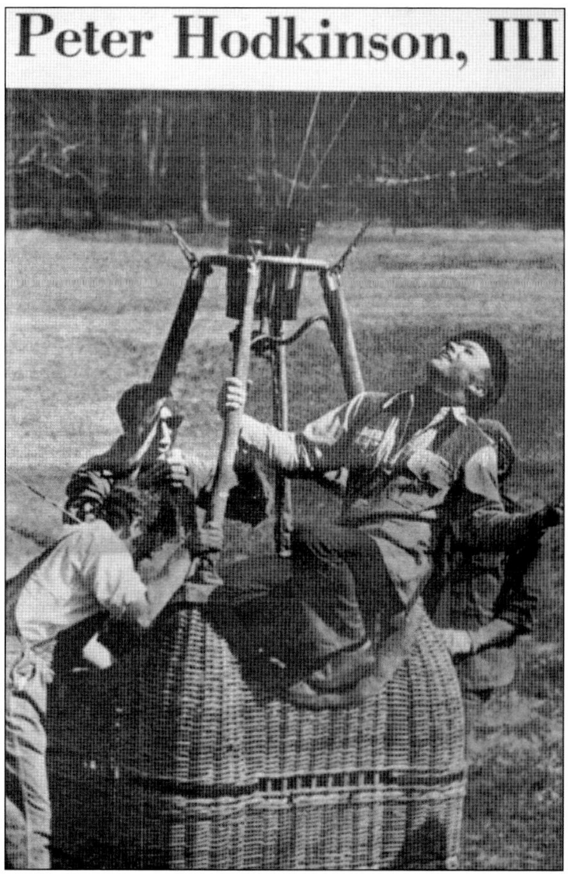

The exuberant, free-spirited Pete Hodkinson died May 18, 1976, on the eve of the third annual Helen to the Atlantic Balloon Race. After lifting off from Helen, he and passenger Hugh Rainey were attempting to land near Toccoa, when a sudden gust of wind tossed Rainey from the basket then lifted Hodkinson and the balloon into high-voltage power lines. Hodkinson was also ejected from the basket and fell nearly 80 feet to the ground. At the time of Pete's death, writer Phil Garner said, "We do not have to erect a statue to Pete. The city of Helen is his monument."

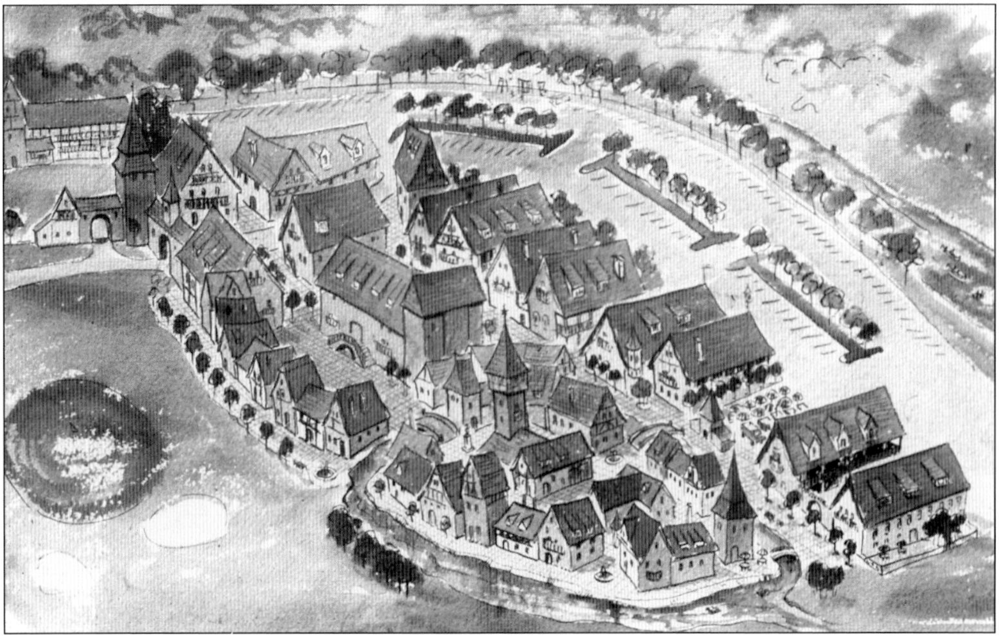

In John Kollock's rendering of the Island area, the Helendorf Motel is seen in the upper left. It was called the Island because of the mote that encircled the shops in the foreground. The first buildings constructed were a kite shop and Kubler's Hayloft Pub. After Pete Hodkinson died, the project lost its main promoter and faltered. The mote was abandoned, and only Kubler's Hayloft Pub and a few other buildings were completed. The golf course gave way to what are now the Festhalle, Wendy's, United Community Bank, Huddle House, and the Super 8 Motel.

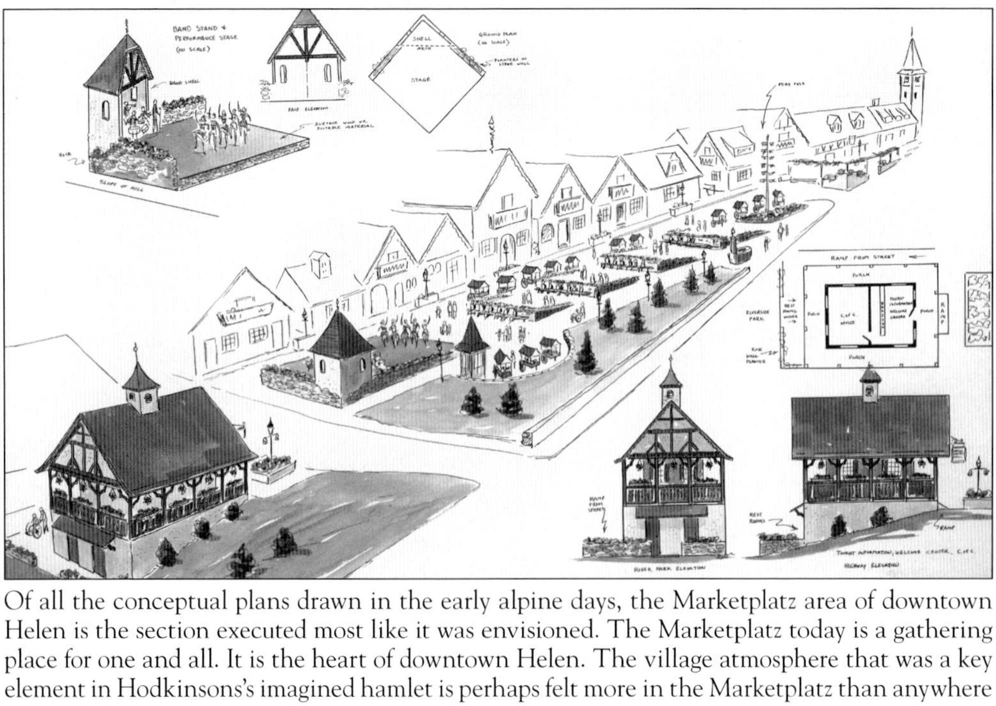

Of all the conceptual plans drawn in the early alpine days, the Marketplatz area of downtown Helen is the section executed most like it was envisioned. The Marketplatz today is a gathering place for one and all. It is the heart of downtown Helen. The village atmosphere that was a key element in Hodkinsons's imagined hamlet is perhaps felt more in the Marketplatz than anywhere else in Helen.

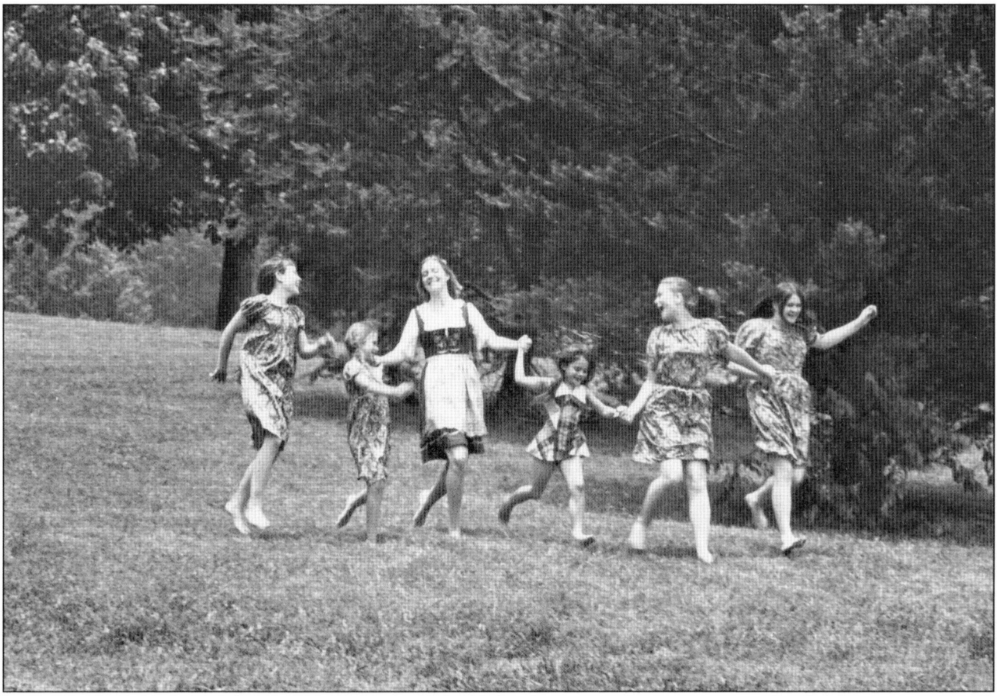

Beginning in 1972, a summer theater production of *The Sound of Music* was offered in the building formerly occupied by Wilco Hosiery Mills. Professional actors from New York City as well as acting students from local colleges were recruited for the musical production of the popular Von Trapp family. Performances garnered good reviews and a faithful following, but productions proved too costly and ended in 1978.

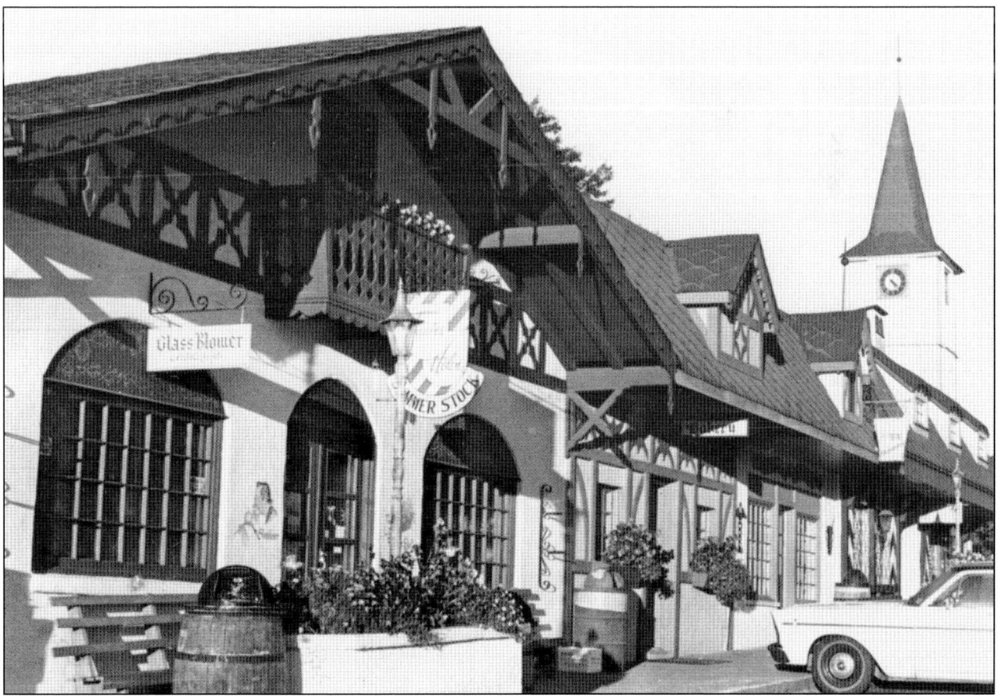

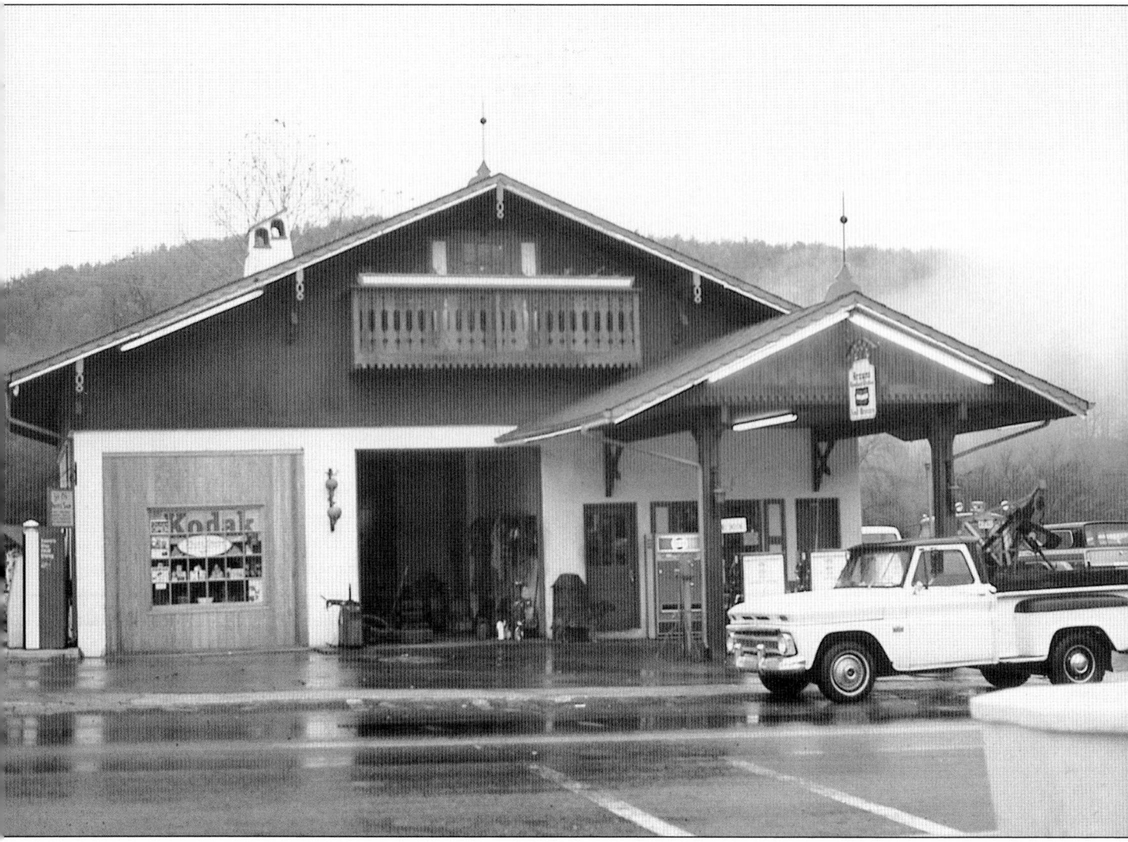

With a sense of what the future had in store, Warren Brown leased out one of the bays of his service station, which became Ye Ole Photo Shop in 1978. Realizing it was more profitable to rent space to new vendors than to fix tires, Brown's property eventually transformed into retail shops catering to tourism.

Facing fog-shrouded Hamby Mountain in 1974, this image captures the second phase of the Helendorf Motel enlargement. The parking lot and main building are about where the millpond for the Byrd-Matthews sawmill once stood. The structure across Highway 17/75 at the end of the bridge is Paul's Steak House, close to where the Helen train station was 60 years before.

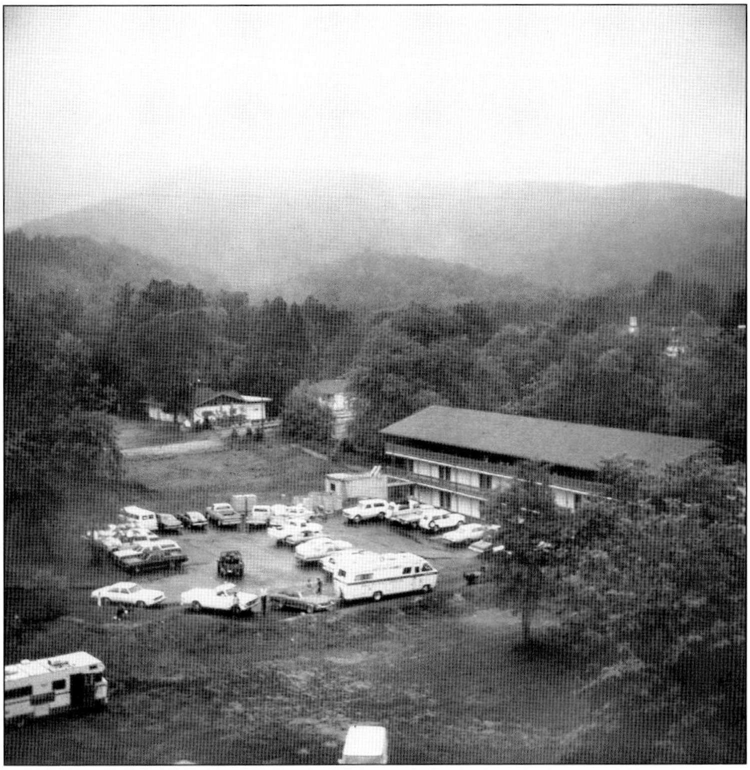

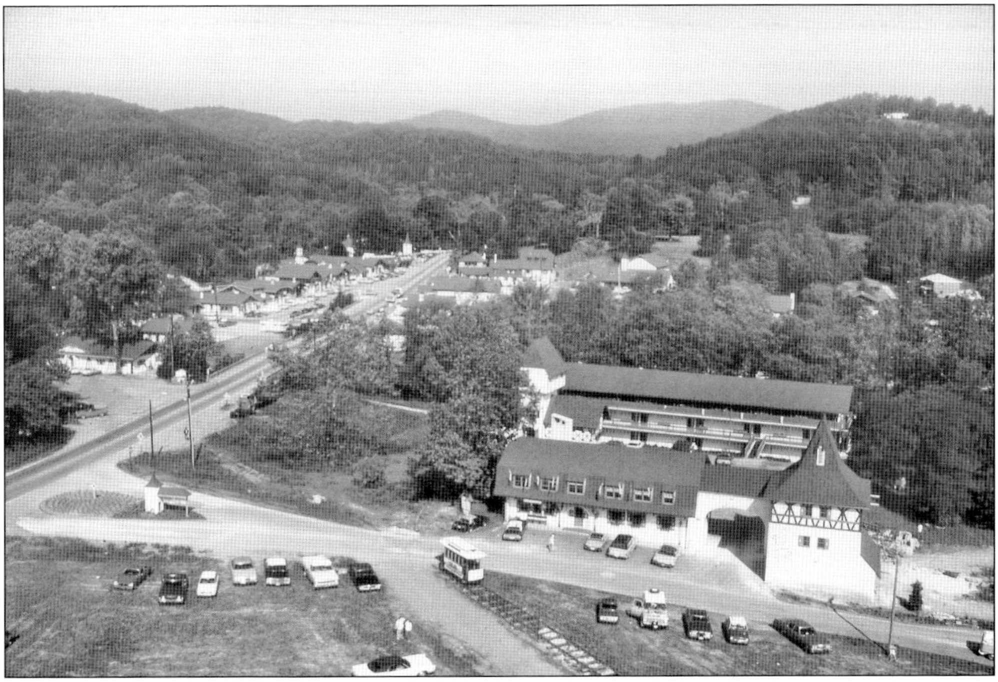

This 1978 image of the Helendorf Motel, taken from a hot air balloon, faces north toward Tray Mountain. By the mid-1970s, the alpine transformation was complete, and the buildings that would become the Riverhaus Pizza area were under construction, all designed in alpine style.

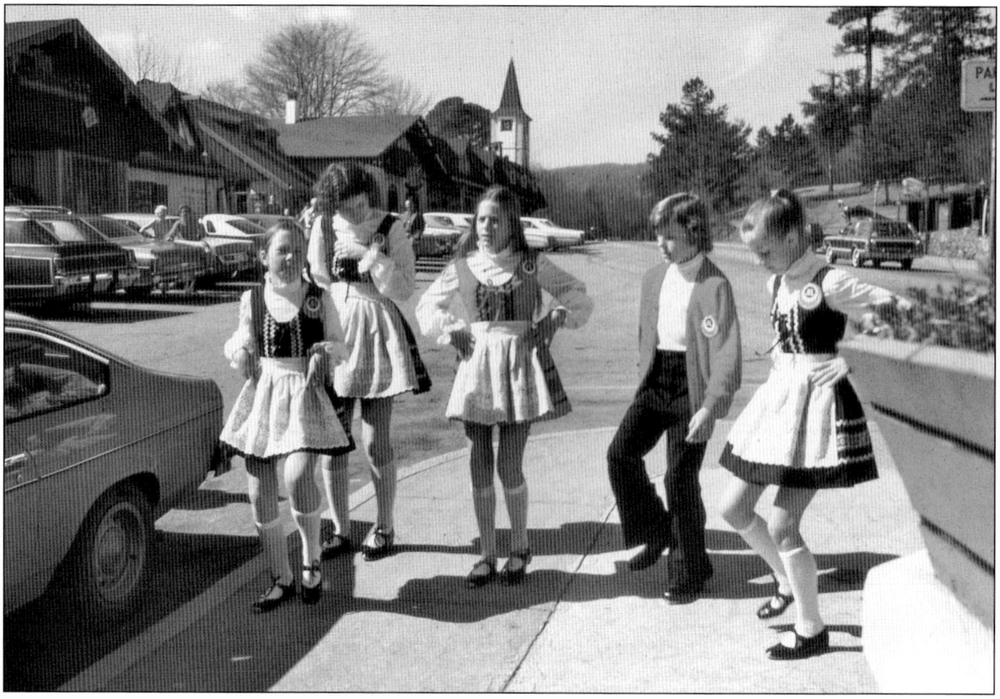

In tourism promotions, clogging was featured. The word *clog* comes from Gaelic *cloc*, meaning "clock." Clogging is a dance that is done in time with music's downbeat. For Appalachian settlers with Gaelic roots, clogging was a means of personal expression in a land of newfound freedoms. American tap dancing is a hybrid of British clogging and West African step dance.

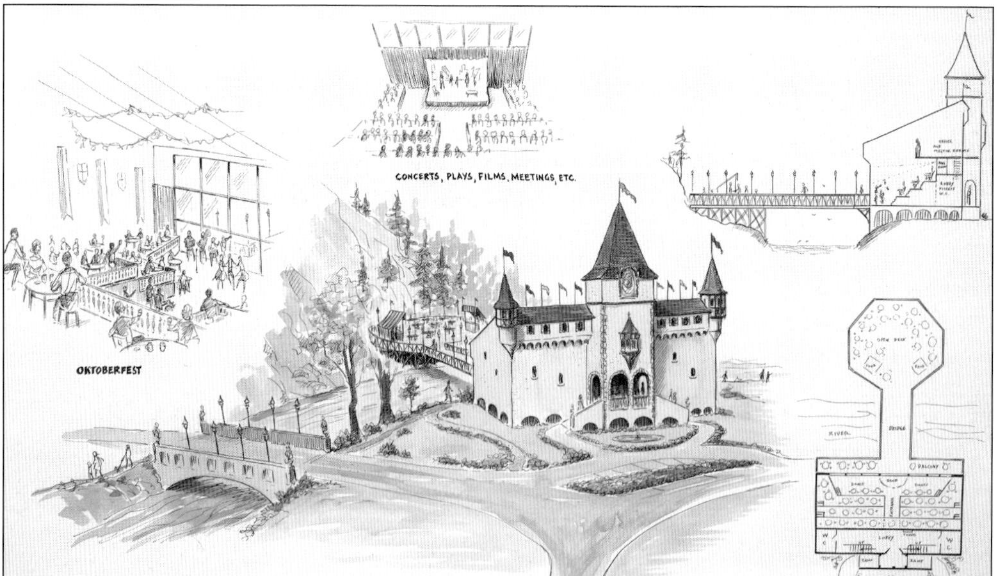

The Helen Festhalle, as conceived by John Kollock, was another project that did not quite achieve full fruition. Envisioned as a riverside venue with towers and a bridge over the Chattahoochee River that led to a separate, open-air dining pavilion, today the Festhalle, while riverside, is a much less ambitious structure, hosting Helen's Oktoberfest and other events throughout the year.

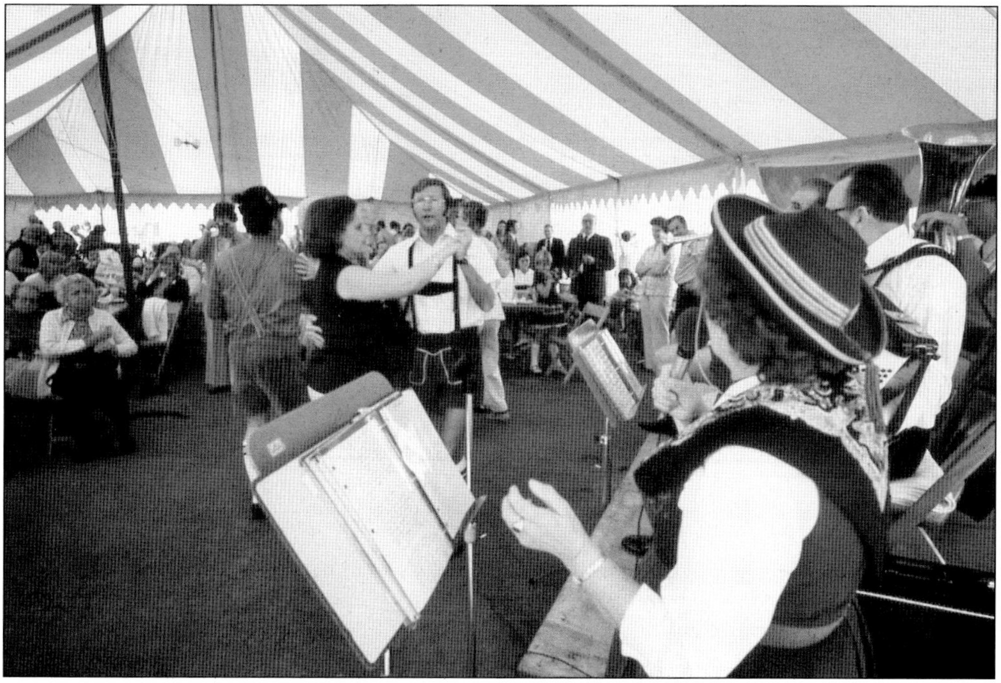

Between 1970 and 1980, the Oktoberfest event had evolved essentially from a sidewalk to a parking lot, to a large tent, to its own venue, Festhalle, by the river. Thousands of visitors gather for the two-month event each year to enjoy German-style oompah music, eat wursts, drink beer, and dance the chicken. Though probably not for the Teutonic purists, the event does give guests a taste of Heidelberg.

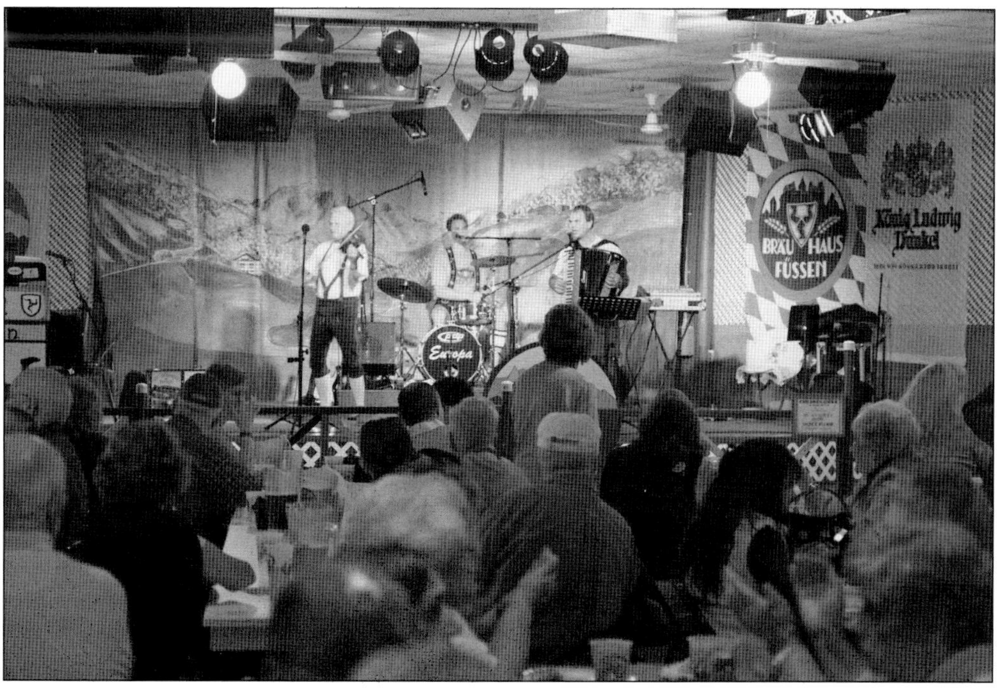

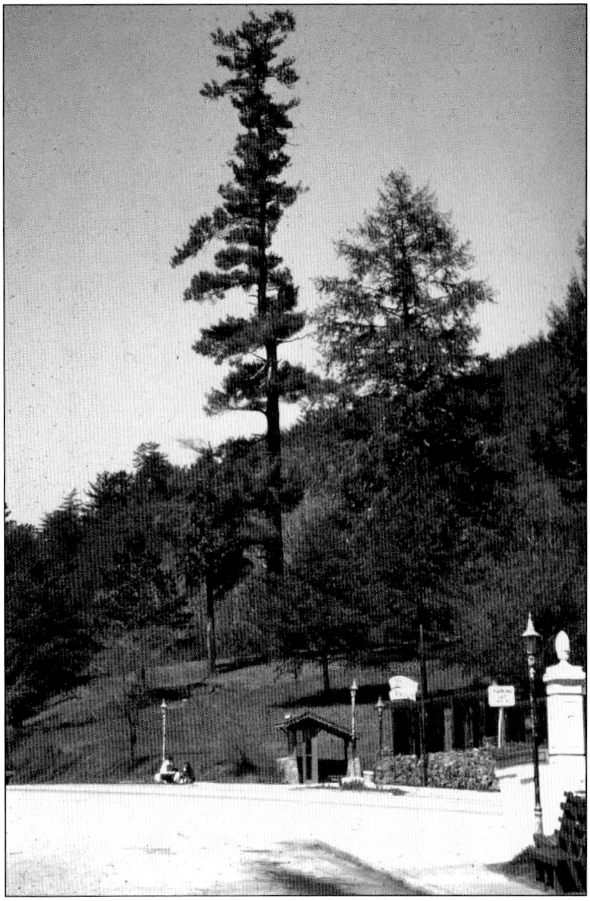

Perhaps one of the last remnants of the good old days was the huge white pine that once stood on Unicoi Hill, site of the Mountain Ranch Hotel. It stood over 100 feet tall and was nearly 100 years old when it was removed in the early 1980s. The majestic conifer survived Helen's sawmill era, the Depression, and the town's quiet years, only to be removed because it posed a threat to passing cars and pedestrians.

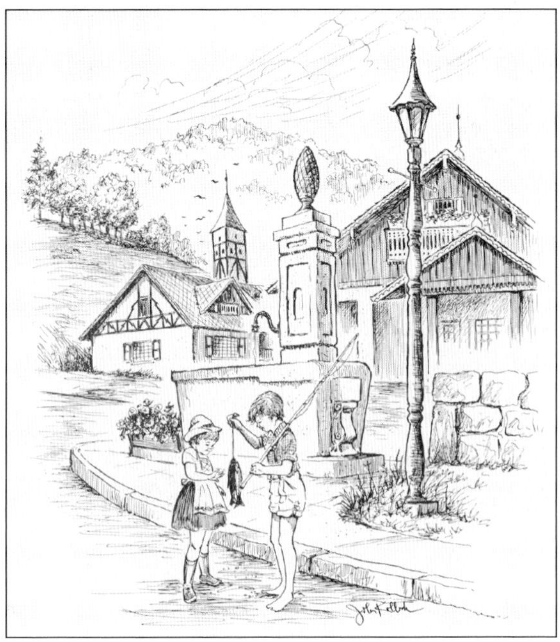

Recognizing the importance of joining the old with the new, many of John Kollock's illustrations and renderings fused alpine features with those of traditional Appalachia. Here, a Swiss miss admires a string of fish caught by a Blue Ridge boy. Because of Kollock's family ties to the area and his interest in local history, his designs honored the past and embraced the new.

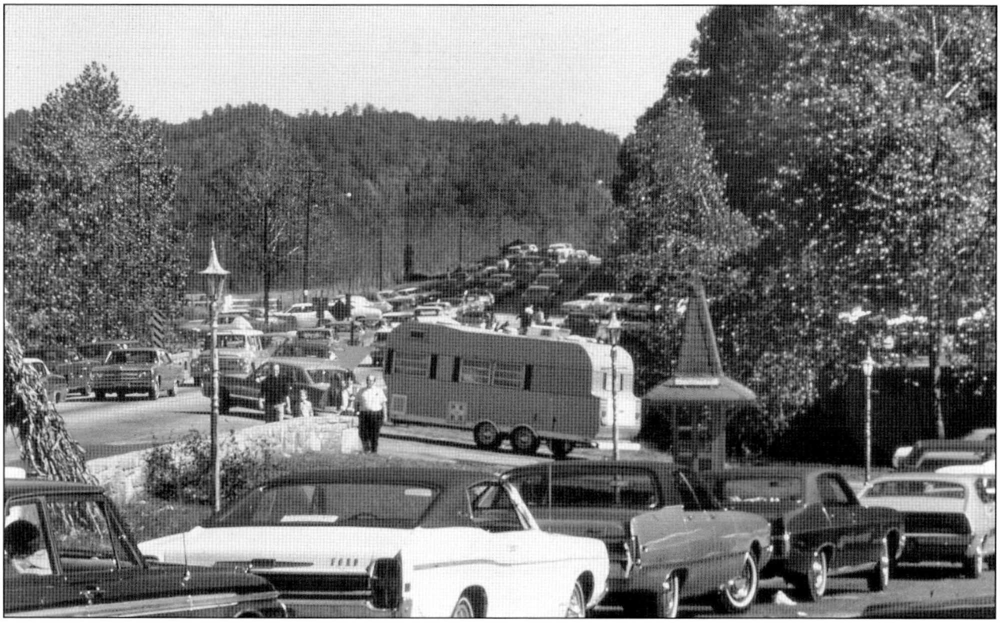

If traffic was any indication of success, Helen had achieved its growth objectives by the mid-1970s. Particularly in the fall, day-trippers and overnighters flocked to the mountains to see the new alpine hamlet. Freeways funneled down to four-lane highways, which narrowed to two-lane roads, and the two lanes led to the gridlock that was Helen. In the minds of many it was a welcome problem to have, but a problem nonetheless that remains today.

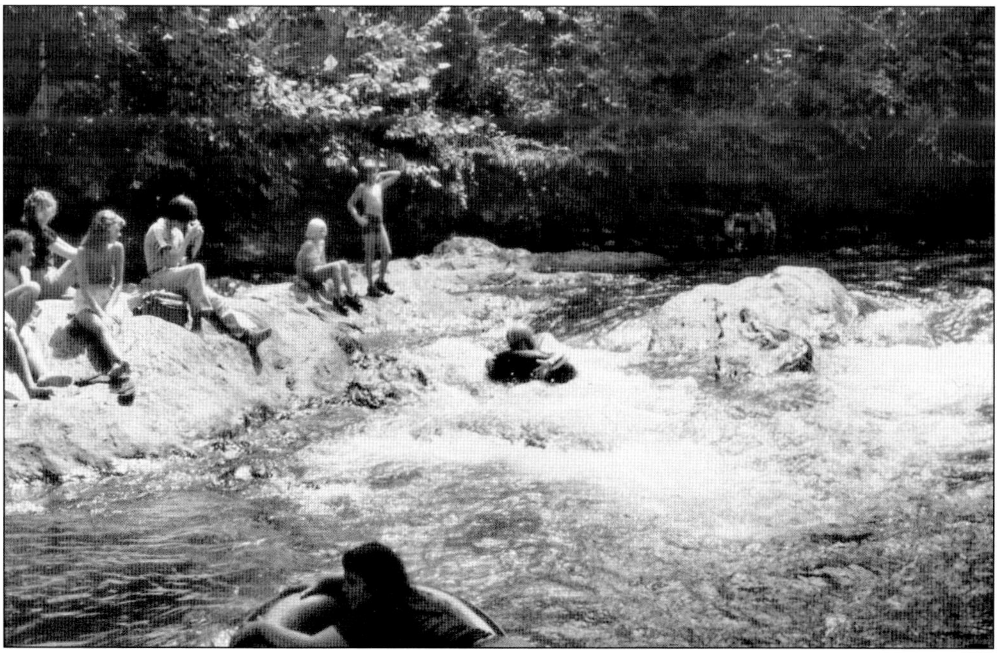

Before tubing became big business, individuals would bring their own tubes or buy used tubes from Warren Brown's service station. Kids could buy a used tube at Brown's service station for $2, fill it with air for free, and tube all summer. However, by mid-July, the inevitable tube patch kit cost a kid another dollar. In this c. 1980 image, a cautious tuber wears a protective helmet.

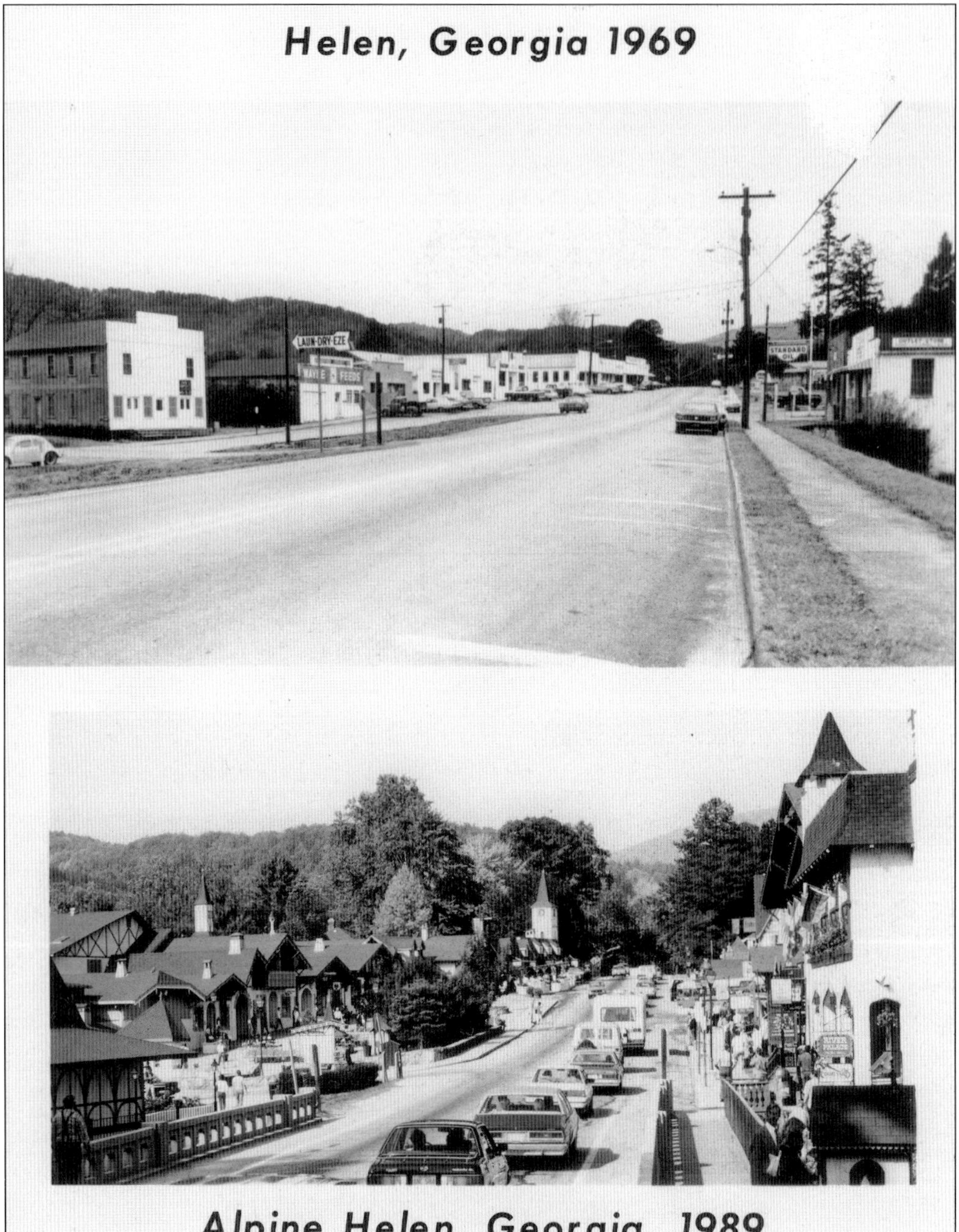

This oft-published before-and-after composite compares Main Street in 1969 and 1989. It had been 20 years since Helen's alpine rebirth, 76 years since the sawmill era, and almost 175 years since the Unicoi Turnpike opened for travelers. While the meaning of success means something different to each person, by all accounts Helen has experienced a remarkable renaissance.

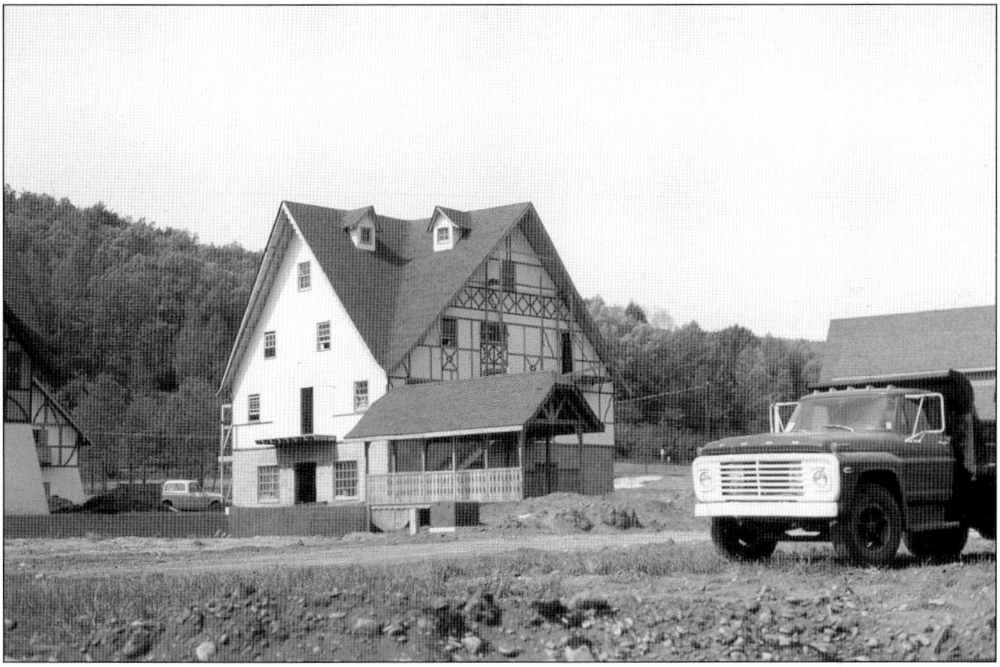

Helen's growth continued through the 1980s, 1990s, and 2000s. The Island area added more shops around Kubler's Hayloft Pub, five more hotels were built, and the timeshare resorts Loreley and Alpine Crest were developed. Innsbruck Golf Club opened, and outlet mall buildings were constructed. Though some ventures failed to thrive in the challenging post-2000 economy, Helen continues to move forward. Most of those who live and work in the area develop a deep bond to the valleys, rivers, creeks, and mountains that transcends monetary challenges.

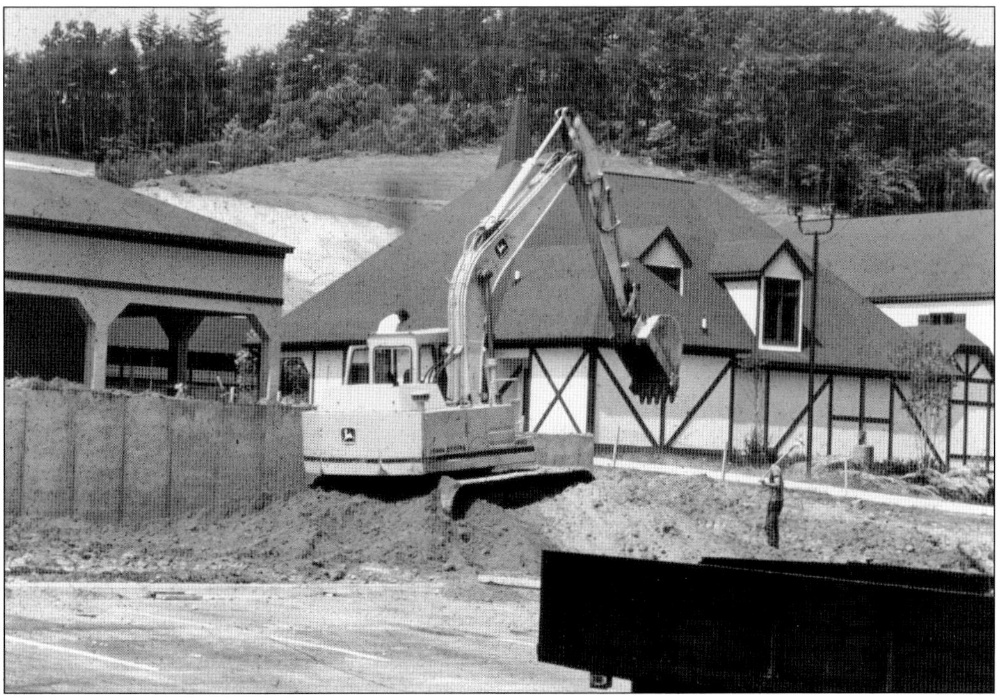

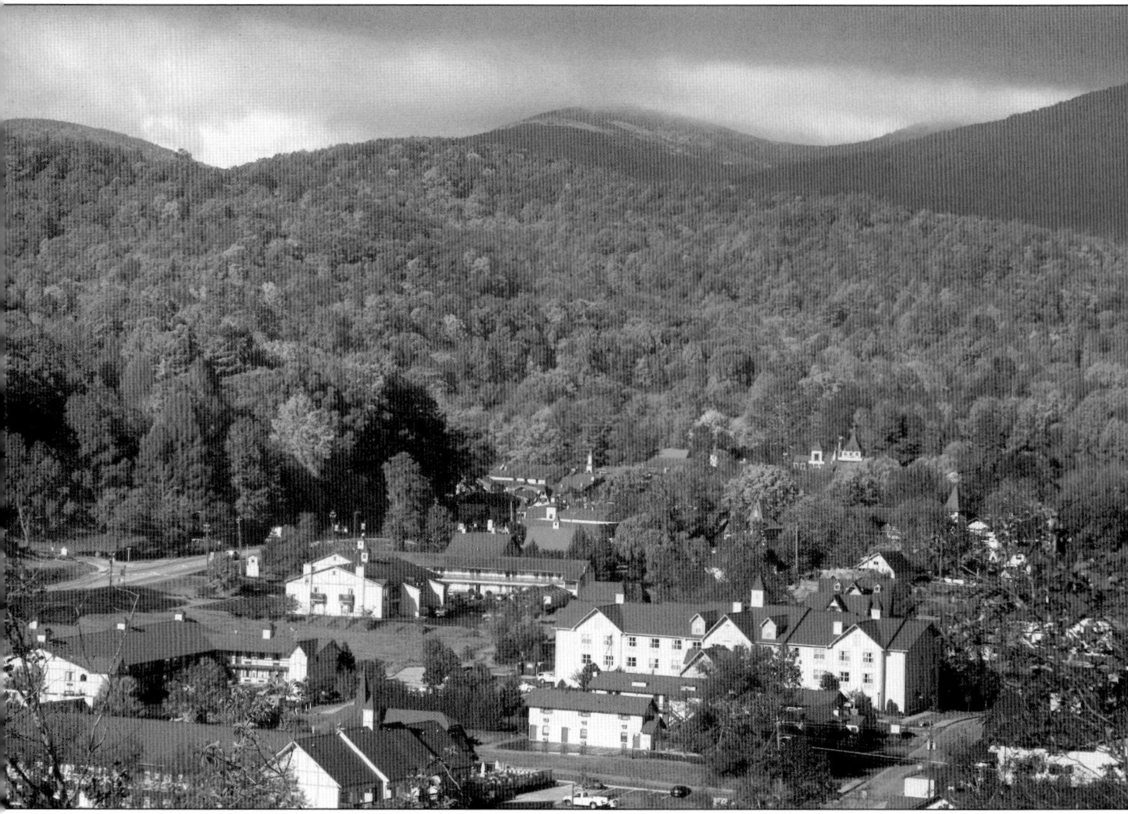

This autumn 2008 view of the Helen Valley, in many ways, is not much different than that seen in the early settlement years. While the valley bottom is considerably more developed, the mountains beyond the city remain timeless. Bordered by the Chattahoochee National Forest to the north and the Nacoochee Valley Historic district to the south, with the Chattahoochee River running though the center, the town does have limited room for growth. But these geographical boundaries are what help make Helen so distinctive, keeping the town concentrated and compact, like a hidden alpine treasure.

BIBLIOGRAPHY

Anderson, Barbara and Garland Vandiver. *Memories of Helen.* Self-published.

Baker, Garrison. *In the Shadow of Yonah: A History of White County, Georgia.* Cleveland, GA: Brasstown Creek, 2005.

Gedney, Matthias J. *Living on the Unicoi Road: Helen's Pioneer Century and Tales from the Georgia Gold Rush.* Marietta, GA: Little Star Press, 1997.

———. *The Story of Helen and Thereabouts.* Marietta, GA: Little Star Press, 2005.

Lumsden, Thomas N. *Nacoochee: Her Times and Places.* Self-published.

Matthews, Edward C. III. *Matthews: The Historic Adventures of a Pioneer Family.* Cape Girardeau, MO: Southeast Missouri State University, 2004.

Van Veelen, Douglas. *The Gainesville Midland and Her Sister Short Lines.* Bloomington, IN: AuthorHouse, 2006.